Mometrix
TEST PREPARATION

I0868266

MCA

Success Strategies
Grade 7
Reading

Dear Future Exam Success Story

First of all, **THANK YOU** for purchasing Mometrix study materials!

Second, congratulations! You are one of the few determined test-takers who are committed to doing whatever it takes to excel on your exam. **You have come to the right place.** We developed these study materials with one goal in mind: to deliver you the information you need in a format that's concise and easy to use.

In addition to optimizing your guide for the content of the test, we've outlined our recommended steps for breaking down the preparation process into small, attainable goals so you can make sure you stay on track.

We've also analyzed the entire test-taking process, identifying the most common pitfalls and showing how you can overcome them and be ready for any curveball the test throws you.

Standardized testing is one of the biggest obstacles on your road to success, which only increases the importance of doing well in the high-pressure, high-stakes environment of test day. Your results on this test could have a significant impact on your future, and this guide provides the information and practical advice to help you achieve your full potential on test day.

Your success is our success

We would love to hear from you! If you would like to share the story of your exam success or if you have any questions or comments in regard to our products, please contact us at **800-673-8175** or **support@mometrix.com**.

Thanks again for your business and we wish you continued success!

Sincerely,
The Mometrix Test Preparation Team

Copyright © 2026 by Mometrix Media LLC. All rights reserved.
Written and edited by the Mometrix Test Preparation Team
Printed in the United States of America

TABLE OF CONTENTS

Introduction

Thank you for purchasing this resource! You have made the choice to prepare yourself for a test that could have a huge impact on your future, and this guide is designed to help you be fully ready for test day. Obviously, it's important to have a solid understanding of the test material, but you also need to be prepared for the unique environment and stressors of the test, so that you can perform to the best of your abilities.

For this purpose, the first section that appears in this guide is the **Success Strategies**. We've devoted countless hours to meticulously researching what works and what doesn't, and we've boiled down our findings to the most impactful steps you can take to improve your performance on the test. We start at the beginning with study planning and move through the preparation process, all the way to the testing strategies that will help you get the most out of what you know when you're finally sitting in front of the test.

We recommend that you start preparing for your test as far in advance as possible. However, if you've bought this guide as a last-minute study resource and only have a few days before your test, we recommend that you skip over the first two Success Strategies since they address a long-term study plan.

If you struggle with **test anxiety**, we strongly encourage you to check out our recommendations for how you can overcome it. Test anxiety is a formidable foe, but it can be beaten, and we want to make sure you have the tools you need to defeat it.

Copyright © Mometrix Media. You have been licensed one copy of this document for personal use only. Any other reproduction or redistribution is strictly prohibited. All rights reserved.
This content is provided for test preparation purposes only and does not imply an endorsement by Mometrix of any particular political, scientific, or religious point of view.

Strategy #1 – Plan Big, Study Small

There's a lot riding on your performance. If you want to ace this test, you're going to need to keep your skills sharp and the material fresh in your mind. You need a plan that lets you review everything you need to know while still fitting in your schedule. We'll break this strategy down into three categories.

Information Organization

Start with the information you already have: the official test outline. From this, you can make a complete list of all the concepts you need to cover before the test. Organize these concepts into groups that can be studied together, and create a list of any related vocabulary you need to learn so you can brush up on any difficult terms. You'll want to keep this vocabulary list handy once you actually start studying since you may need to add to it along the way.

Time Management

Once you have your set of study concepts, decide how to spread them out over the time you have left before the test. Break your study plan into small, clear goals so you have a manageable task for each day and know exactly what you're doing. Then just focus on one small step at a time. When you manage your time this way, you don't need to spend hours at a time studying. Studying a small block of content for a short period each day helps you retain information better and avoid stressing over how much you have left to do. You can relax knowing that you have a plan to cover everything in time. In order for this strategy to be effective though, you have to start studying early and stick to your schedule. Avoid the exhaustion and futility that comes from last-minute cramming!

Study Environment

The environment you study in has a big impact on your learning. Studying in a coffee shop, while probably more enjoyable, is not likely to be as fruitful as studying in a quiet room. It's important to keep distractions to a minimum. You're only planning to study for a short block of time, so make the most of it. Don't pause to check your phone or get up to find a snack. It's also important to **avoid multitasking**. Research has consistently shown that multitasking will make your studying dramatically less effective. Your study area should also be comfortable and well-lit so you don't have the distraction of straining your eyes or sitting on an uncomfortable chair.

The time of day you study is also important. You want to be rested and alert. Don't wait until just before bedtime. Study when you'll be most likely to comprehend and remember. Even better, if you know what time of day your test will be, set that time aside for study. That way your brain will be used to working on that subject at that specific time and you'll have a better chance of recalling information.

Finally, it can be helpful to team up with others who are studying for the same test. Your actual studying should be done in as isolated an environment as possible, but the work of organizing the information and setting up the study plan can be divided up. In between study sessions, you can discuss with your teammates the concepts that you're all studying and quiz each other on the details. Just be sure that your teammates are as serious about the test as you are. If you find that your study time is being replaced with social time, you might need to find a new team.

Copyright © Mometrix Media. You have been licensed one copy of this document for personal use only. Any other reproduction or redistribution is strictly prohibited. All rights reserved.
This content is provided for test preparation purposes only and does not imply an endorsement by Mometrix of any particular political, scientific, or religious point of view.

Strategy #2 – Make Your Studying Count

You're devoting a lot of time and effort to preparing for this test, so you want to be absolutely certain it will pay off. This means doing more than just reading the content and hoping you can remember it on test day. It's important to make every minute of study count. There are two main areas you can focus on to make your studying count.

Retention

It doesn't matter how much time you study if you can't remember the material. You need to make sure you are retaining the concepts. To check your retention of the information you're learning, try recalling it at later times with minimal prompting. Try carrying around flashcards and glance at one or two from time to time or ask a friend who's also studying for the test to quiz you.

To enhance your retention, look for ways to put the information into practice so that you can apply it rather than simply recalling it. If you're using the information in practical ways, it will be much easier to remember. Similarly, it helps to solidify a concept in your mind if you're not only reading it to yourself but also explaining it to someone else. Ask a friend to let you teach them about a concept you're a little shaky on (or speak aloud to an imaginary audience if necessary). As you try to summarize, define, give examples, and answer your friend's questions, you'll understand the concepts better and they will stay with you longer. Finally, step back for a big picture view and ask yourself how each piece of information fits with the whole subject. When you link the different concepts together and see them working together as a whole, it's easier to remember the individual components.

Finally, practice showing your work on any multi-step problems, even if you're just studying. Writing out each step you take to solve a problem will help solidify the process in your mind, and you'll be more likely to remember it during the test.

Modality

Modality simply refers to the means or method by which you study. Choosing a study modality that fits your own individual learning style is crucial. No two people learn best in exactly the same way, so it's important to know your strengths and use them to your advantage.

For example, if you learn best by visualization, focus on visualizing a concept in your mind and draw an image or a diagram. Try color-coding your notes, illustrating them, or creating symbols that will trigger your mind to recall a learned concept. If you learn best by hearing or discussing information, find a study partner who learns the same way or read aloud to yourself. Think about how to put the information in your own words. Imagine that you are giving a lecture on the topic and record yourself so you can listen to it later.

For any learning style, flashcards can be helpful. Organize the information so you can take advantage of spare moments to review. Underline key words or phrases. Use different colors for different categories. Mnemonic devices (such as creating a short list in which every item starts with the same letter) can also help with retention. Find what works best for you and use it to store the information in your mind most effectively and easily.

Copyright © Mometrix Media. You have been licensed one copy of this document for personal use only. Any other reproduction or redistribution is strictly prohibited. All rights reserved.
This content is provided for test preparation purposes only and does not imply an endorsement by Mometrix of any particular political, scientific, or religious point of view.

Strategy #3 – Practice the Right Way

Your success on test day depends not only on how many hours you put into preparing, but also on whether you prepared the right way. It's good to check along the way to see if your studying is paying off. One of the most effective ways to do this is by taking practice tests to evaluate your progress. Practice tests are useful because they show exactly where you need to improve. Every time you take a practice test, pay special attention to these three groups of questions:

- The questions you got wrong
- The questions you had to guess on, even if you guessed right
- The questions you found difficult or slow to work through

This will show you exactly what your weak areas are, and where you need to devote more study time. Ask yourself why each of these questions gave you trouble. Was it because you didn't understand the material? Was it because you didn't remember the vocabulary? Do you need more repetitions on this type of question to build speed and confidence? Dig into those questions and figure out how you can strengthen your weak areas as you go back to review the material.

Additionally, many practice tests have a section explaining the answer choices. It can be tempting to read the explanation and think that you now have a good understanding of the concept. However, an explanation likely only covers part of the question's broader context. Even if the explanation makes perfect sense, **go back and investigate** every concept related to the question until you're positive you have a thorough understanding.

As you go along, keep in mind that the practice test is just that: practice. Memorizing these questions and answers will not be very helpful on the actual test because it is unlikely to have any of the same exact questions. If you only know the right answers to the sample questions, you won't be prepared for the real thing. **Study the concepts** until you understand them fully, and then you'll be able to answer any question that shows up on the test.

It's important to wait on the practice tests until you're ready. If you take a test on your first day of study, you may be overwhelmed by the amount of material covered and how much you need to learn. Work up to it gradually.

On test day, you'll need to be prepared for answering questions, managing your time, and using the test-taking strategies you've learned. It's a lot to balance, like a mental marathon that will have a big impact on your future. Like training for a marathon, you'll need to start slowly and work your way up. When test day arrives, you'll be ready.

Start with the strategies you've read in the first two Success Strategies—plan your course and study in the way that works best for you. If you have time, consider using multiple study resources to get different approaches to the same concepts. It can be helpful to see difficult concepts from more than one angle. Then find a good source for practice tests. Many times, the test website will suggest potential study resources or provide sample tests.

Copyright © Mometrix Media. You have been licensed one copy of this document for personal use only. Any other reproduction or redistribution is strictly prohibited. All rights reserved.
This content is provided for test preparation purposes only and does not imply an endorsement by Mometrix of any particular political, scientific, or religious point of view.

Practice Test Strategy

If you're able to find at least three practice tests, we recommend this strategy:

Untimed and Open-Book Practice

Take the first test with no time constraints and with your notes and study guide handy. Take your time and focus on applying the strategies you've learned.

Timed and Open-Book Practice

Take the second practice test open-book as well, but set a timer and practice pacing yourself to finish in time.

Timed and Closed-Book Practice

Take any other practice tests as if it were test day. Set a timer and put away your study materials. Sit at a table or desk in a quiet room, imagine yourself at the testing center, and answer questions as quickly and accurately as possible.

Keep repeating timed and closed-book tests on a regular basis until you run out of practice tests or it's time for the actual test. Your mind will be ready for the schedule and stress of test day, and you'll be able to focus on recalling the material you've learned.

Copyright © Mometrix Media. You have been licensed one copy of this document for personal use only. Any other reproduction or redistribution is strictly prohibited. All rights reserved.
This content is provided for test preparation purposes only and does not imply an endorsement by Mometrix of any particular political, scientific, or religious point of view.

Strategy #4 – Pace Yourself

Once you're fully prepared for the material on the test, your biggest challenge on test day will be managing your time. Just knowing that the clock is ticking can make you panic even if you have plenty of time left. Work on pacing yourself so you can build confidence against the time constraints of the exam. Pacing is a difficult skill to master, especially in a high-pressure environment, so **practice is vital**.

Set time expectations for your pace based on how much time is available. For example, if a section has 60 questions and the time limit is 30 minutes, you know you have to average 30 seconds or less per question in order to answer them all. Although 30 seconds is the hard limit, set 25 seconds per question as your goal, so you reserve extra time to spend on harder questions. When you budget extra time for the harder questions, you no longer have any reason to stress when those questions take longer to answer.

Don't let this time expectation distract you from working through the test at a calm, steady pace, but keep it in mind so you don't spend too much time on any one question. Recognize that taking extra time on one question you don't understand may keep you from answering two that you do understand later in the test. If your time limit for a question is up and you're still not sure of the answer, mark it and move on, and come back to it later if the time and the test format allow. If the testing format doesn't allow you to return to earlier questions, just make an educated guess; then put it out of your mind and move on.

On the easier questions, be careful not to rush. It may seem wise to hurry through them so you have more time for the challenging ones, but it's not worth missing one if you know the concept and just didn't take the time to read the question fully. Work efficiently but make sure you understand the question and have looked at all of the answer choices, since more than one may seem right at first.

Even if you're paying attention to the time, you may find yourself a little behind at some point. You should speed up to get back on track, but do so wisely. Don't panic; just take a few seconds less on each question until you're caught up. Don't guess without thinking, but do look through the answer choices and eliminate any you know are wrong. If you can get down to two choices, it is often worthwhile to guess from those. Once you've chosen an answer, move on and don't dwell on any that you skipped or had to hurry through. If a question was taking too long, chances are it was one of the harder ones, so you weren't as likely to get it right anyway.

On the other hand, if you find yourself getting ahead of schedule, it may be beneficial to slow down a little. The more quickly you work, the more likely you are to make a careless mistake that will affect your score. You've budgeted time for each question, so don't be afraid to spend that time. Practice an efficient but careful pace to get the most out of the time you have.

Copyright © Mometrix Media. You have been licensed one copy of this document for personal use only. Any other reproduction or redistribution is strictly prohibited. All rights reserved.
This content is provided for test preparation purposes only and does not imply an endorsement by Mometrix of any particular political, scientific, or religious point of view.

Test-Taking Strategies

This section contains a list of test-taking strategies that you may find helpful as you work through the test. By taking what you know and applying logical thought, you can maximize your chances of answering any question correctly!

It is very important to realize that every question is different and every person is different: no single strategy will work on every question, and no single strategy will work for every person. That's why we've included all of them here, so you can try them out and determine which ones work best for different types of questions and which ones work best for you.

Question Strategies

✓ Read Carefully

Read the question and the answer choices carefully. Don't miss the question because you misread the terms. You have plenty of time to read each question thoroughly and make sure you understand what is being asked. Yet a happy medium must be attained, so don't waste too much time. You must read carefully and efficiently.

✓ Contextual Clues

Look for contextual clues. If the question includes a word you are not familiar with, look at the immediate context for some indication of what the word might mean. Contextual clues can often give you all the information you need to decipher the meaning of an unfamiliar word. Even if you can't determine the meaning, you may be able to narrow down the possibilities enough to make a solid guess at the answer to the question.

✓ Prefixes

If you're having trouble with a word in the question or answer choices, try dissecting it. Take advantage of every clue that the word might include. Prefixes can be a huge help. Usually, they allow you to determine a basic meaning. *Pre-* means before, *post-* means after, *pro-* is positive, *de-* is negative. From prefixes, you can get an idea of the general meaning of the word and try to put it into context.

✓ Hedge Words

Watch out for critical hedge words, such as *likely, may, can, often, almost, mostly, usually, generally, rarely*, and *sometimes*. Question writers insert these hedge phrases to cover every possibility. Often an answer choice will be wrong simply because it leaves no room for exception. Be on guard for answer choices that have definitive words such as *exactly* and *always*.

✓ Switchback Words

Stay alert for *switchbacks*. These are the words and phrases frequently used to alert you to shifts in thought. The most common switchback words are *but, although*, and *however*. Others include *nevertheless, on the other hand, even though, while, in spite of, despite*, and *regardless of*. Switchback words are important to catch because they can change the direction of the question or an answer choice.

Copyright © Mometrix Media. You have been licensed one copy of this document for personal use only. Any other reproduction or redistribution is strictly prohibited. All rights reserved.
This content is provided for test preparation purposes only and does not imply an endorsement by Mometrix of any particular political, scientific, or religious point of view.

✓ Face Value

When in doubt, use common sense. Accept the situation in the problem at face value. Don't read too much into it. These problems will not require you to make wild assumptions. If you have to go beyond creativity and warp time or space in order to have an answer choice fit the question, then you should move on and consider the other answer choices. These are normal problems rooted in reality. The applicable relationship or explanation may not be readily apparent, but it is there for you to figure out. Use your common sense to interpret anything that isn't clear.

Answer Choice Strategies

✓ Answer Selection

The most thorough way to pick an answer choice is to identify and eliminate wrong answers until only one is left, then confirm it is the correct answer. Sometimes an answer choice may immediately seem right, but be careful. The test writers will usually put more than one reasonable answer choice on each question, so take a second to read all of them and make sure that the other choices are not equally obvious. As long as you have time left, it is better to read every answer choice than to pick the first one that looks right without checking the others.

✓ Answer Choice Families

An answer choice family consists of two (in rare cases, three) answer choices that are very similar in construction and cannot all be true at the same time. If you see two answer choices that are direct opposites or parallels, one of them is usually the correct answer. For instance, if one answer choice says that quantity *x* increases and another either says that quantity *x* decreases (opposite) or says that quantity *y* increases (parallel), then those answer choices would fall into the same family. An answer choice that doesn't match the construction of the answer choice family is more likely to be incorrect. Most questions will not have answer choice families, but when they do appear, you should be prepared to recognize them.

✓ Eliminate Answers

Eliminate answer choices as soon as you realize they are wrong, but make sure you consider all possibilities. If you are eliminating answer choices and realize that the last one you are left with is also wrong, don't panic. Start over and consider each choice again. There may be something you missed the first time that you will realize on the second pass.

✓ Avoid Fact Traps

Don't be distracted by an answer choice that is factually true but doesn't answer the question. You are looking for the choice that answers the question. Stay focused on what the question is asking for so you don't accidentally pick an answer that is true but incorrect. Always go back to the question and make sure the answer choice you've selected actually answers the question and is not merely a true statement.

✓ Extreme Statements

In general, you should avoid answers that put forth extreme actions as standard practice or proclaim controversial ideas as established fact. An answer choice that states the "process should be used in certain situations, if..." is much more likely to be correct than one that states the "process should be discontinued completely." The first is a calm rational statement and doesn't even make a definitive, uncompromising stance, using a hedge word *if* to provide wiggle room, whereas the second choice is far more extreme.

Copyright © Mometrix Media. You have been licensed one copy of this document for personal use only. Any other reproduction or redistribution is strictly prohibited. All rights reserved.
This content is provided for test preparation purposes only and does not imply an endorsement by Mometrix of any particular political, scientific, or religious point of view.

⊘ BENCHMARK

As you read through the answer choices and you come across one that seems to answer the question well, mentally select that answer choice. This is not your final answer, but it's the one that will help you evaluate the other answer choices. The one that you selected is your benchmark or standard for judging each of the other answer choices. Every other answer choice must be compared to your benchmark. That choice is correct until proven otherwise by another answer choice beating it. If you find a better answer, then that one becomes your new benchmark. Once you've decided that no other choice answers the question as well as your benchmark, you have your final answer.

⊘ PREDICT THE ANSWER

Before you even start looking at the answer choices, it is often best to try to predict the answer. When you come up with the answer on your own, it is easier to avoid distractions and traps because you will know exactly what to look for. The right answer choice is unlikely to be word-for-word what you came up with, but it should be a close match. Even if you are confident that you have the right answer, you should still take the time to read each option before moving on.

General Strategies

⊘ TOUGH QUESTIONS

If you are stumped on a problem or it appears too hard or too difficult, don't waste time. Move on! Remember though, if you can quickly check for obviously incorrect answer choices, your chances of guessing correctly are greatly improved. Before you completely give up, at least try to knock out a couple of possible answers. Eliminate what you can and then guess at the remaining answer choices before moving on.

⊘ CHECK YOUR WORK

Since you will probably not know every term listed and the answer to every question, it is important that you get credit for the ones that you do know. Don't miss any questions through careless mistakes. If at all possible, try to take a second to look back over your answer selection and make sure you've selected the correct answer choice and haven't made a costly careless mistake (such as marking an answer choice that you didn't mean to mark). This quick double check should more than pay for itself in caught mistakes for the time it costs.

⊘ PACE YOURSELF

It's easy to be overwhelmed when you're looking at a page full of questions; your mind is confused and full of random thoughts, and the clock is ticking down faster than you would like. Calm down and maintain the pace that you have set for yourself. Especially as you get down to the last few minutes of the test, don't let the small numbers on the clock make you panic. As long as you are on track by monitoring your pace, you are guaranteed to have time for each question.

⊘ DON'T RUSH

It is very easy to make errors when you are in a hurry. Maintaining a fast pace in answering questions is pointless if it makes you miss questions that you would have gotten right otherwise. Test writers like to include distracting information and wrong answers that seem right. Taking a little extra time to avoid careless mistakes can make all the difference in your test score. Find a pace that allows you to be confident in the answers that you select.

Copyright © Mometrix Media. You have been licensed one copy of this document for personal use only. Any other reproduction or redistribution is strictly prohibited. All rights reserved.
This content is provided for test preparation purposes only and does not imply an endorsement by Mometrix of any particular political, scientific, or religious point of view.

⊘ Keep Moving

Panicking will not help you pass the test, so do your best to stay calm and keep moving. Taking deep breaths and going through the answer elimination steps you practiced can help to break through a stress barrier and keep your pace.

Final Notes

The combination of a solid foundation of content knowledge and the confidence that comes from practicing your plan for applying that knowledge is the key to maximizing your performance on test day. As your foundation of content knowledge is built up and strengthened, you'll find that the strategies included in this chapter become more and more effective in helping you quickly sift through the distractions and traps of the test to isolate the correct answer.

Now that you're preparing to move forward into the test content chapters of this book, be sure to keep your goal in mind. As you read, think about how you will be able to apply this information on the test. If you've already seen sample questions for the test and you have an idea of the question format and style, try to come up with questions of your own that you can answer based on what you're reading. This will give you valuable practice applying your knowledge in the same ways you can expect to on test day.

Good luck and good studying!

Copyright © Mometrix Media. You have been licensed one copy of this document for personal use only. Any other reproduction or redistribution is strictly prohibited. All rights reserved.
This content is provided for test preparation purposes only and does not imply an endorsement by Mometrix of any particular political, scientific, or religious point of view.

Reading

Using Print and Digital Resources

Dictionary

A print or digital dictionary can be used to find out many things about a word. A dictionary will show the correct pronunciation of a word, provide its meaning, and identify what part of speech the word is. It will also tell how the word was derived—that is, what words it came from originally. A dictionary will have a guide that shows how to sound out the words; it will use symbols to indicate sounds, and will also use sample sounds (the "a" in "bad," for instance). A dictionary lists all of the meanings of a word and the parts of speech the word can be used as.

Example:

Philippe used his dictionary to check the various meanings of the word *eliminate*. He found this entry:

> eliminate \ i-ˈli-mə-ˌnāt \ verb
> 1. to put an end to or get rid of
> 2. to expel from the living body
> 3. to cause to disappear by combining two or more equations

Identify which definition of *eliminate* is used in the following sentence:

> Harold couldn't wait to *eliminate* the other team from the playoffs by winning the first two games.

The correct answer is meaning 1: "to put an end to or get rid of." If you substitute that definition for the word, the sentence makes sense. Meanings 2 and 3 do not fit with the context of the sentence. When considering which meaning is being used, always check for context clues in the sentence or in the sentences before or after the sentence in which the word is used. Dictionaries also tell you how to pronounce words and often the derivation of the word, although that is not given here.

Thesaurus

A thesaurus is a reference book that gives synonyms of words. It is different from a dictionary because a thesaurus does not give definitions. A thesaurus can be helpful in finding the meaning of an unfamiliar word when reading. If the meaning of a synonym is known, then the meaning of the unfamiliar word will be known. Another time in which a thesaurus can be helpful is when writing. Using a thesaurus helps authors to vary their word choice.

Glossary

A glossary is a list of terms and their definitions that can be found at the back of certain types of books, such as textbooks or reference books. A glossary does not have the definitions of all words, like a dictionary, but instead gives the definitions of the important terms within that particular book which are either uncommon or newly introduced. One may use a glossary when reading a book about economics or a chapter in a science textbook, for example, to define some of the technical terms within the text.

Copyright © Mometrix Media. You have been licensed one copy of this document for personal use only. Any other reproduction or redistribution is strictly prohibited. All rights reserved.
This content is provided for test preparation purposes only and does not imply an endorsement by Mometrix of any particular political, scientific, or religious point of view.

Denotative and Connotative Meaning

The **denotative meaning** of a word is the exact dictionary definition of the word. The **connotative meaning** of a word is the emotion conveyed by the use of the word in context. The word may have associated meaning in addition to its dictionary definition. A good way to remember the difference between denotative and connotative is to think "direct" or "dictionary" in relation to denotative.

An example of a denotative meaning for the adjective *ablaze* would be "burning", as in the logs burning in a fireplace. A connotative meaning for the adjective *ablaze*, based on the context of the word, may indicate a level of comfort while sitting in front of a fireplace. For instance, in the context: "A logs were *ablaze* in the fireplace, radiating heat out into the corners of the snow-enclosed room", the word *ablaze* implies comfort and coziness within the space described. The connotative meaning of a word can often have an emotional association for the reader.

Example

Define the denotative and connotative meaning of the word *palace* in the following sentence:

> The golden *palace* gates opened slowly to reveal an expansive garden that was well-tended by precise gardeners all wearing the king's insignia.

In the example, the denotative meaning of the word is that a *palace* is literally a place where royalty lives. A *palace* implies, or connotes, a place of riches and is usually associated with wealth. The words "golden", "expansive garden", and "king's insignia" all give clues that the *palace* can be viewed as a place of importance, one that is well taken care of.

When looking for the denotative meaning of a word, remember to think "direct", or the literal meaning of the word. The connotative meaning of the word is implied and not directly stated; the connotative meaning is often associated with emotion and feeling about the typical context of the word.

Derivative of a Word

The derivative of a word is the final product after a word has undergone a change from its original form. For example, the word *fruit* refers to seed-containing products of a tree or plant that are often consumed by humans. If a prefix or suffix is added onto the root word *fruit*, the meaning of the word is changed. The suffix *-ful* added onto *fruit* to form the word *fruitful* would mean "full of fruit" or, more accurately, "abundant growth". Note that the meaning of the derivative, or final word form, changed from the meaning of the root word. If a word has been changed from its original form, it can have an entirely different meaning based on what prefixes or suffixes have been added onto the root word.

Using Specialized Reference Materials to Determine the Pronunciation of a Word

A print or digital dictionary can be used as a means to find the correct pronunciation of words. The dictionary will have a **phonetic** spelling that uses symbols to show how to correctly pronounce the words.

Example

This chart shows three common symbols used in phonetic spellings of words along with a word the phoneme appears in

ʊ	ə	ŋ
g<u>oo</u>d	teach<u>er</u>	si<u>ng</u>

Copyright © Mometrix Media. You have been licensed one copy of this document for personal use only. Any other reproduction or redistribution is strictly prohibited. All rights reserved.
This content is provided for test preparation purposes only and does not imply an endorsement by Mometrix of any particular political, scientific, or religious point of view.

Use Context to Clarify Word Meaning

FINDING WORD MEANINGS

Readers of all levels will encounter words that they have either never seen or that they have seen before but still don't know what it means. The best way to define a word in **context** is to look for nearby words that can assist in learning the meaning of the word.

CONTEXT CLUES

Context clues are hints about the meaning of a word. They are the words or phrases in the sentence or sentences before and after a new or unfamiliar word. Context clues give the reader an idea about what a word means. A context clue may also contain words that help define the new word or an example of what the new word means. A context clue in the form of an example may contain the words including 'such as', a dash, or a colon before stated information.

Using context clues to figure out meaning can be helpful when learning a new set of vocabulary words or reading a difficult text. The dictionary definition of a word can always be looked up to double-check intended meaning.

Review Video: Reading Comprehension: Using Context Clues
Visit mometrix.com/academy and enter code: 613660

SYNONYMS AND ANTONYMS

When you understand how words relate to each other, you will discover more in a passage. This is explained by understanding **synonyms** (words that mean the same thing) and **antonyms** (words that mean the opposite of one another). As an example, *dry* and *arid* are synonyms, and *dry* and *wet* are antonyms.

EXAMPLE 1

Using context clues, determine the meaning of *gregarious* in the following excerpt.

> Beverly is the most *gregarious* person I have ever known. She loves people and spends a lot of her time talking to her friends and arranging get-togethers. She doesn't mind spending hours cooking as long as she knows that her house will be filled with people.

This excerpt says Beverly loves people and spends a lot of her time talking with friends and arranging get-togethers. It also says that she likes her house filled with people. These clues in the sentence help the reader determine that *gregarious* means Beverly is someone who likes to talk with other people, so she is "sociable."

EXAMPLE 2

Read the sentence and explain the meaning of *sense of foreboding:*

> All day long Ron kept thinking about Sue. For some unknown reason he was worried about her. He had a strong *sense of foreboding* that something was about to go wrong in Sue's city. Then he heard about the earthquake there. Luckily Sue was not injured.

To figure out the meaning of the phrase *sense of foreboding*, the reader needs to look for context clues in just the same way the reader would do to figure out the meaning of a single word. The excerpt says that Ron was "worried" about Sue for "some unknown reason." It also says that he felt

Copyright © Mometrix Media. You have been licensed one copy of this document for personal use only. Any other reproduction or redistribution is strictly prohibited. All rights reserved.
This content is provided for test preparation purposes only and does not imply an endorsement by Mometrix of any particular political, scientific, or religious point of view.

that "something was going to go wrong in Sue's city." Ron also heard about an earthquake taking place in Sue's city. A "sense of foreboding" must mean that Ron had an idea that something bad was going to happen. The context clues help the reader figure out the meaning of the phrase.

EXPERIENCE TO DETERMINE WORD MEANING

The more words a person is exposed to, the greater their vocabulary will become. By reading on a regular basis, a person can increase the number of ways they have seen a word in context. Based on experience, a person can recall how a word was used in the past and apply that knowledge to a new context.

For example, a person may have seen the word *gull* used to mean a bird that is found near the seashore. However, a *gull* can also be a person who is easily tricked. If the word is used in context in reference to a character, the reader can recognize that the character is being called a bird that is not seen as extremely intelligent. Using what the reader knows about a word can be useful when making comparisons or figuring out the meaning of a new use of a word, as in figurative language, idioms, analogies, and multiple-meaning words.

EXAMPLE 3

Using experience, determine the definition of the multiple-meaning word *basin* in the following sentence:

> The *basin* had filled with water over the summer months, so that the rocky bottom was no longer visible to the casual hiker.

A *basin* can be either a bowl filled with water or a depression in the earth. Looking at the context of the word in the sentence, the second definition is correct in this case. Knowing multiple definitions of a word can help when figuring out which definition applies in a sentence. If the definition of a word is not known, however, look at the context of the word. In the example, the reader knows that the *basin* had to be deep enough to fill with water. The reader also knows that the bottom of the *basin* had been filled with rock, and that the location is outdoors. Hikers are normally able to see the bottom of the *basin*, so it must be a large depression in the earth.

SUBSTITUTION TO FIND MEANING

One way to find out if you have figured out the correct meaning of a new word is to substitute the meaning for the word. Using the example for *basin*, if the reader substituted in "depression in the earth," the sentence would read:

> The "depression in the earth" had filled with water over the summer months, so that the rocky bottom was no longer visible to the casual hiker.

This is a way for the reader to confirm that they have used the context clues in the sentence correctly.

MULTIPLE-MEANING WORDS

A multiple-meaning word has different definitions, depending on the contextual use of the word. A multiple-meaning word is also called a **homonym**. A homonym is defined as a word that has more than one meaning, but is spelled and pronounced the same for all of them. For example, look at the word *leaves* in the following two sentences:

1. Michelle *leaves* the building at 5 o'clock every day.
2. The *leaves* fell off the oak tree in September.

Copyright © Mometrix Media. You have been licensed one copy of this document for personal use only. Any other reproduction or redistribution is strictly prohibited. All rights reserved.
This content is provided for test preparation purposes only and does not imply an endorsement by Mometrix of any particular political, scientific, or religious point of view.

In the first sentence, *leaves* means exits. In the second sentence, *leaves* refers to parts of a tree. By looking at the rest of each sentence, the reader can understand which definition of the multiple-meaning word the author is referring to.

Similar Words

Homophones are words that are pronounced the same, but may be spelled differently. An example of two homophones would be *heir* (someone due to inherit an estate) and *air* (the invisible substance people breathe).

Homographs are words that are spelled the same, but may be pronounced differently. An example of a homograph is the word *row*, which is pronounced one way when used to mean a horizontal grouping and is pronounced another way when used to mean an argument.

Using Roots to Determine Meaning

Affixes and Roots

A **root word** is a word that can be added onto. An **affix** is a prefix or suffix that is added onto a root word. Often, the affixes in the English language come from Latin or Greek origins. A **prefix** is added to the beginning of a root word and a **suffix** is added to the end of a root word.

For example, the word "inscription" is made up of three sections. The root *script* means "write" or "writing." There are two affixes in the word. The prefix *in-* can mean various things such as "not," but also "on." In this case it means "on." The suffix *-tion* means "action" or "process." So, put together, the word "inscription" means "the act of writing on." Studying roots and affixes is important because it allows you to decode words you might not otherwise understand with relative ease.

Common Prefixes

Prefix	Meaning	Example
Dis-	Not	Disagree
Im-	Not	Impossibly (not possible)
In-	In, into, not	Injustice (not just)
Mis-	Wrongly	Misspell
Non-	Not	Nonpaid (not paid)
Pre-	Before	Preview (to view before)
Sub-	Under	Submerge (to sink below the surface)
Super-	Over or greater than	Superhuman (greater than a regular human)
Trans-	Across, through, or change	Translate (to write or say in a different language)

Common Suffixes

Suffix	Meaning	Example
[illegible]	[illegible]	[illegible]

Copyright © Mometrix Media. You have been licensed one copy of this document for personal use only. Any other reproduction or redistribution is strictly prohibited. All rights reserved.
This content is provided for test preparation purposes only and does not imply an endorsement by Mometrix of any particular political, scientific, or religious point of view.

Latin Root Words

Latin Root	Meaning	Example
[illegible]	[illegible]	[illegible]
[illegible]	[illegible]	[illegible]
[illegible]	[illegible]	[illegible]
[illegible]	[illegible]	[illegible]
[illegible]	[illegible]	[illegible]
[illegible]	[illegible]	[illegible]
[illegible]	[illegible]	[illegible]
[illegible]	[illegible]	[illegible]

Greek Root Words

Root	Meaning	Example
[illegible]	[illegible]	[illegible]
[illegible]	[illegible]	[illegible]
[illegible]	[illegible]	[illegible]
[illegible]	[illegible]	[illegible]
[illegible]	[illegible]	[illegible]

Example

Use knowledge of affixes to figure out the meaning of the word *mournful* in the following sentence:

> "Well, it being away in the night and stormy, and all so mysterious-like, I felt just the way any other boy would a felt when I see that wreck laying there so *mournful* and lonesome in the middle of the river." (From *The Adventures of Huckleberry Finn* by Mark Twain).

Mourn means to grieve for something, while *-ful* refers to being "full of". Putting the two components together, *mournful* means "full of grief or sadness". This definition makes sense in the context of the sentence. The "wreck" in the sentence is sad looking because it is in the river by itself.

When trying to determine the meaning of a word, always look for a root word and any prefixes or suffixes that have been added on to the root word. If a component of a word is not familiar, decipher what is clear about the word, then look at the word as used in context.

Main Idea and Supporting Details

Main Idea and Supporting Details

The main idea in a passage is usually located in the first paragraph or two of text. Having the main idea near the beginning of the passage allows the author to grab the reader's attention and let them know what the rest of the passage will discuss.

To find the main idea in a passage, there are questions the reader can ask while reading: What is this passage about? What does the author want the reader to know about the topic? The supporting details will provide evidence that the main idea is correct and are found in the body of a passage. The supporting details often provide examples of the main idea.

For example, a passage may contain the main idea: "Ellis Island was an entry-point to America for many immigrants during the Industrial Revolution." A supporting detail for the main idea may be "Immigrants were examined for contagious diseases at Ellis Island before being granted entry to America."

Review Video: Thesis Statements
Visit mometrix.com/academy and enter code: 691033

Copyright © Mometrix Media. You have been licensed one copy of this document for personal use only. Any other reproduction or redistribution is strictly prohibited. All rights reserved.
This content is provided for test preparation purposes only and does not imply an endorsement by Mometrix of any particular political, scientific, or religious point of view.

EXAMPLE 1

Determine the main idea the following sentence tells the reader and indicate what details support the main idea:

> Her breath billowed out in clouds of white and disappeared into the quiet air.

The main idea is what the author wants the reader to understand about the text. Details help to explain or support that main idea. A main idea usually states the point of an entire essay, article, or book, but can be simply stated in one sentence. The main idea in the sentence above is that a girl is outside in the cold. Details to support this statement include the word 'her,' showing that the character is a girl, and 'clouds of white,' which indicate that the air is cold. In order to conclude that the girl is out in the cold, the reader needs to understand that breath can be seen when the air is cold.

SUPPORTING DETAILS

Provide evidence and backing for the main point. All texts contain details, but they are only classified as supporting details when they serve to reinforce some larger point. Supporting details are most commonly found in informative and persuasive texts. In some cases, they will be clearly indicated with words like **for example** or **for instance**, or they will begin with words like **first**, **second**, and **last**. However, these special words are not a requirement. As a reader, it is important to consider whether the author's supporting details really back up his or her main point. Supporting details can be factual and correct but still not relevant to the author's point. Sometimes, supporting details can seem important but they might not support the main idea in the story well because they are based on opinion that cannot be proven.

EXAMPLE 2

Decide whether the following sentence is the main point or a supporting point of a text, and state where the information would be placed in an outline:

> One type of horseback riding, bareback horseback riding, involves sitting on a moving horse without a saddle and grasping the horse's mane.

This sentence is a supporting point, with the main point of the entire text likely about horseback riding in general. As a supporting point, this sentence would go further down in an outline, next to any numeral after numeral I. This sentence can be followed by additional sub-points that further explain the concept of bareback horseback riding. When a supporting point is used to clarify a main point or topic, the supporting point helps to break the topic down into smaller pieces.

OPPOSITE POINT OF VIEW

After identifying the main idea, readers can increase their understanding of the text if they think about what the opposite point of view would be.

Read the following topic sentence. Describe what the opposite point of view would include:

> The new bike path at the public park provides families in the community with a safe opportunity to get some fresh air on the weekends.

This topic sentence could be taken in several different directions. The main focus of the sentence is that the bike path is safe and allows for families to get out and enjoy some fresh air on the weekends. The opposite point of view may state that the new bike path is unsafe and the air is polluted. An example of a topic sentence with the opposite point of view may state: The new bike

Copyright © Mometrix Media. You have been licensed one copy of this document for personal use only. Any other reproduction or redistribution is strictly prohibited. All rights reserved.
This content is provided for test preparation purposes only and does not imply an endorsement by Mometrix of any particular political, scientific, or religious point of view.

path at Primer School is unsafe for families in the community to travel on the weekends and goes through a polluted area.

When looking for the main point in a sentence, look for keywords that define the sentence. In the sentence about the bike path, we know that the path is new, seems safe, and has fresh air. By changing around these keywords, the entire meaning of the sentence can be shifted.

Central Argument

A **central argument** is the main point of a book or essay. It is the author's **opinion** and is usually the **reason** they are writing the book or essay. It can be structured in several different ways including argument by cause and effect, argument by analogy, and argument by authority. When an author uses argument by cause and effect, they are trying to convince the reader that a certain cause will produce a specific effect. An argument by analogy uses perceived similarities as a basis in order to argue for some further similarity that has not yet been observed. Finally, an argument by authority is being used when an author argues for something on the basis of someone's authority. This can be a positive thing when the referenced person's authority involves having a great deal of knowledge on the subject, but would be considered a logical fallacy if the person's authority is unrelated to the subject of the argument.

Themes

Theme

The **theme** of a story is a unifying idea that is used throughout the text; it can take the form of a common setting, idea, symbol, design, or recurring event. The theme of a story may vary according to place, time, and characters, but theme is often based on common human experience. A plot line is built around the theme of a story. Most themes are about life, society, or human nature. The theme is often why a passage is written. It helps give a passage unity. The theme is created through the development of the story. The events of a story help shape the kind of theme the passage. A theme is not usually stated explicitly. The reader **infers** the theme from the topic, information, or plot of a passage.

For example, a series of events in a story may be based upon people being willing to trust the actions of others. The story may be centered on why people need to trust others in order to carry out important actions. For example, a character may trust that a bus driver will stay on the road while the bus driver, in turn, trusts that the passengers stay in their seats so that they do not distract him.

The theme of a story is not the same as the topic of a story. The topic is what the story is about, but the theme is what a reader is meant to learn. When readers are discussing theme, they can determine both theme topics as well as theme statements.

Theme topics are broad ideas that apply to the text. Examples include:

- Love changes people
- Man versus man
- Man versus nature
- Man versus himself
- Fate versus free will
- Triumph over adversity
- Coming of age

Copyright © Mometrix Media. You have been licensed one copy of this document for personal use only. Any other reproduction or redistribution is strictly prohibited. All rights reserved.
This content is provided for test preparation purposes only and does not imply an endorsement by Mometrix of any particular political, scientific, or religious point of view.

- The importance of friendship
- Good vs. evil
- The circle of life

Theme statements are specific ideas that must be written in sentence form, and usually contain the name of the work and the author. Examples include:

- In *The City of Ember* by Jeanne DuPrau, the author shows how acts of courage can bring positive changes to the world.
- The author of *Uglies*, Scott Westerfeld, introduces readers to a futuristic world where the idea of what makes a person beautiful is explored.

EXAMPLE 1

Tell why the theme of the following excerpt should be "Overconfidence can lead to a fall."

> Bella was happy. She auditioned for the starring role in the school play and she felt sure she'd got the part. Afterwards, she told her friends she would be starring in the play. But on Tuesday when the director said they had offered the part to Sara Goodwin, she started crying.

The excerpt tells the story of a girl who has an audition and thinks she got the starring role. She is so confident that she even tells her friends that she has the part. But then she learns that the role was offered to someone else and she starts to cry. She was overly confident about her success and was subsequently devastated when she learned of her failure, and that is the lesson of the story. If you are overly confident you may have a fall. That is the theme of the story. A theme is the lesson that a story teaches. This particular theme is found often in literature. A theme is not stated in a passage: the reader must deduce it from the plot of the story.

UNIVERSAL THEMES

Some themes are fairly common. These themes are called **universal themes** and they suggest things about life, society, and human nature. If a reader is trying to decide whether a theme is universal or not, they must consider whether the theme they have identified can be applied to other works as well. Some examples of universal theme topics are

GOOD VERSUS EVIL

- The universal theme of a small number of people invested in doing good works becoming a powerful force against those doing evil works can be seen in multiple texts, including the *Harry Potter* series by J.K. Rowling, *The Hunger Games* by Suzanne Collins, and *Cinder* by Marissa Meyer.

CHANGE VERSUS TRADITION

- *The Giver* by Lois Lowry, the *Divergent* series by Veronica Roth, and *Children of Eden* by Joey Graceffa all reveal the universal theme of the ongoing struggle for societies to welcome change rather than being stuck in tradition.

MAN VERSUS MAN

- Learning that people are capable of committing horrifying acts against other people is a universal theme evident in *The Boy in the Striped Pajamas* by John Boyne, *A Long Walk to Water* by Linda Sue Park, and *All the Light We Cannot See* by Anthony Doerr.

Copyright © Mometrix Media. You have been licensed one copy of this document for personal use only. Any other reproduction or redistribution is strictly prohibited. All rights reserved.
This content is provided for test preparation purposes only and does not imply an endorsement by Mometrix of any particular political, scientific, or religious point of view.

Paraphrasing and Summarizing

Paraphrasing and Summarizing

Paraphrasing and summarizing are two ways readers can work to understand what they read. Both involve reading a text and recalling the main points in an accurate way, but they differ in several ways.

How to Paraphrase	How to Summarize
State the message in the text in the reader's own words, while keeping the original meaning of the text Take all of the original ideas and word them in a way that the reader can better understand Put what the reader has read into their own words, rephrasing what the author has written	State main points of the text clearly and to-the-point. Take information and state it simply, in a much shorter form. Put information in a short form that keeps the main points of the whole text. Do not include many details, just the main idea of the text

Paraphrasing is often done for individual ideas, while summarizing is done for an entire block of text or ideas. Often times, a summary can be done in just one sentence, boiling down the author's words into just main idea.

Review Video: Summarizing Text
Visit mometrix.com/academy and enter code: 172903

Paraphrasing Main Point of a Sentence

Paraphrase the main point of the following two sentences:

> Emmanuel went swimming in the lake by his house, where the water reached a depth of twenty feet in the middle. He did not venture out more than six feet into the water, however.

When paraphrasing a couple sentences or an entire paragraph, always include the main point of the text being reviewed, this is what the reader needs to know about the text. In the example, the reader needs to know that Emmanuel went swimming in the lake, but not more than six feet out. A paraphrase of the text may include: Emmanuel went swimming six feet out in the lake by his house. That is the main point that the audience needs to know.

Recall that a paraphrase is stating the author's ideas in the reader's own words. A summary typically involves including the main points of a longer text, such as a novel or full story.

Summarizing Literature to Support Comprehension

When reading literature, especially demanding works, summarizing helps readers identify important information and organize it in their minds. They can also identify themes, problems, and solutions, and can sequence the story. Readers can summarize before, during, and after they read. They should use their own words, as they do when describing a personal event or giving directions. Previewing a text's organization before reading by examining the book cover, table of contents, and illustrations also aids summarizing. So does making notes of key words and ideas in a graphic organizer while reading. Graphic organizers are another useful method; readers skim the text to determine main ideas and then narrow the list with the aid of the organizer. Unimportant details

Copyright © Mometrix Media. You have been licensed one copy of this document for personal use only. Any other reproduction or redistribution is strictly prohibited. All rights reserved.
This content is provided for test preparation purposes only and does not imply an endorsement by Mometrix of any particular political, scientific, or religious point of view.

should be omitted in summaries. Summaries can include description, problem-solution, comparison-contrast, sequence, main ideas, and cause-and-effect.

Evaluation of Summaries

A summary of a literary passage is a condensation in the reader's own words of the passage's main points. Several guidelines can be used in evaluating a summary. The summary should be complete yet concise. It should be accurate, balanced, fair, neutral, and objective, excluding the reader's own opinions or reactions. It should reflect in similar proportion how much each point summarized was covered in the original passage. Summary writers should include tags of attribution, like "Macaulay argues that" to reference the original author whose ideas are represented in the summary. Summary writers should not overuse quotations: they should only quote central concepts or phrases they cannot precisely convey in words other than those of the original author. Another aspect in evaluating a summary is whether it can stand alone as a coherent, unified composition. In addition, evaluation of a summary should include whether its writer has cited the original source of the passage so that readers can find it.

Example Summary

Read the following paragraph and then give a one sentence summary statement:

> When choosing a pet, people need to think about what type of home they can offer the animal. For example, a small apartment might not be a good fit for a large dog, but could be a comfortable home for a kitten. A house that has a big yard would be great for a puppy, but a rabbit does not need a large yard.

In order to summarize, one has to identify the main idea and any supporting ideas in the author's work. The summary is an overview of the author's paragraph and will tell what it is about without getting into any of the details. The summary needs to be broad enough to cover all of the information in the author's paragraph. Here is a possible summary statement for the above paragraph:

> People need to consider a number of factors, particularly the available space they have, when choosing a pet.

Example Paraphrasing

Read the following sentences and then paraphrase the material:

> The government is debating a new health care system for our country. The Senate and the House of Representatives have both passed bills; now they need to resolve these two bills into one bill that a majority can agree on.

When paraphrasing information, one needs to read carefully and pay attention to details, then put the material away and write or tell it in their own words. One does not want to look at the material while paraphrasing to avoid plagiarizing by accident. Here is one example of a way to paraphrase the sentences:

> Our government is trying to adopt a new health care system. The Senate has passed a bill and so has the House of Representatives. Their bills are different so now they have to compromise on one bill that can be passed.

Copyright © Mometrix Media. You have been licensed one copy of this document for personal use only. Any other reproduction or redistribution is strictly prohibited. All rights reserved.
This content is provided for test preparation purposes only and does not imply an endorsement by Mometrix of any particular political, scientific, or religious point of view.

Objective Summary

An objective summary of an informational text tells what the main idea of the text is and includes the important details. It tells what the text is mostly about and includes the most important supporting details. A summary should not include too much information; it is not a paraphrase of the information. It is important to select only the most important details to include. A summary should also be objective. This is achieved by focusing on the main idea rather than any opinions that might be in the text but that are not related to the main idea. It would also not include any personal opinions on the subject.

Example 1

Read the summary and explain how to improve it.

> Edgar Degas was a great artist who broke with tradition and became an Impressionist. His paintings and sculptures are included in the collections of major museums everywhere. In his forties, his vision became poor and he worked more on sculptures because he could feel them. He died in 1917 at the age of 83. His father was a banker.

This summary is quite good. It has a main idea and includes some of the important details. The main idea is that Degas was a great artist. Supporting details include that his paintings and sculpture are included in collections of major museums as well as the fact that he had poor vision and turned to sculpting because he could feel the sculptures. While the information about his death is not perhaps the most important, it is of interest that he lived to the age of 83. The one glaring error with the summary is that it mentions the fact that his father was a banker. This does not directly relate to the main idea. It is not a supporting detail and is unimportant to the central thesis of the passage. It should be deleted.

Example 2

Read the summary and discuss how it could be improved.

> This story is about a man and a woman who moved to the West many years ago. There was a lot of information about covered wagons or "prairie schooners," as they called them. I liked the story because of that.

The summary tells the main idea of the story, but it doesn't include the details of what happens in the story. It does not include the main characters and what they did or what challenges they faced. It does not summarize the plot. Another problem with the summary is that it is not objective; it is subjective. The writer describes what he thinks about the story. But personal opinions have no place in an objective summary of a story. To improve it, the writer should remove his personal opinion and add descriptions of who was in the story, what important things happened to them, and how the story ended.

Copyright © Mometrix Media. You have been licensed one copy of this document for personal use only. Any other reproduction or redistribution is strictly prohibited. All rights reserved.
This content is provided for test preparation purposes only and does not imply an endorsement by Mometrix of any particular political, scientific, or religious point of view.

Plot Elements

Plot

The storyline of any text is also called a **plot**. The characters and events in the story determine what the plot will be. Readers may find a **plot line** useful as they try to put the events in the text in order and determine the relationships between events.

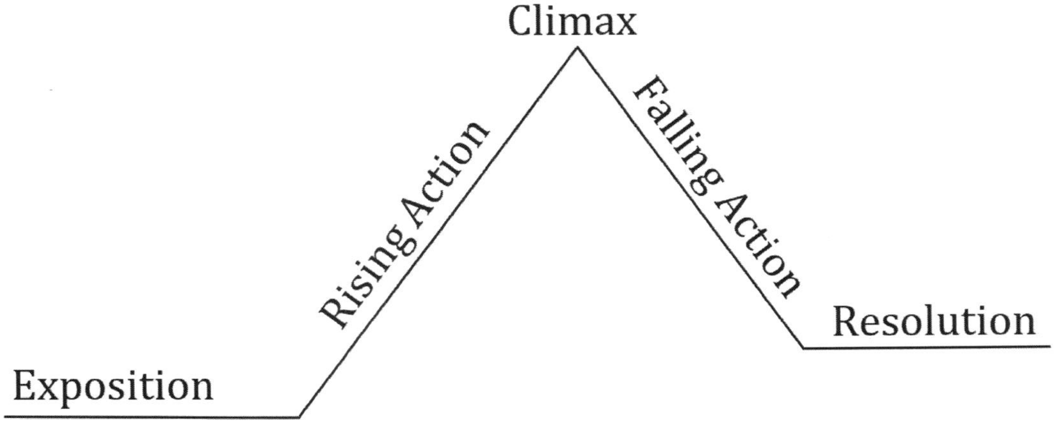

Review Video: Plot Line
Visit mometrix.com/academy and enter code: 944011

Every plot will begin with **exposition**, which introduces the characters and the setting of the story. The plot will continue to develop as new ideas and events centered on the main conflict in the story are revealed, which is called the **rising action**. The action in the story will rise until a **climax** is reached within the conflict. The climax can also be referred to as the turning point in the story, since the climax is where each character makes an important decision. After the climax, the action starts to wind down during the **falling action**. At this point, the characters begin to follow the paths they chose in during climax. The events of the story reach **resolution** in some way by the end of the story. Some conflicts are left open-ended, so that the reader is left to decide what really happened at the end of the story. Keep in mind that not all resolutions are happy or peaceful.

Example

Read the following plot and analyze what event is missing from the plot sequence.

> Martin's family decided to go camping at the local park over the weekend. They packed all the camping necessities and drove to the park. Thick sheets of rain poured down all day, so they were stuck in their tent.

Martin and his family forgot to check the weather forecast before they left for their camping trip. to fill in the missing detail, the author may write: "Martin and his family checked the forecast and saw that it was going to rain, but decided to go camping anyway." the flow of the story is broken up by the sudden realization that it is raining, something that could be prevented by adding in the missing detail.

When details are missing from a plot sequence, the audience has trouble following the action in a story. By adding in additional details, the point of each step in a story can be made clearer to the audience.

Copyright © Mometrix Media. You have been licensed one copy of this document for personal use only. Any other reproduction or redistribution is strictly prohibited. All rights reserved.
This content is provided for test preparation purposes only and does not imply an endorsement by Mometrix of any particular political, scientific, or religious point of view.

IDENTIFYING THE MAIN CONFLICT

An important part of analyzing the plot of a passage is identifying the **main conflict**. There will likely be many smaller conflicts in the story, but there will be one main problem that influences the characters and events. to identify the main conflict, first look at who the main character is. Now ask yourself what they want. They may want to something to happen or not happen, another character to do or not do something, or to confront or avoid a problem, among other things. Once you know what they want, now ask yourself what is standing in the character's way. It may be a person, an event, or something less tangible like the passing of time. Combining what the main character wants and why they do not currently have leaves the reader with a summary of the main conflict.

EXAMPLE 1

Read the following sentence from the *Call of the Wild* by Jack London and describe the main conflict in the sentence. Explain how the conflict may be resolved.

> The breaking down of discipline likewise affected the dogs in their relations with one another.

Based on the information in the sentence, an event has caused the dogs, the characters in the story, to not follow their regular routine. The sentence indicates that there has been a breaking down of discipline which is affecting how the dogs relate to each other. in order to solve this conflict, discipline needs to be restored. However, in order to return to previous relations between the dogs, any problems that are in the way of conflict resolution need to be taken care of. The word *likewise* means *also*, which tells the reader that other parts of the story are being affected besides the relations between the dogs.

EXAMPLE 2

Read the following sentence and explain the main conflict between the two characters:

> Joe stared angrily at Jamie's retreating back as Jamie raced away down the field with Joe's soccer ball.

The main conflict in the sentence is that Jamie has Joe's soccer ball. There may be additional conflicts between the two characters, but none are evident from the evidence shown in the sentence. in any story, a conflict may be minor and only affect part of the story, or be the main focus, taking an entire story to solve a conflict between characters. in the context of the sentence, it is not clear whether or not the entire story will revolve around Jamie taking Joe's soccer ball.

RESOLUTION

The term **resolution** usually indicates the result of a conflict in a story. Conflict between characters, within a character, or against an external element is necessary in order to have a plot for a story. without conflict, no events would occur to form the story. A conflict will come to a climax, and then conclude in some way. The resolution of a problem may be open-ended, end tragically, or end in a way that is good for everyone involved. The problem resolution typically occurs near the end of a story, after the climax has happened. A problem may be resolved by the characters involved within the conflict or by an external event; an upcoming resolution may be foreshadowed in the text, or may be completely unexpected by the reader. If the resolution is completely unexpected, it is considered to be a **twist** in the story.

Copyright © Mometrix Media. You have been licensed one copy of this document for personal use only. Any other reproduction or redistribution is strictly prohibited. All rights reserved.
This content is provided for test preparation purposes only and does not imply an endorsement by Mometrix of any particular political, scientific, or religious point of view.

Effect of Plot On Theme

The plot builds one event at a time and over time, the plot of the story helps the reader understand the **theme**. The theme of a story is its underlying message, and should not be confused with the story's topic. For example, in a story about a man who goes to war to fight for his country, the topic is war. The theme would be what the author is saying about going to war, perhaps that patriotism should be encouraged in a nation. Themes are most often expressed as a complete sentence in what is called a **theme statement**. an example of a theme statement is "War is a necessary evil and the able-bodied citizens of a nation should fight to defend their freedoms." Themes are always based on the opinions and beliefs of the writer, so an author who does not support war might write a story that could be described by a very different theme statement, such as "War is never an acceptable choice, and citizens should peacefully protest the use of violence to solve problems."

Example

Discuss how the following sentence would impact the theme of the passage it belongs to:

> Wanda realized then that she had made a terrible mistake and she would be haunted by this experience for the rest of her life.

This sentence would impact the theme because it suggests that Wanda would never recover from something that she did and that she would remember it for the rest of her life. This ties into a theme because it is saying something about life and what Wanda realizes about her life. We do not know what she did, but the sentence clearly states that it was a mistake. We would have to read the entire passage to understand why it was a mistake and why she would be haunted, but the sentence gives us a good idea that she learned a lesson from what happened.

Effect of Plot On a Story's Characters

The plot of a story unfolds as each event follows another, shaping the characters as they react to the various events that occur. Some characters are able to resolve their problems by the end of the story, while some characters fail to overcome their predicaments. As characters respond to the events around them, they reveal more and more about their personalities. Some grow and some do not. The reader can use the events of the plot to interpret the meaning of the story and understand its characters.

Example

Read the excerpt and explain how finding the chest affects Marta.

> The map said this was the spot. Marta held her breath. Her fists were clenched into two tight balls. She lifted the shovel and scooped more sand out of the hole. There it was; she had found the chest with the diamonds. She opened the top. She would never need to work again. She smiled. It was really happening.

The event affects Marta by making her happy. The reader gets several clues that she is anxiously waiting ("Marta held her breath" and "her fists were clenched"), and that she is happy with what she found ("She smiled"). Events can cause characters to have all kinds of feelings. Here, something wonderful happened. However, events in stories are not always quite so happy. For instance, if a robber had suddenly seen Marta and the chest, he might have stolen the chest. That event would have had a very different effect on her. Readers need to pay attention to how characters are reacting to events, whether they are simply hinted at or stated in the story. in this way a reader will learn what characters are like.

Copyright © Mometrix Media. You have been licensed one copy of this document for personal use only. Any other reproduction or redistribution is strictly prohibited. All rights reserved.
This content is provided for test preparation purposes only and does not imply an endorsement by Mometrix of any particular political, scientific, or religious point of view.

Setting in Story

Setting

The setting is where a story takes place. The setting of a story may stay the same for the entire story, or change as events in the story unfold. For example, an entire story may take place in one room or cross continents as the reader follows the characters along on a trail of events.

The setting of a story is described by the author in terms of what it looks like, how the character feels, and anything else that is happening at that location at the time. For example, a character may be caught on a doorstep on a cold, rainy day. The character may feel frustrated as they shiver in the doorway, waiting for the heavy rain to let up a bit.

Shaping a Character with Setting or Plot

The setting of a story shapes character because it helps to define the situation that a character finds herself in. A character is limited to the setting of a story. For example, if a story takes place in a cold environment filled with snow and ice, this is certain to impact what actions a character can and will take. Frequently, the setting changes the way characters behave based on time. For example, the character of a woman who is a single mother in 1920 would be seen and behave very differently than a single mother in 2020.

Example

Read the excerpt and determine how the setting influences the character in this excerpt.

> She had swum too far out. The waves were higher than she thought. She was struggling hard to get to shore. She wondered if she would make it. She thought of her childhood. Had she been right to run away from home, she wondered? Just then, a lifeguard grabbed her and helped her to shore.

The setting of the ocean and the high waves creates a conflict in the character. She is worried. She thinks about her childhood and her parents. She doesn't know if she will make it to shore. This is how the setting affects the character in this excerpt. Without the high waves and the struggle, she would not become so worried and start to think about her past. She probably would not have questioned herself. This is an example of how a setting influences a character. If the waves had not been high, there probably would not have been a struggle or any self-searching of the swimmer's past.

Perception of a Story Based on Setting

The setting of a story can allow the reader to draw on personal experience about where the story takes place. If a story takes place on a farm, the reader will likely picture a rural, peaceful setting, which may go along with (or be in contrast to) the actual plot of the story. For example, a reader would not expect a scary story to occur on a farm on a sunny day. Conversely, a reader may view a dark subway as a dangerous place, while the plot of a story set there may be based on a very calm series of events. When an author is crafting a story, they need to consider what the audience may already think about a particular setting in order to properly present the events of a story for greatest impact.

Historical and Cultural Setting

Historical context influences literature in a number of ways. The style of the author's writing can be impacted by the historical period during which it was written (e.g., Dickens wrote at a time when authors were paid by the word; this is why his novels are so long). Obviously, the setting of the

Copyright © Mometrix Media. You have been licensed one copy of this document for personal use only. Any other reproduction or redistribution is strictly prohibited. All rights reserved.
This content is provided for test preparation purposes only and does not imply an endorsement by Mometrix of any particular political, scientific, or religious point of view.

book includes its historical context. In addition, dialect may be a function of the historical period of the book. When a reader understands the historical context of a particular book, he or she can have a deeper understanding of the novel. Knowing about the time period during which the author wrote, as well as the time period discussed in the novel, helps the reader understand some of the author's choices, including character motivations.

EXAMPLE

Slavery used to be the norm in Southern states. One of the major ways in which the historical context of slavery impacted literature coming out of the South was the birth of the slave narrative. Slaves wanted to have their experiences documented. After the Civil War, former slaves wrote their stories. These slave narratives have given historians valuable firsthand accounts of life in the South. From a literary perspective, slave narratives are one of the most important genres of African-American writing. Slavery influenced literature by delving into themes of power, racial injustice, and equality. Literature from this time period can help the reader better understand the perspectives and experiences of the slaves themselves, as well as the slave holders.

Mood, Voice, and Tone

STYLE, TONE, AND MOOD

Style, tone, and mood all play an important role in the development of a story. The reader's impression of a story can vary based on the *style*, *tone*, and *mood* established by the author.

- **Style** - Refers to the way an author uses words, phrases, and sentence structure. The style of the text can change depending on whether the author uses short, choppy sentences, long, elaborate sentences, formal language, or informal language.
- **Tone** - Refers to the attitude of the writer toward the subject matter. The tone can change throughout the text or stay the same. There are many ways to describe the tone of the text, such as light, playful, questioning, humorous, serious, solemn, or tense.
- **Mood** - Refers to the overall feeling conveyed by a setting. For example, a story may be dark in terms of setting, characters, and events that occur. If a story is presented in a picturesque countryside location where the characters are content and the style of speaking is elaborate, the reader will have a different impression of the story than if the setting is in a rundown house with a pale, unhappy caretaker that rarely speaks.

EXAMPLE 1

Read the following sentences. Describe how the mood of the sentences could be changed by the author.

> The waves crashed loudly against the rough peaks of the shore, sending shivers up Madeleine's spine. Dark clouds rolled in from the open sea, signaling an incoming storm.

The author uses adjectives and adverbs in the sentence to build a mood of worry and dark suspense in the setting. To change the mood of the text, the author can simply change the adjectives and adverbs used to describe the scene. For example, the following revision would make the mood of the sentences feel calmer and inviting:

> The waves lapped softly up the rounded dunes of the shore, soothing Madeleine's thoughts. Sun rays shone down from the open sky, signaling a day of calm waters.

Copyright © Mometrix Media. You have been licensed one copy of this document for personal use only. Any other reproduction or redistribution is strictly prohibited. All rights reserved.
This content is provided for test preparation purposes only and does not imply an endorsement by Mometrix of any particular political, scientific, or religious point of view.

The way an author chooses to describe a scene sets the mood of the story. An author will plan how he or she wants the scene to sound to the reader, then use the necessary adjectives and adverbs to describe the scene he or she envisions.

Example 2

Read the following sentences. Describe the style and tone that are used by the author.

> At precisely 8:55 am, he arrived at the heavy front door of the library. He glanced at the gold watch on his left wrist before pausing to tap his polished black shoes with impatience.

The style used by the author in the sentences is matter-of-fact and descriptive. The author uses proper grammar and full sentences, making the tone very formal. The reader gets a sense of urgency from the tone of the sentences, based on the character arriving "precisely" at a certain time, "glancing at his watch", and "tapping his shoes with impatience".

An author can choose the type of words to include in a paragraph based upon the image that he or she wants to portray to the audience. The author builds anticipation by using words in the example that show urgency. The audience is encouraged to read more and find out what happens next by the author's choice of words in the selection.

Characters and their Roles in Story

Conflict

The conflict in a text occurs when something goes wrong. The are many different kinds of conflicts, but they often occur either because of external forces that characters can't control (like catching a cold) or because of interactions between characters (like arguing over who to invite). Usually, the conflict is solved by the end of the story.

Review Video: Conflict
Visit mometrix.com/academy and enter code: 559550

Example 1

Read the following sentence and explain the main conflict between the two characters:

> Joe stared angrily at Jamie's retreating back as Jamie raced away down the field with Joe's soccer ball.

The main conflict in the sentence is that Jamie has Joe's soccer ball. There may be additional conflicts between the two characters, but from the evidence shown in the sentence, Joe seems to be angry that Jamie has his soccer ball.

In any story, a conflict may be minor and only affect part of the story, or be the main focus of the story. An entire story may entail solving a conflict between characters. In the context of the sentence, it is not clear whether or not the entire story will revolve around Jamie taking Joe's soccer ball. However, the current conflict is based upon that information in the sentence.

Example 2

Read the following sentence and analyze how the problem can be resolved:

> Jason had homework in five subjects over the weekend, but he also had a basketball game to attend on Saturday evening.

Copyright © Mometrix Media. You have been licensed one copy of this document for personal use only. Any other reproduction or redistribution is strictly prohibited. All rights reserved
This content is provided for test preparation purposes only and does not imply an endorsement by Mometrix of any particular political, scientific, or religious point of view.

The main problem, or conflict in the story, is that Jason has multiple obligations. He needs to complete work for school over the weekend, but he also has to, or wants to, attend a basketball game. In order to solve the problem, Jason needs to figure out how long each obligation will take. He also needs to take into account that time will be spent on daily activities, such as eating and sleeping. Once Jason figures out how much time it will take to complete homework for each subject and how much time the basketball game will take (including preparation time), he can figure out how to divide up his weekend hours. For example, Jason may say that the homework for one subject will take an hour to complete, while the homework for the other four subjects will take half an hour each. That means that Jason will need to set aside at least three hours of time to complete homework over the weekend.

Example 3

Read the following sentence from *The Call of the Wild* by Jack London and describe the main conflict in the sentence and how the conflict may be resolved:

> The breaking down of discipline likewise affected the dogs in their relations with one another.

Based on the information in the sentence, an event has caused the dogs, the characters in the story, to not follow their regular routine. The sentence indicates that there has been a breaking down of discipline which is affecting how the dogs relate to each other. In order to solve this conflict, discipline needs to be restored in the story. There may be another conflict that needs to be resolved in order to re-establish discipline. However, in order to return to previous relations between the dogs, any problems that are in the way of conflict resolution need to be taken care of. The word "likewise" means also, which tells the reader that other avenues are being affected in the story besides the relations between the dogs.

Character Relationships and Changes

Characters can change in a multitude of ways throughout a story; however, there are main aspects of a character that change. A character's identifying characteristics, such as personality or behavior traits, may change as the result of a prominent event in the story, current motivations, and conflicts. As conflicts change or are resolved, a character may no longer be motivated by striving toward a goal that was previously important to them. As the plot of a story moves along, characters can constantly change in relation to events that occur. Relationships between characters and the points of view of characters may change throughout a story as well.

Each story will have many different types of characters and each of these characters will have a different relationship with other characters. Stories usually have a protagonist, antagonist, and a variety of other characters including round, flat, and stock characters.

Protagonist

The main character in a drama, movie, novel, or other fictional text. The author portrays the protagonist in a way that the audience is most like to identify with themselves. The protagonist is generally undertaking some type of personal challenge throughout the story. The author writes the story so that the reader becomes aware of the protagonist's emotions and is generally able to empathize with the personal challenge.

Antagonist

The character that actively opposes the protagonist by trying to prevent them from succeeding. The antagonist is usually presented in such a way as to make the audience dislike them, and want them

Copyright © Mometrix Media. You have been licensed one copy of this document for personal use only. Any other reproduction or redistribution is strictly prohibited. All rights reserved.
This content is provided for test preparation purposes only and does not imply an endorsement by Mometrix of any particular political, scientific, or religious point of view.

to fail at stopping the protagonist. The protagonist and antagonist oppose each other, so their relationship is almost always one of dislike.

Flat Character

Does not have any substantial changes throughout the story. They stay the same despite the conflict, and do not learn any lessons. They are usually minor characters that might interact with the main character in some way.

Round Character

Major characters in the story that will be more fully developed than other minor characters. They will usually encounter some type of conflict that they must overcome, and usually learn a lesson about life or themselves along the way.

Stock Characters

Often get their characteristics and mannerisms from stereotypes of people that are widely recognized. These types of characters are often repeated and well-known. Readers should be aware that stereotypes are rarely accurate in reality, and are generally intended to be humorous or dramatic. Some examples are evil stepmothers, unintelligent blondes, rude athletes, and loyal servants.

Driving the Action

There are many ways in which the action of a story may be driven. Dialogue is one of them. What a character says either to another character or about a situation may propel the action by revealing what a character is thinking or what he may do. Similarly, what a character says will tell the audience what he is like. His manner of speaking, what he says, and how he says it are all clues to his personality. Dialogue can also provoke a decision by showing what the character intends to do in the future. Incidents in a story also propel the action because the plot is made up of events that build on events. Incidents such as a confrontation could reveal aspects of a character or provoke a decision.

Example 4

Read the excerpt and tell how this incident propels the action of the story and provokes a decision.

> It was a perfect day it seemed, until Sam saw the thunderheads roll in. He knew that it would be dangerous to be in a rowboat in the middle of the lake during a thunder and lightning storm. Suddenly the sky became darker and he heard a clap of thunder.

This incident certainly propels the action of the story. It would appear that Sam is in a rowboat in the middle of the lake having a lovely time when he hears a clap of thunder. He realizes that a lake is a dangerous place to be so this event means that Sam must take action. What that action is would be of interest to the reader because it will help form the plot of the story. The incident also forces Sam to make a decision about what he should do. This will help the reader better understand Sam as a character.

Character Trait

The traits of a character may include how they act and physical characteristics; a character trait is a behavior or physical characteristic that is unique to a specific character. For example, a character may be outgoing, which means he or she likes to talk a lot, or they may have bright red hair. These are both character traits.

Copyright © Mometrix Media. You have been licensed one copy of this document for personal use only. Any other reproduction or redistribution is strictly prohibited. All rights reserved.
This content is provided for test preparation purposes only and does not imply an endorsement by Mometrix of any particular political, scientific, or religious point of view.

An author uses character traits to describe a character in a story and help the reader to learn more about how the character acts and what they look like. By comparing the character traits in a story, the reader can see similarities and differences between characters. The author includes character traits to help the reader understand why a character may act a certain way in the story. For example, a character who is shy may not want to talk with a lot of people in a new classroom, but a character who is outgoing may want to talk with many people.

An author typically provides many details about a character so that the reader can learn more about the character's traits, motivations, relationships, and any conflicts they may have in the story. The traits of a character may include how they act and how they look. Characters are often motivated by things that have already happened in their life or how they feel about a topic. The author will often give the reader enough information about the character so that the reader can figure out why the character responds to a situation in a certain way. The author will also often give details about the relationships between characters and points they may conflict on. For example, a character may be good friends with another character; however, the two characters may disagree on where to play outside if one character likes being near the water and the other character does not.

Example 5

Read the following description of a character and decide, logically, whether the character is likely to go hiking outdoors:

> Jeremy lived in a high-rise in Chicago. He was studious, and not very athletic. Jeremy preferred to stay indoors and read a book, rather than enjoy outdoor weather.

Based on the description of the character's traits, preferences, and personality, he is not likely to go hiking outdoors. The description indicates that the character prefers reading, rather than enjoying outdoor weather. In addition, the character lives in a tall building in the middle of a large city, in order for him to enjoy the outdoors, he would have to travel away from where he lives. The character is not likely to change his preferences. A situation may lead the character to go hiking, but he is not likely to initiate the action on his own. A description of a character that is likely to go hiking outdoors may include a preference for outdoor activity and living near trails.

Literary Devices

Point of View

An author may use first, second, or third person point of view in a text.

- First person point of view is written from the perspective of one character. Use of the pronouns 'I', 'me', 'we', and 'my' indicate that the author is using first person point of view.
- Second person point of view uses the pronoun 'you' when telling the story to another person. Second person point of view is the least commonly used point of view.
- Third person point of view tells a story from an all-knowing, or omniscient, perspective. The reader can get into the thoughts and points of view of multiple characters in a story when third person point of view is used.

Developing and Contrasting the Points of View of Different Characters or Narrators in a Text

An author uses many writing skills to develop a character's point of view in a piece of literature. By having a character respond to an event in a particular way, an author can show what the character

Copyright © Mometrix Media. You have been licensed one copy of this document for personal use only. Any other reproduction or redistribution is strictly prohibited. All rights reserved.
This content is provided for test preparation purposes only and does not imply an endorsement by Mometrix of any particular political, scientific, or religious point of view.

thinks about it. Similarly, an author can choose to display a character's viewpoint through dialogue or actions. Various characters will have differing viewpoints and these can be shown in the conflict in a story or drama or even in a poem. Authors often display the narrator's point of view about characters, events, or the plot of a literary piece. The manner in which the author does this may be subtle or it may be overt. It is important to observe the language of the author, in order to analyze the author's and narrator's viewpoints about a character, an event, or a topic.

Example 1

Read the following excerpt.

> Clarisse went to the window. She looked out. As was her habit, she dismissed the entire scene. To her it was no more than two people showing off. She failed to notice the severity of the matter, nor could she foresee the outcome of this untimely fight.

Analyze the narrator's viewpoint of Clarisse.

> The narrator seems to have a rather dim view of Clarisse. She says that Clarisse dismissed the "entire scene" of the two people who were outside her window showing off. This seems to suggest that the narrator thinks she doesn't really relate to what is going on. The narrator also says that Clarisse "failed to notice the severity of the matter," which also suggests that Clarisse doesn't have a deep understanding of what is happening. From these comments, the reader can figure out that the narrator is not praising Clarisse, but instead is somewhat critical of Clarisse. When determining a narrator's viewpoint of a character, be sure to watch for clues that tell you the narrator's opinion, such as the clues in this excerpt.

Establishing a Point of View

When writing a narrative, a story line or plot should be conceived that will allow for a narrator and characters as well as the point of view of the narrator as well as the author. The author's viewpoint will not necessarily be the same as the narrator's viewpoint. Points of view can be shown through dialogue or the way the narrator reacts to what characters do in the story. The characters will need to be drawn very clearly through both their descriptions; the author can hide his own perspective in the characters' thoughts or actions. The narrator's point of view is usually more overtly seen in what is said in the narrative by the narrator.

Example 2

Discuss the character and point of view in the following passage.

> The mouse ran through the hole. She saw the cheese. She grabbed it, but then she heard noises. She couldn't make it back to the hole. She was terrified. She ran under a chair and remained there until it was quiet. Then she ate the cheese.

The author has chosen to tell the narrative from the point of view of the mouse. This makes the mouse more human and more attractive to the reader. The author gives the mouse human characteristics; the mouse feels and can also reason. The author has created a character out of the mouse by concentrating on it and telling what it does. This is one way an author can establish the point of view of a character in a narrative. It is not clear what the point of view of the author is, but this could come later in the narrative.

Subjective and Objective Point of View

The point of view of a character or narrator can either be **subjective** or **objective**. When a character or narrator is describing a person, object, or idea using phrases that are based on

Copyright © Mometrix Media. You have been licensed one copy of this document for personal use only. Any other reproduction or redistribution is strictly prohibited. All rights reserved.
This content is provided for test preparation purposes only and does not imply an endorsement by Mometrix of any particular political, scientific, or religious point of view.

opinions or motivated by feelings, their point of view is subjective. When they use phrases based on facts or something that can be proven, their point of view is objective. For example, if a character describes a person walking toward them and they say "Her shirt was a beautiful shade of yellow, which made her blonde hair shine even brighter" they are speaking in subjective point of view. The yellow color they think is beautiful could be someone else's least favorite color. If the same character described the situation objectively, they might say "As she walked by, I noticed her shirt was yellow and her hair was blonde." The narrator doesn't comment on his opinion of the color, just that it is factually yellow.

Example 1

Determine whether the following excerpt from Jordan Sonnenblick's novel *Drums, Girls & Dangerous Pie* is written using subjective or objective point of view:

> 'Did you really JUST fall, Jeffrey?'
> Why does everybody in my family talk in these dramatic CAPITAL LETTERS all the time?
> Why am I the only calm one?

In this excerpt, the narrator's point of view is subjective. Steven describes himself as the "only calm one" in his family, and while he may honestly feel this way, it is a statement based on feelings, not on facts. Steven cannot prove that he is the only calm one, and a different member of the family would likely view the situation differently, which makes his point of view subjective.

Connecting to a Text

Making Connections to Enhance Comprehension

Reading involves thinking. For good comprehension, readers make text-to-self, text-to-text, and text-to-world connections. Making connections helps readers understand text better and predict what might occur next based on what they already know, such as how characters in the story feel or what happened in another text. Readers can make connections before, during, and after reading. Venn diagrams and other graphic organizers can help readers visualize connections.

Text-to-Self

Reading while looking for connections with the reader's life and experiences makes literature more personally relevant and meaningful to readers. Sentences showing text-to-self connections may begin with these examples

- This is similar to a time when...
- I understand how the character feels because...
- The setting makes me think of...
- I experienced this same thing when...

Text-to-Text

Reading while looking for connections to other texts helps the reader learn to identify the way authors use genre, setting, characters, plot elements, literary structure and devices, and themes to create meaning. Sentences showing text-to-text connections may begin with these examples

- The character in this story reminds me of the character in...
- These two stories are alike because...
- The conflict in this story is similar to the conflict in...
- The relationship between the friends in this story is different than the relationship in...

Copyright © Mometrix Media. You have been licensed one copy of this document for personal use only. Any other reproduction or redistribution is strictly prohibited. All rights reserved.
This content is provided for test preparation purposes only and does not imply an endorsement by Mometrix of any particular political, scientific, or religious point of view.

TEXT-TO-WORLD

Reading while looking for connections to the world helps the reader begin to see literature as a reflection of real life and notice patterns in history and current events. Sentences showing text-to-world connections may begin with these examples

- The event in this story sounds like the event in history when...
- The actions of this character sound like...
- This is like what happened in real life when...
- I heard about this on the news when...

Making Inferences

INFERENCE

An **inference** is a **conclusion** or generalization that the reader makes based on the information provided within a text. Certain facts are included to help a reader come to a specific conclusion. It is what the story may hint about, and what a reader can conclude as a result of what the author says in the passage. It is also the best guess that a reader can make based on what happened or was said or in a story. A good inference is based on or supported by details in the passage.

Readers may come to their own conclusion about a topic, or the author may state a conclusion at the end of a story. When readers are in the middle of a story, they can predict what will happen at the end of it based on the events that have occurred so far and the typical characteristics that have been presented by the author up to that point. A reader needs to consider all of the information that an author has presented, including the main point and supporting points, to make logical conclusions and inferences about the story.

For instance, if a passage says that Joan is holding her mouth and moaning, you might conclude, or **infer,** that she has a sore mouth or a toothache. You cannot be sure of this, but it is the best conclusion that you can reach using the information at hand. Inferences are considered **implicit information**. They are not found directly in a passage.

EXPLICIT INFORMATION

Explicit information is information that is stated in a passage. It is stated right in the text; it is not suggested or hinted at. Explicit information can be facts or details about a topic. Frequently this information supports a main idea or thesis. Explicit information can be found just by reading a text, especially an informational passage. The explicit information in passages can, however, be used to form the basis for an inference. When making an inference, you need to put together the explicit information to form a conclusion. It is the best guess that a reader can make based on the information given in a passage.

Review Video: Inference
Visit mometrix.com/academy and enter code: 379203

EXAMPLE 1

Read the following excerpt. Tell whether it contains explicit information or not.

> I think the most famous person in the Old West is Annie Oakley. Annie is the best rifle shot who ever lived. She almost never missed. Many men challenged her to contests of speed and accuracy. She won them all.

Copyright © Mometrix Media. You have been licensed one copy of this document for personal use only. Any other reproduction or redistribution is strictly prohibited. All rights reserved.
This content is provided for test preparation purposes only and does not imply an endorsement by Mometrix of any particular political, scientific, or religious point of view.

Most of the information in the excerpt is explicit information. The information tells the reader about Annie Oakley: that she was the best rifle shot who ever lived and that she almost never missed. It also says that many men challenged her to contests and she won them all. This information is found right in the excerpt. It is not suggested or hinted at. Everything that is said is clearly what it means. The first sentence is a personal opinion; it is also explicit because the reader does not have to guess what the author thinks of Annie Oakley.

Example 2

Read the passage and discuss why the conclusion that the Vikings were searching for new farmland is valid.

> The Vikings set out in their boats in summer. The number of people in Scandinavia was growing fast. They needed to grow more food. In the late 900s, Eric the Red sailed across the Atlantic to Greenland. In 985, Viking farmers settled in Greenland.

The passage says that the Viking population was growing and that they needed to be able to grow more food. It is logical to guess that they sailed in search of new farmland. There is really not another possibility. Remember, inferences are assumptions that are hinted at or suggested by the text. They are not like explicit information; they are implicit in the text based on the explicit information that is found there. They are the best guess a reader can make.

Example 3

Read the following sentence and draw a conclusion based upon the information presented:

> "You know the reason Mother proposed not having any presents this Christmas was because it is going to be a hard winter for everyone; and she thinks we ought not to spend money for pleasure, when our men are suffering so in the army." (from *Little Women* by Louisa May Alcott, p. 3)

Based on the information in the sentence, the reader can conclude, or infer, that the men are away at war while the women are still at home. The pronoun 'our' gives a clue to the reader that the character is speaking about men she knows. In addition, the reader can assume that the character is speaking to a brother or sister, since the term Mother is used by the character while speaking to another person. The reader can also come to the conclusion that the characters celebrate Christmas, since it is mentioned in the context of the sentence. In the sentence, the Mother is presented as an unselfish character who is opinionated and thinks about the well-being of other people.

Example 4

Draw a conclusion based on the following sentence from *The Adventures of Tom Sawyer* by Mark Twain:

> He had discovered a great law of human action, without knowing it—namely, that in order to make a man or a boy covet a thing, it is only necessary to make the thing difficult to attain.

The reader can conclude from the sentence that the character did not set out to learn something, but through an action, the character learned that people will want what is hard to attain. The character learned a fact about human nature: that a person will value something more if they have to work hard for it, than if it is simply given to them. The word *covet* means to desire, which the character learns can be manipulated by making an item or an outcome more difficult to grasp. In everyday life, this could apply toward taking a hard test and doing well. If someone studies for a

Copyright © Mometrix Media. You have been licensed one copy of this document for personal use only. Any other reproduction or redistribution is strictly prohibited. All rights reserved.
This content is provided for test preparation purposes only and does not imply an endorsement by Mometrix of any particular political, scientific, or religious point of view.

hard test and does well, the person will value their score more than if the test was very easy and he or she did not study for the test.

Using Evidence to Support a Response

TEXT EVIDENCE

The term **text evidence** refers to information included in a text that supports the main point of the paper. A reader can draw conclusions or generalizations based upon information found in a text, in which the author will deliberately include key points that serve as supporting details for the main point. For example, the main point of a paper may state: The average yearly rainfall in the city has risen by 2 inches per year in the past five years. The paper would go on to include the amount of rainfall for each month or season and any contributing factors that may be causing an increase in yearly rainfall. Additional facts, or text evidence to support the point that yearly rainfall is rising in the city would help to prove that the author's main point is correct. In fiction, details about characters, events, and setting can be both explicit and implicit.

Review Video: Textual Evidence
Visit mometrix.com/academy and enter code: 486236

EXPLICIT INFORMATION

Explicit information includes facts and statements that are found directly in a passage or a story. It is not information that is hinted at or information you need to make a conclusion about. Explicit information may be found in many forms; it can be contained in a quote as well as in a description. It can be found in dialogue and in actions. This information can sometimes be used to support an inference. The answers to questions about explicit information are found through careful reading of the text. Attention is given to important facts or other information.

EXAMPLE:

Read the following excerpt and tell what information is explicit:

> Carlos didn't really speak Spanish. His parents often spoke to him in that language, which he understood, but he always replied in English. As a result, his Spanish pronunciation was very bad, and he had trouble picking the right word. But then he fell in love with Alicia, who didn't understand English. Carlos changed very quickly.

The explicit information in the excerpt is all about Carlos. The passage says that he didn't really speak Spanish. It says that while his parents spoke to him in Spanish and that he understood it, he always responded in English. It also says his Spanish pronunciation was bad and he didn't pick the right words. This is explicit information. So is the fact that Carlos fell in love with Alicia and that Carlos changed quickly.

IMPLICIT INFORMATION

Implicit information is information that is not directly stated in a text, but can be inferred from something that the author explicitly states. For instance, the author may say "Seth buys a new TV, laptop, and home theater system every year." From this the reader could infer several things. For instance, Seth probably likes electronics and has a lot of spending money.

Copyright © Mometrix Media. You have been licensed one copy of this document for personal use only. Any other reproduction or redistribution is strictly prohibited. All rights reserved.
This content is provided for test preparation purposes only and does not imply an endorsement by Mometrix of any particular political, scientific, or religious point of view.

Example

Draw a conclusion based on the implicit information in the following sentence from *The Adventures of Tom Sawyer* by Mark Twain:

> He had discovered a great law of human action, without knowing it—namely, that in order to make a man or a boy covet a thing, it is only necessary to make the thing difficult to attain.

The reader can clearly see from the sentence that the character did not set out to learn something, but through an action, the character learned that people will want what is hard to attain. Although it's not explicitly stated, the reader can draw the conclusion that the character gained the experience of coveting (or desiring) something that was hard to get.

Drawing Conclusions Based on Text Evidence

Readers often need to use prior experience and background information to draw an accurate conclusion about the passage they are reading. Sometimes interpreting the information in a sentence can be difficult, especially if the reader is unfamiliar with some of the words used in a sentence. Looking at the words that the reader does understand in the sentence can help. By taking a pen or pencil and underlining important information in a sentence, the reader can better understand what the author is trying to say and draw a clearer conclusion from that.

Example 1

Draw a conclusion based on the following sentence:

> New Orleans then was a mere huddle of buildings around Jackson Square; but with the purchase of the Louisiana territory from France, and the great influx of American enterprise that characterized the first quarter of the last century, development was working like yeast...

The sentence describes how New Orleans grew after the "purchase of the Louisiana territory" and how "development was working like yeast". Yeast multiplies rapidly, so the reader can conclude that New Orleans was growing rapidly.

Example 2

Read the following sentence. Draw a conclusion based upon the information presented.

> "A rosy-faced servant-maid opened the door, and smiled as she took the letter which he silently offered."

The reader can conclude, based on the sentence, that the servant-maid is friendly. The words "rosy-faced" and "smiled" lead the reader to this conclusion. People who are friendly are often described as having rosy complexions and smiling as a common sign of pleasantness. The reader can also assume, from the sentence, that the letter does not present any threat or unpleasantness to the servant-maid. The person presenting the letter does not have anything to say upon offering it, so perhaps he is waiting to see how the servant-maid will react.

When interpreting a sentence, always look for key words that describe a character. The author carefully crafts a description of each character, to form a picture in the reader's mind about what the character is like.

Copyright © Mometrix Media. You have been licensed one copy of this document for personal use only. Any other reproduction or redistribution is strictly prohibited. All rights reserved.
This content is provided for test preparation purposes only and does not imply an endorsement by Mometrix of any particular political, scientific, or religious point of view.

Synthesizing Information

SYNTHESIZING A TEXT WITH EXISTING KNOWLEDGE

Synthesizing is similar to summarizing but it takes it one step further. Synthesizing involves taking the main points of a text and comparing it with existing knowledge to create a new idea, perspective, or way of thinking.

Another term for knowledge that you already have is **schema**. The plural form of this word is **schemata**. Schemata contain all the ideas you have about something. Synthesizing is all about how schemata change over time with the introduction of new information.

EXAMPLE

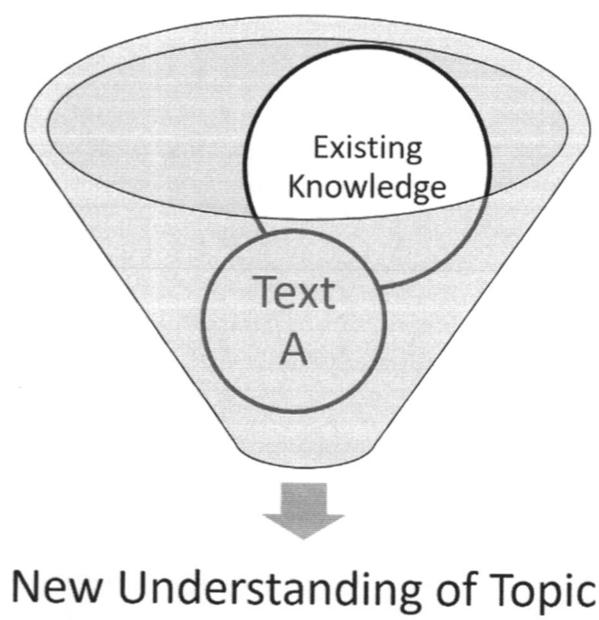

Using self-questioning strategies can help readers synthesize texts with their schemata to increase or change their understanding of topics. These questions include

- What do I already know about this topic?
- Is any of this new information?
- Has my perspective changed now that I've read this?
- What do I understand now that I didn't before?
- What are the main ideas of this text?
- How do the parts of the text fit together to create meaning?
- Are there any text-to-text, text-to-self, or text-to-world connections here?

SYNTHESIZING TEXTS WITHOUT EXISTING KNOWLEDGE

If the reader is completely unfamiliar with the topic, they will have no background knowledge. In this case, instead of using existing knowledge, synthesizing may instead be done by combining the

Copyright © Mometrix Media. You have been licensed one copy of this document for personal use only. Any other reproduction or redistribution is strictly prohibited. All rights reserved.
This content is provided for test preparation purposes only and does not imply an endorsement by Mometrix of any particular political, scientific, or religious point of view.

ideas provided in two or three different texts. The reader must make connections between the texts, determine how the ideas fit together, and gather evidence to support the new perspective.

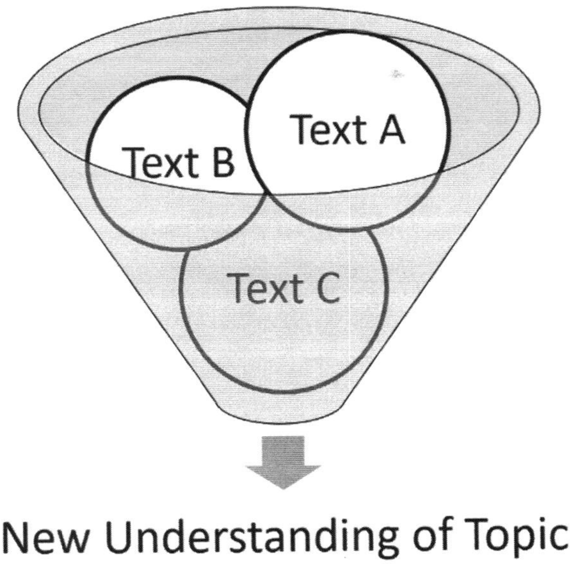

Using self-questioning strategies can help readers synthesize texts to increase their understanding of topics. In this case, readers are creating new schemata as they read. These questions include

- What do these texts have in common?
- What is different between these texts?
- What new information have I learned?
- What do I understand now that I didn't before?
- How do these texts relate to one another?
- If I think of these texts as parts of one whole, what meaning do they create together?
- What predictions can I make about this topic?

Literary Genres

LITERARY GENRES

Literature contains many different **genres**, which are categories that texts can be divided into. Genres are used to group types of writing together for purposes of study, reading, or simple organization. Some common literary genres are

- **Realistic fiction** -A story that could actually happen and reflects life in a realistic way.
- **Adventure stories** -Short, mostly fictional stories that follow characters as they go on an adventure or quest.
- **Historical fiction** -Often strays from historical reality in order to tell a story and make a true historical event more interesting to the reader.
- **Mysteries** -Fiction stories about solving crimes or revealing secrets.
- **Humor** –Stories, mostly fictional, full of fun and excitement meant to entertain readers. Can be seen in stories from all genres.
- **Myth** -A legend or traditional narrative, often based on a historical event. The story reveals something about human behavior or the natural world, and often involves actions of gods.

Copyright © Mometrix Media. You have been licensed one copy of this document for personal use only. Any other reproduction or redistribution is strictly prohibited. All rights reserved.
This content is provided for test preparation purposes only and does not imply an endorsement by Mometrix of any particular political, scientific, or religious point of view.

- **Fantasy** -Fictional stories that contain unusual and other worldly settings and characters. The sense of "realness" in other stories is not present.
- **Science fiction** -Fiction based on what could happen if actual, imagined, or possible scientific advances occurred. Usually set in the future, a modified past, or on other planets.

Review Video: Literary Genres
Visit mometrix.com/academy and enter code: 587617

Drama

Drama

Dramas are texts that are written to be performed by people reading the lines or acting the stories out. They can also be presented as monologues (one character speaks), dialogues (two character speak to each other), or pantomimes (body movements are used instead of spoken words). Dramatic texts are called plays or **scripts**, and they are written differently than other texts.

Text Structure in Drama

Plays are divided into **acts** (large units) and **scenes** (small sections inside acts) instead of chapters. There are also **stage directions**, which are instructions from the playwright about where items go, where actors should move, and what the characters should be doing during the scene. Stage directions are usually in italics to set them apart from other parts of the play. When it is time for a character in a play to speak, there will be **character tag** on the left side of the page which shows the name of the character (all letters of the name are capitalized) followed by a colon.

Here is an example of how a page from a play might look:

Title of Play

Act Number

Scene Number

The setting of the scene is being described here. The reader is being introduced to the characters and the things happening around them. Characters will enter speak to one another during the scene.

CHARACTER 1:
I am speaking. These are words I say. *(stage directions)* I am still speaking.

CHARACTER 2 *enters and does something.*

CHARACTER 2:
Now I am speaking. This is my dialogue.

Dialogue and Stage Directions

Dialogue refers to what the characters say in a play when they are talking to each other, talking to themselves, or even talking to the audience. The type of speech, word choice, and accent a character uses is specific to the role he is playing. For example, a person cast to play a cowboy would have certain words in his vocabulary that a character from a big city in the North would not have.

A playwright also uses stage directions to make the play flow smoothly. Character interaction helps the viewer to understand the mood of the scene. If two characters are confrontational, the viewer is

Copyright © Mometrix Media. You have been licensed one copy of this document for personal use only. Any other reproduction or redistribution is strictly prohibited. All rights reserved.
This content is provided for test preparation purposes only and does not imply an endorsement by Mometrix of any particular political, scientific, or religious point of view.

aware that there is some type of conflict occurring. Stage directions create order when all the characters are on stage together.

Soliloquy

A moment when a character is speaking alone on stage is called a **soliloquy**. Oftentimes characters reveal something personal or dramatic in soliloquies because no other characters in the play can hear them. Of course, the audience is listening, so these are opportunities for the character to be one on one with the audience. Soliloquies play a large role in shaping a play or drama because they allow the audience to have first-hand knowledge of what a character is feeling or thinking without having the interference of the other characters in the play. They are a chance for a character to bare his or her soul to the world in general. This experience creates an intensity of feeling between the character and the audience that leads to greater understanding of the character's personal plight and the meaning of the play.

Literary Elements in Poetry

Meter, Rhyme, and Repetitions of Sounds

The **meter** of a poem refers to the number of syllables per line as well as the pattern of emphasis on those syllables. The use of meter gives a poem a rhythmic context and contributes to the poem's flow. Certain types of meter can also make a poem more appealing to the reader or represent natural speech rhythms.

Rhymes repeat the ending sound of words: "So very soon/We will fly to the moon." Here the "oo" sound is repeated in the words *soon* and *moon*. Rhymes are frequently used in poetry, mostly older forms of poetry rather than modern poems.

Another type of repetition is **alliteration**. Alliteration repeats beginning sounds, usually consonants: "Rah, rah, rah," the crowd cried, "rah, rah, rah." It is often used in poetry as well as in spoken forms of writing.

Rhyme Scheme

When determining what a poem's rhyme scheme is, readers should look at the last word of each line to see which words rhyme with each other. Words that rhyme are assigned a letter of the alphabet, beginning with "a." The next time words rhyme, if the rhyme is different than the last one, they assigned a new letter, going forward in order of the alphabet until the poem is over or there are no more rhymes. This sounds complicated, but it's easy with practice.

Let's take a look at an excerpt from Dylan Thomas' poem "Do not go gentle into that good night":

> Do not go gentle into that good night,
> Old age should burn and rave at close of day;
> Rage, rage against the dying of the light.
>
> Though wise men at their end know dark is right,
> Because their words had forked no lightning they
> Do not go gentle into that good night.

Copyright © Mometrix Media. You have been licensed one copy of this document for personal use only. Any other reproduction or redistribution is strictly prohibited. All rights reserved.
This content is provided for test preparation purposes only and does not imply an endorsement by Mometrix of any particular political, scientific, or religious point of view.

The words at the end of the lines are *night, day, light, right, they,* and *night.*

We know that the first rhyme is assigned the letter "a," and can clearly see that *night, light,* and *right* all rhyme, so we can mark the poem like this

Do not go gentle into that good night,	**a**	
Old age should burn and rave at close of day;		
Rage, rage against the dying of the light.		**a**
Though wise men at their end know dark is right,		**a**
Because their words had forked no lightning they		
Do not go gentle into that good night.	**a**	

Now, we'll look at the only other rhyme in the poem, which is made up of the words *day* and *they*. This rhyme does not rhyme with the first set of words, so it gets a new letter, "b."

Do not go gentle into that good night,	**a**	
Old age should burn and rave at close of day;	**b**	
Rage, rage against the dying of the light.		**a**
Though wise men at their end know dark is right,		**a**
Because their words had forked no lightning they	**b**	
Do not go gentle into that good night.	**a**	

After looking at all six lines and determining how they rhyme, we can confidently say that the rhyme scheme for this excerpt is a, b, a, a, b, a.

Rhymes are used at the discretion of the poet and are not always mandatory. Many modern poems—actually, most of them—use a blank verse, where there are no rhyme schemes. However, there are many formal poetic types, such as the sonnet, that have a specific rhyme scheme that poets must follow to achieve that kind of poetic form.

EXAMPLE

Explain the rhyme scheme of the following excerpt from a poem entitled "Alone" by Edgar Allan Poe.

From childhood's hour I have not been
As others were; I have not seen
As others saw; I could not bring
My passions from a common spring.
From the same source I have not taken
My sorrow; I could not awaken
My heart to joy at the same tone;
And all I loved, I loved alone.

The rhyme scheme that Edgar Allan Poe uses in this excerpt from his poem "Alone" is: a, a, b, b, c, c, d, d, e, e. Every two lines rhyme, but the rhyme is not repeated in the other lines. This is a rather unusual rhyme scheme; many others have lines that repeat the rhyme scheme, but not in a consecutive order, such as a, b, a, b or a, b, c a, b, c.

Copyright © Mometrix Media. You have been licensed one copy of this document for personal use only. Any other reproduction or redistribution is strictly prohibited. All rights reserved.
This content is provided for test preparation purposes only and does not imply an endorsement by Mometrix of any particular political, scientific, or religious point of view.

Graphical Elements in Poem

Graphic elements in a poem such as capitalization, line length, and word position can call special attention to words or phrases. Capitalization can signal the beginning of a sentence, or all caps may be used to provide emphasis. Line length can be used to help create a shape, like in concrete poems, or to create a bold statement, like a one-word line. A poet can create tension by using line length and punctuation independently of one another. Word position can be used to contribute to a feeling, or it can also be used to help create a shape, so poets are often careful where they end lines.

Poetic Form Contributes to Meaning

The form or structure of a poem is extremely important to the meaning of the text. Poetry comes out of guidelines that were developed in Europe and England and then were brought to the United States, where they were used and sometimes changed to serve a different purpose. For example, strict rhyming poetry has given way to blank verse, and the choice of the structure of the poem or play can give the reader a hint as to its meaning.

Organization of Informational Texts

Introducing a Topic

When writing an informational or explanatory text, the author will need to introduce the topic that the text will be about. There are numerous strategies that can help improve the reader's comprehension of the subject. An author may choose to define key words that a reader may not be familiar with, classify information or compare and contrast it, or use a cause and effect relationship in the report. Charts and tables are extremely useful for displaying complicated information and the use of headings can help signify where certain information will be found. Multimedia devices, including video and audio, can also improve the way in which an author displays his material because they are appealing to the audience or reader.

Developing a Topic

To develop a topic in an informational or explanatory text, an author needs to use relevant facts that support details related to the main topic. The topic may be included in a topic sentence or opening statement and then followed by supporting details. Some of the supporting details should be concrete facts that have been researched and confirmed. Quotations of experts in the field of the topic are another good source for supporting material. Quoting experts gives variety and credence to a text. Examples, charts, and multimedia techniques can also be used to enhance the presentation, but these extras should not be used as a substitute for solid supporting details.

Example

Analyze the beginning of this informational text and tell what could be added to improve it.

> The journey of the salmon from salt water to fresh water to breed is one of the wonders of nature. This journey, called the salmon run, is difficult because the fish must swim upriver against the current. Some even leap up waterfalls as they make their way back to their original breeding grounds.

This seems like a good start to an informational text. The first sentence establishes the topic. It tells what the report is going to be about. It also includes two supporting details to tell more about the topic. This is one way to introduce and develop a topic in a report or other informational or explanatory text. What should come next are more supporting details and also sources for the information that is cited; a quotation from an authority of the salmon run would make the report

Copyright © Mometrix Media. You have been licensed one copy of this document for personal use only. Any other reproduction or redistribution is strictly prohibited. All rights reserved.
This content is provided for test preparation purposes only and does not imply an endorsement by Mometrix of any particular political, scientific, or religious point of view.

stronger and give it credence. Some statistics, facts, figures about how many salmon make the run each year and how many survive would also be of interest.

Using Appropriate Transitions

When writing an informational or explanatory text it is important to use appropriate transitions that will clarify the relationships among ideas and concepts. For example, to show causality between ideas, use transition words or phrases, such as "therefore," "consequently," and "as a result of." To show comparison or contrast relationships, words such as "however," "on the other hand," "but," "in contrast," and "similarly" should be used. Transition words and expressions to introduce examples include "for example, "for instance," "namely" and "that is." The order of importance can also be shown through transitions, such as "at first," "former," "latter," "primarily" and "second."

Importance of Using Precise Language and Domain-Specific Vocabulary

When writing informational or explanatory texts it is of utmost importance to use precise language and domain-specific vocabulary to explain your main idea and supporting details. Generalized vocabulary will not help the audience grasp the points that you are attempting to make because they will not accurately reflect your main idea and supporting details. Domain-specific vocabulary is important to use because it will accurately describe or explain the ideas or processes that are central to your text. When you research a subject, make sure to familiarize yourself with any vocabulary that is involved in its explanation. Use context clues, dictionaries, or, if necessary, a technical dictionary to decode any words that you are not familiar with. Also include definitions of domain-specific vocabulary in your text to enlighten readers.

Establishing and Maintaining a Formal Style

When writing an informational or explanatory text it is important to establish and maintain a formal style of writing. Do not use a colloquial or casual tone. It is necessary to use the third person and to make the sentences longer and more complex. It is also important not to use contractions when you write. A formal style announces that the writer is serious about his or her subject and wants to write an objective paper. This can be done by keeping the main ideas and supporting details clear, to the point, but as complex as they need to be. A formal style also means that the writer will not include a personal opinion that is not justified.

Example

Discuss why the following excerpt is an example of formal writing.

> Richard Spruce found his life's work in the jungles of South America. Spruce grew up in a part of England that was filled with plants growing wild and free. His love of plants developed early. When he read a book about the Amazon jungle in Brazil, he decided to go there to study the area's plant life.

This is a good example of formal writing. It is objective and unbiased. The author uses the third person perspective, which formal writing is supposed to do. He sets out his main idea in the initial topic sentence, and then gives good supporting details. His sentences are somewhat complex and varied. He does not use any contractions, which are not used in formal writing, and the language is not colloquial or casual. The style of writing matches the subject. At the same time, the writing is not dull; the reader is intrigued and wants to learn more. Formal writing does not have to be uninteresting.

Copyright © Mometrix Media. You have been licensed one copy of this document for personal use only. Any other reproduction or redistribution is strictly prohibited. All rights reserved.
This content is provided for test preparation purposes only and does not imply an endorsement by Mometrix of any particular political, scientific, or religious point of view.

Importance of a Concluding Statement

A concluding statement or section that follows from and supports the information or explanation is important to a text because the conclusion helps to focus the important points in a text and also provides closure to the reader or audience. A good conclusion attempts to sum up the passage and any conclusions that the author makes so that the audience feels they have received a logical ending to the text. An effective conclusion gives the passage the weight it needs to have an effect. The conclusion should not make the reader feel that there is more information to follow, but rather set the tone for the ending of the topic.

Organizational Patterns

When writing there are a variety of ways that an author can choose to organize their text. It is important for them to choose the pattern that best presents their information, as not all patterns will work for every piece of writing. Some examples are

Advantage/Disadvantage

The author chooses a topic or concept and addresses both the advantages and disadvantages (or pros and cons) of the subject. In this type of text the author is not trying to persuade their audience to choose a side, but rather, to inform the reader of all the possible positive and negative effects.

Cause and Effect

The author will write about relationship between two events that occur, where the second event occurs as a result of the first.

For example, a text may discuss a school policy stating that when a student is late to school too many times, they receive a detention. Later in the text, we might see a student repeatedly arriving late to school, after which he is given a detention. In this example, the **cause** is the student being late to school, and the **effect** is the student receiving a detention.

Classification

The author chooses a topic and divides it into smaller parts or groups in order to discuss them individually. These types of texts address how parts work within a whole, or what characteristics can be used to classify a given subject or concept.

Chronological Order

The author organizes the progression of events based upon when they occurred and what was included in each step of the story. By organizing the text in this way the author presents all necessary information about the six questions readers can ask to help themselves understand the text: who, what, when, where, why, and how.

Compare and Contrast

The author will show similarities and differences between items or events.

For example, the author may write about cats and dogs. They might start by giving a brief description of the two. Then they will want to point out all of the similarities, such as; they both have tails, and both are kept as pets. Next, they will explain the differences, such as; dogs are canines, while cats are felines. They will try to provide as much detail as possible about both the similarities and the differences.

Copyright © Mometrix Media. You have been licensed one copy of this document for personal use only. Any other reproduction or redistribution is strictly prohibited. All rights reserved.
This content is provided for test preparation purposes only and does not imply an endorsement by Mometrix of any particular political, scientific, or religious point of view.

DEFINITION

Authors introduce a concept or word and then explain or describe it. This type of text often included examples that will help the reader gain understanding of what is presumably a new concept for them.

INDUCTIVE / DEDUCTIVE

Authors organize ideas from general to specific or specific to general. If ideas are organized **inductively**, they are arranged from specific facts to general conclusions. If ideas are organized from general conclusions to specific facts, they are organized **deductively**. A reader can make a logical assumption about a topic based on the facts that are presented in the text.

For example, in these two sentences the ideas are organized deductively, from general to specific.

> Many canoers use the lake in the summer. Jeff learned how to canoe last summer, and is on his way to the lake now.

The idea that "Many canoers use the lake in the summer" is a general idea. The facts that Jeff already knows how to canoe and is headed to the lake are specific to him as a character.

ORDER OF IMPORTANCE

The author puts the information in the text in order of what is most important. **Order of importance** can be either increasing or decreasing, depending on how the writer wants to structure the work.

PROPOSITION AND SUPPORT

The author states a proposition that they believe to be true, and then provides support for that proposition in the paper. The topics that use this type of structure are generally things that reader might feel uncertain about or might not already have an opinion about. The support that the author gives for the proposition should include facts, statistics, logic, and reasoning. The more hard evidence an author can give the reader, the better it will help convince them to see things from the author's point of view.

IDENTIFYING ORGANIZATIONAL STRATEGIES

EXAMPLE 1

Explain which organization pattern would be the best choice for this writer and why.

> Sara is writing a report on sea turtles. She has researched the various dangers that they face: their predators, the difficulties they encounter in their life cycle starting with their birth, their migration to the ocean, and the dangers that await them as they mature. She is unsure of how to organize her report.

A cause and effect order would seem to be the best idea for Sara because she would be able to identify the causes and effects of the dangers that sea turtles encounter. She could organize the report so that each paragraph deals with a different threat, using headings to identify what would be in each section. A chart would also be useful because it puts the same information in a clear format so that readers would be able to refer to it. She might also consider using a video showing baby turtles migrating towards the open sea, which would give her audience an even greater understanding of the turtles' plight.

Copyright © Mometrix Media. You have been licensed one copy of this document for personal use only. Any other reproduction or redistribution is strictly prohibited. All rights reserved.
This content is provided for test preparation purposes only and does not imply an endorsement by Mometrix of any particular political, scientific, or religious point of view.

Example 2

Identify the text structure that is used in the following sentences:

> Madison and her brother Jake used to live on a wind-torn island in the Chesapeake Bay. Last year they moved to Baltimore, a city in Maryland. Next summer they plan to visit the island where they grew up.

Chronological order is used as a text structure in the example sentences, as they are organized according to the passage of time. Note that each sentence refers to a point in time. The first sentence refers to where the siblings lived in the past. The second sentence refers to the siblings' move to Baltimore last year. The final sentence refers to what the siblings plan to do in the future. By referring to a specific place in time, the reader can see what occurred in the story during that time period. An author will often use flashback to indicate what happened in the past, and foreshadowing to give the reader a glimpse of what may occur in the future.

Example 3

Identify the text structure that is used in the following sentences:

> Three cousins lived in the same small town. One day the cousins decided to journey together to enter a singing contest across the country. The cousins won the contest and made their hometown fans proud.

The information in the story can be organized according to the passage of time, called chronological order. The story will start based in the cousins' hometown, to give some background on where the cousins come from. Subsequent events in the story will occur over time based on the cousins' motivations due to their background. The story will end by referring back to how far the cousins have come from their small-town roots.

Example 4

Read the following thesis statement and discuss the organizational pattern the author will use:

> While many people are content with the DVD players they already have at home, Blu-ray technology provides for better viewing of high definition video.

From this thesis statement the reader can assume that the author is going to use a deductive presentation of ideas. The author starts with the conclusion that Blu-ray technology is a better method for watching high definition video than DVD. The reader can assume that in the rest of the text, the author will discuss the reasons why he arrived at this conclusion, most likely providing details and examples that will support his conclusion. When the conclusion is presented first, then followed by specific examples, the ideas are presented in deductive order.

Example 5

Read the following thesis statement and discuss the organizational pattern that the author will use:

> Throughout his life, Thomas Edison used his questioning and creative mind to become one of America's greatest inventors.

Based on the thesis statement, the reader can assume that the author is going to use chronological order to organize the information in the rest of the essay. The words "throughout his life" clue the reader in to the chronological organizational structure, which presents information in the order than it occurred. The author will probably discuss Edison's childhood and initial inventions first

Copyright © Mometrix Media. You have been licensed one copy of this document for personal use only. Any other reproduction or redistribution is strictly prohibited. All rights reserved.
This content is provided for test preparation purposes only and does not imply an endorsement by Mometrix of any particular political, scientific, or religious point of view.

and then move on to his later queries and inventions. Chronological order is often used as the organizational structure in biographies as a way to logically present the important events in a person's life.

Author's Purpose and Message

Author's Purpose

The purpose of a text is the author's main reason for writing the text. As the reader reads a text, they should always try to figure out the author's purpose for writing as this will help them to better understand the message that the author is trying to convey.

Informational Texts

- Inform the reader on a topic that they previously knew nothing about, such as many non-fiction texts.
- The author will usually include sources of information for an informative piece.
- For example, an informative paper on early Native American Indian tribes would detail where Native American Indians lived, what types of foods they ate, how they bartered for goods, and other aspects of their culture.

Persuasive Texts

- Influence the reader to think a certain way about a topic, calling them to action or pointing them toward resources that would help them to learn more about the topic.
- A Proposition and Support paper would be an example of this, where an author gives their opinion and then tries to convince the reader to see something from their point of view.
- An author will often use positive expert testimonials when trying to persuade the reader to accept a given point-of-view.
- For example, an author may try to persuade the reader that technology is negatively affecting social interaction, and that limits should be set on how much people can use their technological devices.

Expressive Texts

- Express the author or speaker's opinion or emotions about a topic. Generally, expressive texts include descriptive words to clearly show the reader how the author or speaker feels.
- For example, the author may think that history is important for all people to study, and express the opinion that education without history class would be incomplete.

Entertaining Texts

- Entertain the reader, such as in most fictional texts.
- For example, Lois Lowry, the author of *The Giver,* entertains his readers with the story of a young boy named Jonas who is learning how to navigate his unexpected life assignment.

Review Video: Understanding the Author's Intent
Visit mometrix.com/academy and enter code: 511819

Determining the Purpose of a Text

It should be, for the most part, fairly easy to determine the purpose of a text. When reading, ask yourself whether the passage is teaching or instructing you about something, trying to appeal to your emotions, trying to convince you of something, or simply trying to entertain you. There are certain signs that a text is attempting to persuade the reader. The author will offer up an opinion and tell why she thinks this way. If a text is simply informative, it will have many facts that will give details about an event or person, but will not offer an opinion. Examples of texts that entertain are

Copyright © Mometrix Media. You have been licensed one copy of this document for personal use only. Any other reproduction or redistribution is strictly prohibited. All rights reserved.
This content is provided for test preparation purposes only and does not imply an endorsement by Mometrix of any particular political, scientific, or religious point of view.

novels, short stories, and science fiction. Instructional manuals that come with equipment are clearly not persuasive.

During the writing process, the author may decide to **change the purpose of the text**. When this occurs, the entire story is changed. For example, an author may write a story to inform the reader about a given topic, such as the need to stay hydrated during hot weather. If the author decides to change the purpose of the text to persuade the reader to drink a particular type of sports beverage to stay hydrated during hot weather, the text becomes an advertisement. While the original purpose of the text was to inform, the new purpose of the text is to persuade. Changing the purpose of a text can alter the length of the story, the type of words used (descriptive vs. sensational), and the amount of information included. You may be asked to identify the overall purpose of an entire text, or the purpose of a sentence or paragraph within that text.

Example 1

Read the following sentence from *The Tale of Benny Badger*. State the author's point in writing the sentence, whether it is to inform, entertain, persuade, or state an opinion.

> He had a powerful body, short, stout legs, and big feet, which bore long, strong claws.

The author wishes to inform the reader about the character in his story. The example sentence includes a description of the character's physical attributes; describing the character so that the reader can picture what they look like in the scene. The entire story may be meant to entertain the reader, but the sentence is providing factual information about a character. By informing the reader about the character's attributes, the author is giving the reader background information on why the character may act a certain way in an event further along in the story.

The author is not persuading the reader to accept a point of view, the information presented is not an opinion on an issue, and the author does not have a personal motivation for presenting the information. The text is meant to inform the reader through description.

Example 2

Read the following sentence. State the author's point in writing the sentence, whether it is to inform, entertain, persuade, or state an opinion.

> The cat buried itself deep in the crinkled paper bag, until only a soft black nose and long whiskers could be seen by innocent passersby.

The example sentence is meant to **both** entertain and inform the reader. The author uses description to tell the audience where the cat is located and what it looks like. In the example, the reader can picture the cat crouched in a bag, ready to pounce on something that walks by. By using description to paint a picture of the scene in the reader's mind, the author is forming the background for events that occur in the story.

When an author wishes to persuade the audience about a given topic, they will take a single point of view on an issue. If an author is stating their opinion, the sentence will be based on what the author believes to have occurred, not necessarily what is factual.\

Determining an Author's Point of View

The author's point of view may be clear or it may be hidden. It is important to read a text closely to find out exactly what the author thinks about the event, person, topic, or issue that the author is writing about. When reading, look for clues to the author's viewpoint in terms of emotional

Copyright © Mometrix Media. You have been licensed one copy of this document for personal use only. Any other reproduction or redistribution is strictly prohibited. All rights reserved.
This content is provided for test preparation purposes only and does not imply an endorsement by Mometrix of any particular political, scientific, or religious point of view.

statements or critiques of others discussing the topic. Some authors make their viewpoints very clear by stating it at the beginning of a text; but others want to keep their own opinions somewhat secret for many possible reasons. The author may not want to appear biased in one way or another and certainly some authors try very hard to stay objective. Still there are other authors who have a definite viewpoint but choose to conceal it and use other writers' comments to convey their own viewpoint. The reason it is important to ascertain an author's viewpoint is to ensure that you are reading something that gives a total picture of the topic, without bias.

EXAMPLE 3

Read the following excerpt:

> Dear Editor: We must support the "Save-the-Buffalo" bill before Congress. Anyone with any concern about animal life and the environment must support this bill. The people who vote against it are selfish fools who don't care about the environment.

Describe the viewpoint of the author and tell if the letter could be improved.

> The author of the letter's viewpoint is clear; he states what he thinks right away. He is in favor of the "Save-the-Buffalo" bill and he argues that people should support it if they care about the environment. He also insults those who are against by the bill by calling them selfish fools and saying they don't care about the environment. This letter is not subtle in any way. It is the complete opposite. The letter could be improved by the author using facts or figures to back up his argument rather than insulting those who do not agree with him.

EXAMPLE 3

Explain the purpose of the passage below.

> The gray whale is a baleen whale; it has no teeth. Instead, it has sieve-like plates that hang from the upper jaw to filter krill, plankton, and other small organisms from the sea water. The baleen plates are always wearing out and continue to grow throughout the whale's life.

This passage talks about baleen whales and gives details about them. There is nothing in the passage that tries to persuade the reader and there are no statements of opinion in the passage at all. Instead, all of the statements are facts. This is what a passage does that has as its purpose to inform. It states details or facts about a topic. This passage is not funny, so it is not meant to amuse. The passage does not solve any problem, request anything, or narrate a story either. That is how the reader can tell that its purpose is to inform.

AUTHOR'S PERSPECTIVE

The author will always have specific ideas about a story before they draw up a plot line. This is referred to as the **author's perspective** or **author's viewpoint**. The author will know what events they want to take place, how they want the characters to interact, and how the story will resolve. An author will also have an opinion on the topic, or series of events, which is presented in the story, based on their own prior experience and beliefs.

Each story can be taken in whatever direction the author wishes. A story will often make sense based on societal norms, but the author can purposely choose to go against these norms to shock the reader. For example, if an author wrote a story about a man who enjoyed living in the bayous of Louisiana, the audience would not expect the character to promptly move to Alaska. Sometimes an author will put a twist in a story just to surprise the reader.

Copyright © Mometrix Media. You have been licensed one copy of this document for personal use only. Any other reproduction or redistribution is strictly prohibited. All rights reserved.
This content is provided for test preparation purposes only and does not imply an endorsement by Mometrix of any particular political, scientific, or religious point of view.

EXAMPLE 4

Read the following excerpt:

> Dear Editor: We must support the "Save-the-Buffalo" bill before Congress. Anyone with any concern about animal life and the environment must support this bill. The people who vote against it are selfish fools who don't care about the environment.

Describe the perspective of the author and tell if the letter could be improved.

> The perspective of the author of the letter is clear; he states what he thinks right away. He is in favor of the "Save-the-Buffalo" bill and he argues that people should support it if they care about the environment. He also insults those who are against by the bill by calling them selfish fools and saying they don't care about the environment. This letter is not subtle in any way. It is the complete opposite. The letter could be improved by the author using facts or figures to back up his argument rather than insulting those who do not agree with him.

Author's Use of Print and Graphic Features

PRINT AND GRAPHIC FEATURES

An author may show information in a chart, a graph, in paragraph format, or as a list. Information may also be shown in a picture or a diagram. The way an author chooses to show information is often based on the purpose of the text and the audience that the text is meant to reach.

A reader may be asked to answer questions based on the graphic by itself, how the graphic relates to the text, or how the text would best be shown in a graphic form.

CAUSE AND EFFECT GRAPHIC ORGANIZERS

Often used to map the **elements of a story**. A reader might read a story about a string of events and then be asked to correctly fill in either the **cause** or **effect** of an event in the story.

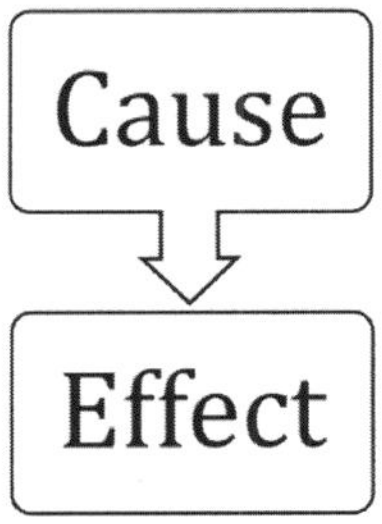

Review Video: Graphic Organizers
Visit mometrix.com/academy and enter code: 665513

EXAMPLE

Read the following excerpt from *Holes* by Louis Sachar and decide what effect Stanley's letter has on his mother.

> Dear Stanley,
> It was wonderful to hear from you. Your letter made me feel like one of the other moms who can afford to send their kids to summer camp. I know it's not the same, but I am very proud of you for trying to make the best of a bad situation.

Copyright © Mometrix Media. You have been licensed one copy of this document for personal use only. Any other reproduction or redistribution is strictly prohibited. All rights reserved.
This content is provided for test preparation purposes only and does not imply an endorsement by Mometrix of any particular political, scientific, or religious point of view.

A **cause and effect** graphic organizer for this excerpt might look something like this:

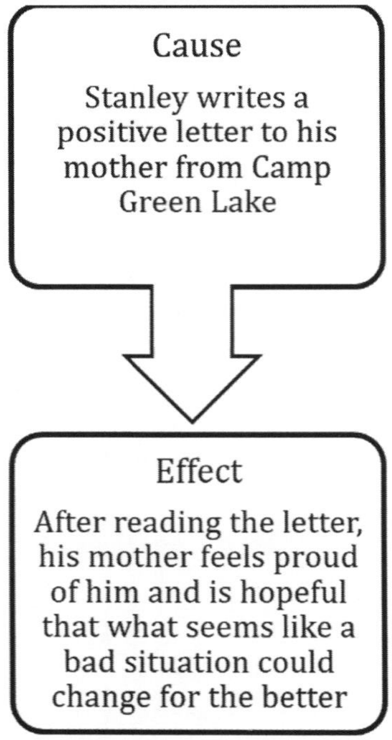

Line Graphs

Used for measuring general **trends over time**. For example, this line graph shows an overall upward trend in the amount of candy bars sold for four weeks.

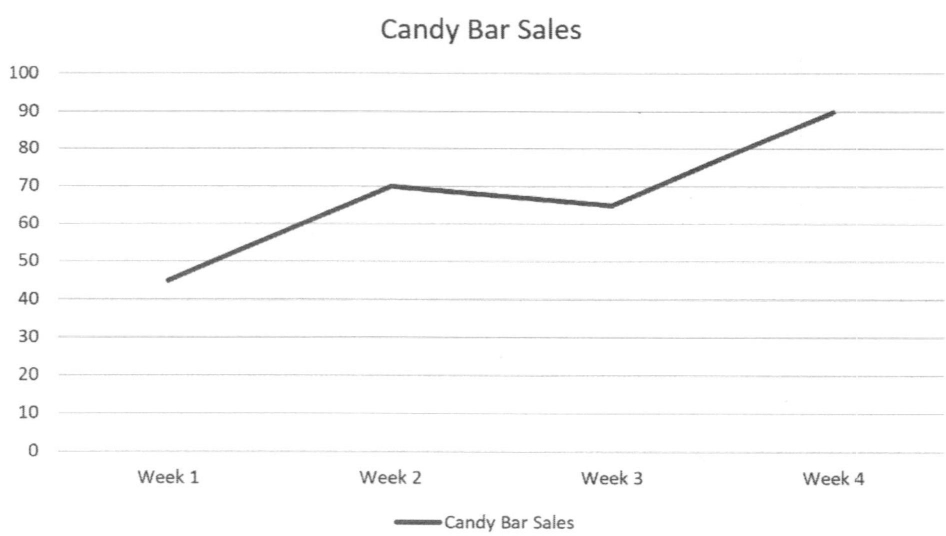

Copyright © Mometrix Media. You have been licensed one copy of this document for personal use only. Any other reproduction or redistribution is strictly prohibited. All rights reserved.
This content is provided for test preparation purposes only and does not imply an endorsement by Mometrix of any particular political, scientific, or religious point of view.

Circle Graphs (also called Pie Charts)

Used to represent information that can be shown as **parts of a whole**. For example, this graph shows the results of people being asked about their favorite color.

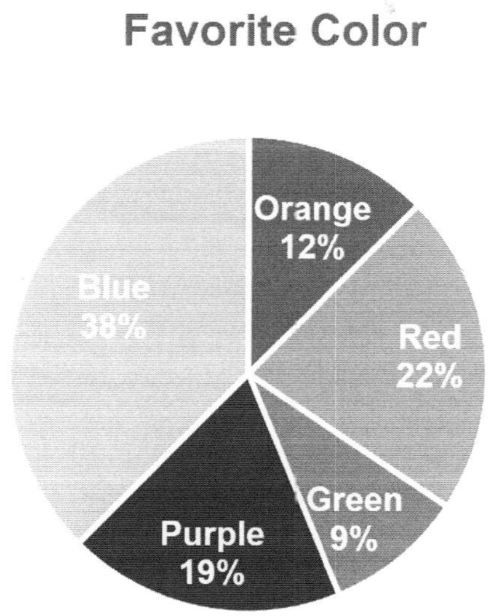

Bar Graphs

Used to illustrate sets of numerical data. The bar graph is one of the most common visual representations of information. For example, this graph is a different way of representing the same results as those in the circle graph.

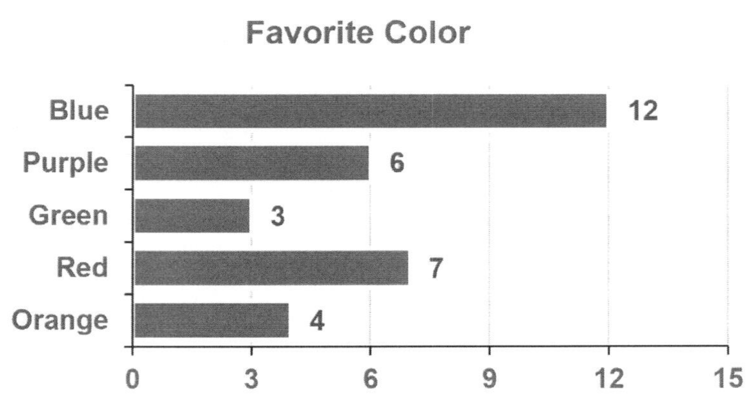

Copyright © Mometrix Media. You have been licensed one copy of this document for personal use only. Any other reproduction or redistribution is strictly prohibited. All rights reserved.
This content is provided for test preparation purposes only and does not imply an endorsement by Mometrix of any particular political, scientific, or religious point of view.

Illustrations and Photographs

Authors may choose to include **illustrations** or **photographs** (or both) with their texts. These two image types both show something from the text or give more information about the text.

Illustrations are drawings of an object. They may be based on reality, or they may represent an artist's abstract idea. For example, this is an illustration of a 1903 automobile.

Photographs are pictures of objects. They are generally extremely realistic, and most often show an object as it actually existed at that moment in time. For example, this is a photograph of a 1917 automobile

Both illustrations and photographs give the reader another way to relate to and understand the text. The reader may be asked how the image relates to the text, what type of caption the image should be given, or why the author chose to include the image with the text.

Diagrams

Used to show information in a visual way. There are many different types of diagrams, including

- Diagrams that show the parts of an object, how they work together, or how they should be put together. This is an example of a diagram which shows how gears turn together

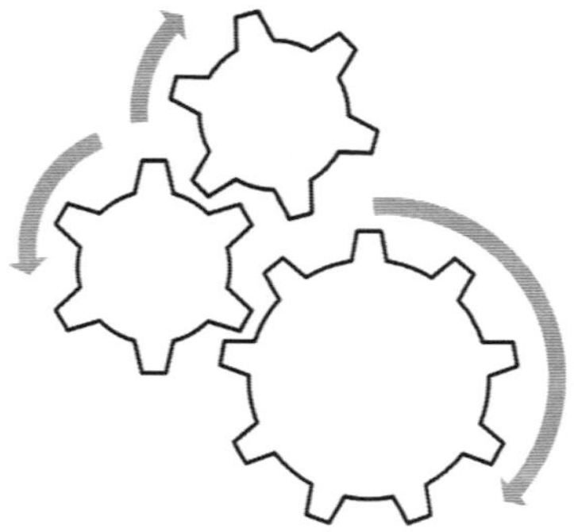

Copyright © Mometrix Media. You have been licensed one copy of this document for personal use only. Any other reproduction or redistribution is strictly prohibited. All rights reserved.
This content is provided for test preparation purposes only and does not imply an endorsement by Mometrix of any particular political, scientific, or religious point of view.

- Diagrams that show how information is related are called **Venn Diagrams**. These are ways to visually see the way in which two different ideas overlap. This is an example of a Venn Diagram comparing cats and dogs

Author's Use of Figurative Language

Literal and Figurative Language

Many types of text use both **literal language**, which means just what it says, and **figurative language**, which allows the writer to expand the way in which he or she uses language. When an author uses figurative language, she connects things in an exaggerated and non-literal way in order to create a memorable image, which helps to describe a situation in a new way for the reader.

Review Video: Figurative Language
Visit mometrix.com/academy and enter code: 584902

Imagery

Imagery is the use of **descriptive language** to add life or feeling to a work of literature. Many authors add literary and sound devices to create vivid pictures in the minds of their readers. Most of the time, imagery is thought to be one of the best ways to help readers fully understand and remember a work.

The most common forms of imagery are those that appeal to the sense of sight and sound. Imagery that appeals to the sense of sight, or **visual imagery**, helps the reader picture an event in their mind, usually by including specific details in the text that are not strictly necessary for the purpose of the story, but allow the reader to more easily envision the scene. Some common forms of figurative language that help create visual imagery include.

Metaphor

- Puts one idea in place of another to draw a parallel between the two ideas.
- For example, an author might write "Her room was a pigsty," to compare a person's bedroom to a dirty spot where pigs sleep.

Simile

- Shows similarity between two ideas or objects, using the words "**like**" or "**as**"
- For example, an author might write "The princess is as beautiful as a rose" to compare the appearance of a woman to a beautiful flower.

Copyright © Mometrix Media. You have been licensed one copy of this document for personal use only. Any other reproduction or redistribution is strictly prohibited. All rights reserved.
This content is provided for test preparation purposes only and does not imply an endorsement by Mometrix of any particular political, scientific, or religious point of view.

Symbolism

- Using one object to stand for something else.
- For example, an author may include a flag flying high throughout a story to show pride in the characters' country and to represent the idea of patriotism.

Hyperbole

- An extreme exaggeration of an idea.
- For example, a character might say "I'm starving to death!" to show that they are really hungry. Most of the time a character who says this is not literally going to die from hunger; they are just ready for a snack.

Irony

- Uses sarcasm or humor (usually with an emphasis on the opposite) to show difference from literal meaning.
- For example, if a character says "Well today must be my lucky day!" after they left their homework on the kitchen table, they are being ironic. The irony used here helps show that it is definitely *not* the character's lucky day.

Personification

- Gives life or human characteristics to an inanimate object
- For example, if an author writes "The trees whispered to each other across the wide blue sky," they are using personification to help the reader imagine the scene. Trees are not human beings, so they do not whisper, but the image created in the reader stands out more than a literal description would.

Example 1

Based on current knowledge, identify whether metaphor, simile, or hyperbole is used in this sentence:

> The chiming bell was a beacon of hope for the downtrodden villagers.

A **metaphor** is used in this sentence to draw a parallel between "the chiming bell" and "a beacon of hope." The bell is being compared to something else in the sentence, which indicates the use of metaphor or simile, but the reader knows that the sentence does not contain a simile, because the words **like** and **as** are not used to show the comparison. The sentence also does not contain an exaggeration of facts, so the reader can see that hyperbole is not used.

Example 2

Discuss the kind of figurative language used in the following poem by the Scottish poet Robert Burns.

> O my luve's like a red, red rose
> That's newly sprung in June;
> O my luve's like the melodie
> That's sweetly played in tune.

The poet uses **similes** to create an image in this poem. The two similes here occur when the speaker says that his love is "**like** a red, red rose" and that she is also "**like** the melodie." These are examples of similes because they use the comparing word 'like' to compare two things. They are not metaphors because metaphors do not use the comparing words 'like' or 'as.' The poem paints an image of the speaker's love by comparing her to a red rose that has newly sprung and a melody that is sweetly played.

Copyright © Mometrix Media. You have been licensed one copy of this document for personal use only. Any other reproduction or redistribution is strictly prohibited. All rights reserved.
This content is provided for test preparation purposes only and does not imply an endorsement by Mometrix of any particular political, scientific, or religious point of view.

Example 3

Read the following excerpt from "The Raven" by Edgar Allan Poe, identify the metaphor, and discuss how it impacts the text:

> And the raven, never flitting, still is sitting, still is sitting
> On the pallid bust of Pallas just above my chamber door;
> And his eyes have all the seeming of a demon's that is dreaming

One **metaphor** in the excerpt from "The Raven" by Edgar Allan Poe is: 'And his eyes have all the seeming of a demon's that is dreaming' The metaphor compares the raven's eyes with a demon, which shows that the speaker thinks there is evil in the bird. This helps contribute to the overall tone of the poem and the reader's understanding of how the speaker views the bird.

Example 4

Read the excerpt from a poem by William Blake and describe what form of figurative language it uses.

> The wild winds weep,
> And the night is a-cold;
> Come hither, sleep,
> And my griefs unfold.

This poem contains several examples of **personification**. In the poem, the speaker says "The wild winds weep," thereby giving the winds the human characteristic of weeping. Later it says "Come hither, sleep," which is another use of personification asking that sleep to go somewhere as though it were a person. The poem gives the winds and sleep human characteristics. This is the definition of personification. It is not an example of simile because there is no comparison using the words "as" or "like." It is not a metaphor because there is no comparison between two things sharing a similar quality. And it is not an example of hyperbole because there is no exaggeration. The poem does contain some alliteration, however; the repetition of the letter "w" in "wild winds weep" qualifies as alliteration, which is another literary technique.

Example 5

Read the excerpt written by Martin Luther King, Jr and identify the type of figurative language Dr. King Jr is using.

> One hundred years later, the Negro is still languishing in the corners of American society and finds himself an exile in his own land.

In this excerpt, Dr. King Jr uses a strong **metaphor** to express what he feels when he compares 'the Negro' to 'an exile in his own land'. An exile is someone who is cast out, but in this case, he is referring to a person living in his own land, so this is an extremely emotional and effective way of demonstrating the problems that African Americans were facing at this time. Figurative language is an effective way to get a point across, as in the case of this metaphor.

Copyright © Mometrix Media. You have been licensed one copy of this document for personal use only. Any other reproduction or redistribution is strictly prohibited. All rights reserved.
This content is provided for test preparation purposes only and does not imply an endorsement by Mometrix of any particular political, scientific, or religious point of view.

Reading Practice Test #1

Questions 1 – 11 pertain to the following passage:

Adventure Land Chase

(1) I had been waiting for Saturday afternoon for what seemed forever. I had the date circled on the calendar in the kitchen, and my mom even let me cross off the days leading up to it. Every day when I would walk into the kitchen, I would see the date circled in a bright green marker and get even more excited.

(2) Saturday was the day that Adventure Land was opening. It is the largest theme park in three states, has massive rollercoaster's that travel at super speed and loop three times, and has a full water park. But it wasn't just the grand opening of Adventure Land about which I was excited. Saturday was also my best friend Riley's birthday, and to celebrate, she was having her birthday party at Adventure Land.

(3) I woke up very early Saturday morning because I could not sleep. I kept thinking about all the rides that we would go on, the games we were going to play, but more than anything, spending time with all of my friends. While I was eating my cereal, my mom packed us a large bag filled with things she said we were going to need at the theme park all day. She packed sunscreen, sunglasses, and water bottles. I didn't pay attention, because I was still too excited about the biggest rollercoaster, the Slithering Cobra. It was the one that shot up really high and had three loops. It was going to be so much fun!

(4) When we first got to the park, my first thought was that it was a lot bigger than I thought it was going to be. It was huge! I could see the tops of the rollercoasters from the car in the parking lot. Inside, everything was made to look like a jungle. There were lots of different kinds of trees, both real and fake, there were long green vines draped across the park like telephone lines, and the workers were dressed up as if they were going on safari. The park was so big, and there was so much to do, but then I noticed one huge problem. There were so many people in the park. Everywhere I looked, there were more people. I was even bumped a few times while we stood at the entrance.

(5) Riley's mom gave all of us wristbands and said that we had to stay with one of our friends at all times.

(6) "Have a buddy," she said. "If anyone gets lost, come to the food court. We will meet at Lickin' Fried Chicken at one o'clock."

(7) Riley was my buddy, and we immediately ran off to go ride the Slithering Cobra.

(8) "Wait up," Charlotte and Ryan called. "We want to come too!"

(9) We stood in line for the ride for over half an hour. There were so many people, and more people kept coming.

(10) "I'm hot," Riley said.

(11) "This is boring," Ryan complained.

Copyright © Mometrix Media. You have been licensed one copy of this document for personal use only. Any other reproduction or redistribution is strictly prohibited. All rights reserved.
This content is provided for test preparation purposes only and does not imply an endorsement by Mometrix of any particular political, scientific, or religious point of view.

(12) When we finally were at the front of the line, the gates opened, and we were allowed to take our seats. Since it was Riley's birthday, they let us ride in the front seats. The rollercoaster took off really fast and went straight into the air. It stopped at the top of the tracks, and it felt as if we were going to fall out of our seats! The rollercoaster tipped over the edge, and soon we were rushing toward the ground. Riley put her arms up, and we both started screaming. The coaster then went straight up and into the three loops. Before we knew it, we were back at the platform, and the ride was over.

(13) "That was awesome!" Charlotte yelled.

(14) "I want to go again!" Ryan added.

(15) We looked at the line, and it had doubled since we had gotten there.

(16) "Maybe later," I said.

(17) When we got off the ride and were walking toward the arcade, our friend Natalie came running up to us. She looked really worried.

(18) "I've lost him," she said. "I lost George! I wasn't supposed to leave him, but I went to the bathroom and now I can't find him!"

(19) "Did you go to the food court?" Ryan asked.

(20) "Yes, and he wasn't there!" she said.

(21) I didn't know what to do. The park was so big, and there were so many people.

(22) "We will have to retrace your steps," Charlotte said. "Where were you the last time you saw him?"

(23) "In the arcade. Playing skee ball."

(24) We all started running toward the arcade, which was shaped like a giant tiger.

(25) "Make sure we all stay together!" Ryan called.

(26) It was really hot, and the sun was beating down right on our faces. I probably should have thought about putting on my sunglasses, but all I could think of was George.

(27) "Who is George?" Riley asked me while we were running.

(28) "I thought you knew!" I said. "I have no idea. Maybe her brother?"

(29) It felt really nice to be inside of the arcade. It looked just like a jungle, too. I kept thinking there was no way we were going to find him, but we had to try. We ran up a flight of stairs and across the room to the skee ball games.

(30) "There he is!" Natalie pointed forward. We didn't see anything. She ran to one of the alleys and picked up a large stuffed monkey. It was George, the stuffed animal from our homeroom that one student has to take home every weekend and write a story about their adventures. We were bewildered.

Copyright © Mometrix Media. You have been licensed one copy of this document for personal use only. Any other reproduction or redistribution is strictly prohibited. All rights reserved.
This content is provided for test preparation purposes only and does not imply an endorsement by Mometrix of any particular political, scientific, or religious point of view.

(31) "That's the George you were talking about?" Riley whined.

(32) "Of course. Mrs. Miller would have killed me if I lost him! But now I have a great adventure to write about!" she said.

(33) We looked at Natalie and laughed.

(34) "Let's go on another ride," I said, and we all started walking back into the jungle.

1. What is the first reason the narrator gives to explain why she was excited about Saturday?

a. It was her best friend's birthday
b. She was going to the beach
c. Adventure Land was opening
d. She was going to have the class's stuffed animal

2. In paragraph 3, the author creates a mood of:

a. Anger
b. Frustration
c. Unease
d. Excitement

3. Paragraphs 1-3 are mainly about:

a. Why the narrator is looking forward to Saturday
b. The fun attractions in the narrator's state
c. Why Adventure Land is fun
d. Who is coming to the party

4. The narrator uses the words "vines" and "safari" to explain that:

a. It is hot outside
b. The theme of the park is the jungle
c. The park is decorated nicely
d. The children are not at home

5. Why did Riley's mom ask that every child have a buddy?

a. So that no one would be lonely
b. So that no one would get lost
c. To make the lines for rides move faster
d. To meet up for lunch

6. Why were the children allowed to ride in the front seat of the rollercoaster?

a. They had been waiting a really long time
b. They were in the line for the front seat
c. They ran and reached the seat the quickest
d. It was their friend's birthday

Copyright © Mometrix Media. You have been licensed one copy of this document for personal use only. Any other reproduction or redistribution is strictly prohibited. All rights reserved.
This content is provided for test preparation purposes only and does not imply an endorsement by Mometrix of any particular political, scientific, or religious point of view.

7. Why does the narrator discuss the number of people at the park?

a. To explain why it was important to not get lost
b. To explain the popularity of the park
c. To justify her complaints about waiting in line
d. To explain that it was hot

8. What is the children's main conflict in this selection?

a. Beating the crowds to get in line for the best ride
b. Wearing sunscreen
c. Trying to find a friend they think is lost
d. Meeting their parents for lunch

9. Why does Ryan ask Natalie if she has been to the food court?

a. He is hungry and wants to know if the food is good
b. It is where they were supposed to go if they were lost
c. It is time to meet up for lunch
d. He thinks she should talk to one of the parents

10. In paragraph 30, what does the word bewildered mean?

a. Happy
b. Upset
c. Confused
d. Numb

11. How is the conflict of the story resolved?

a. The children find George
b. The lines on the rides become shorter
c. The children don't care about a stuffed animal
d. The children leave the park

Questions 12 – 17 pertain to the following passage:

Happily Never After

(1) The tragic story of two star-crossed lovers was first brought to attention in William Shakespeare's play, Romeo and Juliet.

(2) The entire plot of the play is explained in the prologue. It is stated that there are two households of equal status in Verona, Italy. There is an ancient feud between the two families that has progressed into the younger generations, meaning the fight between the parents has now become the fight between the parents' children. The narrator continues, saying, "A pair of star-crossed lovers take their life" and in doing so, end their parents' feud. Romeo and Juliet, a child of each household, fall in love, but cannot live happily together because of the feud. The feud is ended, but it is an act that only the death of these children could make happen.

(3) The majority of stories that audiences enjoy have a happy ending. From childhood, people have grown up with the expectation of an ending that comes with the phrase, "And they lived happily ever after." It is interesting that the story of Romeo and Juliet, a famous tragedy, has extreme popularity and interest among both storytellers and audiences. This raises the question of fascination with tragedy.

Copyright © Mometrix Media. You have been licensed one copy of this document for personal use only. Any other reproduction or redistribution is strictly prohibited. All rights reserved.
This content is provided for test preparation purposes only and does not imply an endorsement by Mometrix of any particular political, scientific, or religious point of view.

(4) In the last act of the play, Juliet has faked her death to escape marriage to another man. A message is supposed to be sent to Romeo explaining that she is alive with a plan for their escape. The message, however, does not reach Romeo. In his despair that he has lost his love, he comes to Juliet's side, drinks poison, and dies. Moments later, Juliet wakes up to find Romeo dead. In her grief, she takes his dagger and kills herself.

(5) Within the prologue, the first moments of the play, the audience is told that the main characters die. It is an interesting way of storytelling. The plot has been ruined, and there is no suspense. The audience is told that Romeo and Juliet die, and in doing so, end their parents' feud. The audience, however, remains, and watches the events take place, even though they know the ending and that it will not be happy.

(6) It is therefore logical to assume that audiences want to believe that a story will end happily, even though they are given evidence that it will not. Audiences will watch the entire play, hoping that something will be done so that the lovers can be saved. And yet, as the prologue stated, the message is not delivered, and the only way that Romeo and Juliet can be together is in death. Their deaths had to take place before the ancient feud would end.

(7) The theme of tragic love has been repeated throughout literary history, although perhaps not brought to the extreme of Romeo and Juliet. Although audiences enjoy stories with a happy ending, the popularity of tragic themes proves that audiences also enjoy stories that do not end happily. It is the hope for happiness that gives tragedies strength, and the hope that things will end differently.

12. Paragraph 2 helps the reader to understand:

a. The characters in Romeo and Juliet
b. The conflict and plot in Romeo and Juliet
c. The mood and tone in Romeo and Juliet
d. The theme of Romeo and Juliet

13. What does the word feud mean in paragraph 5?

a. Fight
b. Happiness
c. Sadness
d. Wealth

14. What is the author's main argument?

a. Romeo and Juliet is a great play
b. Audiences will still hope a tragic story will end happily
c. Tragedies are not as good as stories that have a happy ending
d. Prologues should not ruin the story

15. The author explains that Romeo believes Juliet to be dead because:

a. He watched her take his dagger
b. She drank poison
c. She was ill on her wedding day
d. He never received the message explaining that she faked her death

Copyright © Mometrix Media. You have been licensed one copy of this document for personal use only. Any other reproduction or redistribution is strictly prohibited. All rights reserved.
This content is provided for test preparation purposes only and does not imply an endorsement by Mometrix of any particular political, scientific, or religious point of view.

16. Why does the author think that the prologue in Romeo and Juliet is "an interesting way of storytelling"?

a. The prologue explains that the play is a tragedy
b. The prologue explains how the story will end
c. The prologue is very long
d. The prologue asks the audience a question

17. Why, according to the prologue and author, are Romeo and Juliet's deaths necessary?

a. To make the play a tragedy
b. To show the dangers of poison
c. To end their parents' feud
d. To earn more money and power

Questions 18 – 20 pertain to the following poem:

The Window

Rain spilled like rivers—
the wind whispered
against the window.
Steam rose from the cup
in swirls;
white against the darkness.
Nestled in the warmth
of blankets and tea,
Mother listened to the sounds
knocking outside the window.

18. In the poem, "The Window," what is an example of personification?

a. Spilled
b. Nestled
c. Whispered
d. Rose

19. In the poem, "The Window," the author uses a simile to compare:

a. Steam and swirls
b. Blankets and tea
c. White and darkness
d. Rain and rivers

20. In the poem, "The Window," what is a proper noun?

a. Nestled
b. Mother
c. Rain
d. darkness

Questions 21 – 27 pertain to the following passage:

Musically Inclined

(1) Gibson thought, at least, that it could have been worse. His parents could have named him Fender, given him the middle name Les Paul, or worse yet, Stratocaster.

Copyright © Mometrix Media. You have been licensed one copy of this document for personal use only. Any other reproduction or redistribution is strictly prohibited. All rights reserved.
This content is provided for test preparation purposes only and does not imply an endorsement by Mometrix of any particular political, scientific, or religious point of view.

This was a small comfort to him as he reminded himself that he really never had a chance. It was not he who chose the music. He was born into it, and even named after one of the most famous guitars. It was like the music had found him.

(2) Gibson could not remember a time when he did not know how to play music. His mother was a singer when she was younger, and his father played the lead guitar in the band Mookie Harper. Growing up, he learned to read music at the same time he learned to read words. Music felt as natural to him as walking and was a big part of his life.

(3) There were many instruments in Gibson's house, and over the years, he had learned how to play most of them. He started with a piano when he was very young, moved to the harmonica and drums when he was a bit older, and had just begun learning how to play the violin. But Gibson's favorite instrument was the one he had been playing the longest: his father's Gibson Les Paul guitar.

(4) At school, Gibson felt lonely most days. His family had just moved from Seattle, and the other kids at school thought it was weird that he carried a violin case to school for his fourth period music class. At his old school, he was in the school band, and had a lot of friends who enjoyed playing music with him.

(5) "Why would you play the violin?" Joe asked as he snickered in his chair. "Only girls play that. I bet it was the only thing you could learn," he laughed. The rest of the class laughed behind him.

(6) Gibson sat in his chair and rolled his eyes. He thought that this kid obviously didn't know anything about music, because the violin was one of the most challenging instruments to learn. He left the case on the floor by his chair and waited for his second period history class to begin.

(7) The teacher walked into the classroom pushing a cart. Gibson immediately sat up in his chair. He knew exactly what was in the cases and smiled.

(8) "I was able to borrow these from the music section of the museum to show you today," Ms. Conway said. "Can anyone tell me what these are?" she asked.

(9) "They are guitars, Ms. Conway. Duh," Joe, a boy in the back of the room, said. The class laughed.

(10) Ms. Conway squinted her eyes at Joe. "He is half right," she said. "These are in fact guitars. But can anyone tell me what kind of guitars they are?" She looked around the room. Everyone sat still.

(11) "The one on the right is a 1958 Gibson Les Paul," Gibson said out of the silence. "And the one of the left is a vintage Fender Stratocaster from 1954. Oh, and they are electric guitars," he said.

(12) The class looked at Gibson and stared in silence. Ms. Conway clapped her hands together. "Wow! You're right, Gibson. Great job!"

(13) "How'd you know that?" a girl asked behind him.

Copyright © Mometrix Media. You have been licensed one copy of this document for personal use only. Any other reproduction or redistribution is strictly prohibited. All rights reserved.
This content is provided for test preparation purposes only and does not imply an endorsement by Mometrix of any particular political, scientific, or religious point of view.

(14) "My dad has both of them," he said. "And I've been playing them since I was little."

(15) "You can play the guitar?" Joe laughed. "Yeah right! You play the violin!" He looked around, but no one else was laughing.

(16) "Would you like to play something?" Ms. Conway asked. Gibson looked down at his feet. He didn't know what to say. He just wanted to stay in his seat and have no one look at him.

(17) But then he thought of his dad and smiled. "I'll play the Les Paul," he said. "It's my favorite."

(18) He walked toward the front of the class and picked up the guitar. He played the opening notes of "Gone into the Sun." It was his favorite Mookie Harper song. All of the children sat in awe as they watched him play, and when he was done, they all started clapping and cheering.

(19) "Maybe I'll start playing the violin," the boy next to him said. "If it will get me to play a guitar like that!"

21. Paragraphs 1 through 3 are mainly about:

a. How music has inspired Gibson's family and his life
b. How Gibson will be in a band one day
c. How Gibson wanted to be named after a Fender guitar
d. Why Gibson is moving schools

22. This story is told in what point of view?

a. First-person limited
b. First-person omniscient
c. Third-person omniscient
d. Third-person limited

23. Why did the narrator include the detail that the family was from Seattle?

a. To show why the family loves music
b. To show that Gibson was a new student
c. To show that the family moves a lot because of the father's band
d. To show that the family is on vacation

24. What does Gibson mean when he assumes that he "never really had a chance?"

a. That he was destined to play music because of his family and his name
b. That he was never going to be good at playing the violin
c. That he was never going to be popular at school
d. That he is going to be in a band one day like his father

25. In paragraph 16, why did Gibson want to sit in his seat?

a. He did not like the guitar and did not want to play it
b. He did not want the attention of the other children to be on him
c. He wanted to play the violin instead
d. He thought the guitar was too old to play

Copyright © Mometrix Media. You have been licensed one copy of this document for personal use only. Any other reproduction or redistribution is strictly prohibited. All rights reserved.
This content is provided for test preparation purposes only and does not imply an endorsement by Mometrix of any particular political, scientific, or religious point of view.

26. The author arranges this selection by:

a. Explaining how Gibson grew to like to play the violin
b. Showing how Gibson taught his classmates how to play guitar
c. Listing why the children laughed at Gibson
d. Describing how his love for music helped Gibson be himself at school

27. How is the internal conflict in the story resolved?

a. Gibson is himself and is liked by his classmates
b. Gibson decides not to play in front of everyone
c. Gibson decides to start a band with people in his class
d. Gibson plays a song for his dad

Questions 28 – 36 pertain to the following essay that Timmy has written on why he feels books will soon be a thing of the past:

The Inventions of Technology

(1) Stories have been a part of the world since the beginning of recorded time. For centuries before the invention of the printing press, stories of the world were passed down to generations through oral tradition. With the invention of the printing press, which made written material available to wide ranges of audiences, books were mass-produced and introduced into greater society.

(2) For the last several centuries, books have been at the forefront of education and entertainment. With the invention of the Internet, reliance on books for information quickly changed. Soon, almost everything that anyone needed to know could be accessed through the Internet. Large printed volumes of encyclopedias became unnecessary as all of the information was easily available on the Internet.

(3) Despite the progression of the Internet, printed media was still very popular in the forms of both fiction and non-fiction books. While waiting for an appointment, enduring a several-hour flight, or relaxing before sleep, books have been a reliable and convenient source of entertainment, and one that society has not been willing to give up.

(4) With the progression and extreme convenience of technology, printed books are going to soon become a thing of the past. Inventions such as the iPad from Macintosh and the Kindle have made the need for any kind of printed media unnecessary. With a rechargeable battery, a large screen, and the ability to have several books saved on file, electronic options will soon take over and society will no longer see printed books.

(5) Although some people may say that the act of reading is not complete without turning a page, sliding a finger across the screen or pressing a button to read more onto the next page is just as satisfying to the reader. The iPad and Kindle are devices that have qualities similar to a computer and can be used for so much more than just reading. These devices are therefore better than books because they have multiple uses.

(6) In a cultural society that is part of the world and due to a longstanding tradition, stories will always be an important way to communicate ideas and provide information and entertainment. Centuries ago, stories could only be remembered

Copyright © Mometrix Media. You have been licensed one copy of this document for personal use only. Any other reproduction or redistribution is strictly prohibited. All rights reserved.
This content is provided for test preparation purposes only and does not imply an endorsement by Mometrix of any particular political, scientific, or religious point of view.

and retold through speech. Printed media changed the way the world communicated and was connected, and now, as we move forward with technology, it is only a matter of time before we must say goodbye to the printed past and welcome the digital and electronic future.

28. What is the main argument of this essay?

a. iPad and Kindles are easier to read than books
b. The printing press was a great invention
c. The Internet is how people receive information
d. Technology will soon replace printed material

29. What is the main purpose of paragraph 1?

a. To explain oral tradition
b. To explain the importance of the printing press
c. To explain the progression of stories within society
d. To introduce the essay

30. What does the word enduring mean in paragraph 3?

a. Quitting
b. Undergo
c. Sleeping
d. Thriving

31. According to the essay, what was the first way that stories were communicated and passed down?

a. Oral tradition
b. Printed books
c. Technology
d. Hand writing

32. According to the essay, what changed the reliance on books?

a. Inventions such as the iPad
b. The printing press
c. The Internet
d. Volumes of encyclopedias

33. Which of the following statements is an opinion?

a. Despite the progression of the Internet, printed media was still very popular in the forms of both fiction and non-fiction books
b. Although some people may say that the act of reading is not complete without turning a page, sliding a finger across the screen or pressing a button to read more onto the next page is just as satisfying to the reader
c. With the invention of the Internet, reliance on books for information quickly changed
d. Stories have been a part of the world since the beginning of recorded time

34. What is a secondary argument the author makes?

a. Devices such as the iPad or Kindle are better than books because they have multiple uses
b. Books are still important to have while waiting for an appointment or taking a flight
c. Printed encyclopedias are still used and more convenient that using the Internet
d. With technology, there will soon be no need for stories

Copyright © Mometrix Media. You have been licensed one copy of this document for personal use only. Any other reproduction or redistribution is strictly prohibited. All rights reserved.
This content is provided for test preparation purposes only and does not imply an endorsement by Mometrix of any particular political, scientific, or religious point of view.

35. How is the essay organized?

a. The author explains details as to why he wants to have an iPad
b. The author explains how stories eventually let into oral tradition
c. The author explains technology to explain why books are not needed
d. The author explains the history of stories within society and the ways they progress with time

36. Which of the following statements is not an example of a categorical claim?

a. With a rechargeable battery, a large screen, and the ability to have several books saved on file, electronic options will soon take over and society will no longer see printed books.
b. Soon, almost everything that anyone needed to know could be accessed through the Internet.
c. The iPad and Kindle are devices that have qualities similar to a computer and can be used for so much more than just reading.
d. With the progression and extreme convenience of technology, printed books are going to soon become a thing of the past.

Questions 37 – 42 pertain to the following passage:

The Educational Market Town

(1) Aberystwyth is a market town on the West Coast of Wales within the United Kingdom. A market town refers to European areas that have the right to have markets, which differentiates it from a city or village. The town is located where two rivers meet, the River Ystwyth and River Rheidol and is the best known as an educational center, housing an established university since 1872.

(2) The town is situated between North Wales and South Wales, and is a large vacation destination as well as tourist attraction. Constitution Hill is a hill on the north end of Aberystwyth, which provides excellent views of Cardigan Bay and which is supported by the Aberystwyth Electric Cliff Railway. Although Aberystwyth is known as a modern Welsh town, it is home to several historic buildings, such as the remnants of a castle.

(3) Although there are several grocery, clothing, sporting goods, and various other miscellaneous shops, Aberystwyth is best known for its educational services. Aberystwyth University, formerly known as University College Wales, as well as the National Library of Wales, which is the legal deposit library for Wales and which houses all Welsh publications, are both located within Aberystwyth. The two main languages traditionally spoken in Aberystwyth are English and Welsh. With local live music, arts center, and educational opportunities in gorgeous scenery, Aberystwyth is a hidden luxury within the United Kingdom.

37. What is the purpose of this essay?

a. To explain that the university was established in 1872
b. To explain the legal deposit library in Wales
c. To provide a portrait of a town
d. To explain the views in Aberystwyth

Copyright © Mometrix Media. You have been licensed one copy of this document for personal use only. Any other reproduction or redistribution is strictly prohibited. All rights reserved.
This content is provided for test preparation purposes only and does not imply an endorsement by Mometrix of any particular political, scientific, or religious point of view.

38. What does the word situated mean in paragraph 2?

a. located
b. fighting
c. luxurious
d. hidden

39. Which of the following statements is an opinion?

a. Although Aberystwyth is known as a modern Welsh town, it is home to several historic buildings, such as the remnants of a castle
b. With local live music, arts center, and educational opportunities in gorgeous scenery, Aberystwyth is a hidden luxury within the United Kingdom
c. The two main languages traditionally spoken in Aberystwyth are English and Welsh
d. Aberystwyth is a market town on the West Coast of Wales within the United Kingdom

40. How many languages are traditionally spoken in Aberystwyth?

a. One
b. Two
c. Three
d. More than three

41. What makes Aberystwyth a market town?

a. It is a city
b. It is a village
c. It has the right to have a market
d. There are markets in town every day

42. What is Constitution Hill supported by?

a. Cardigan Bay
b. The ocean
c. North Wales
d. Aberystwyth Electric Cliff Railway

Copyright © Mometrix Media. You have been licensed one copy of this document for personal use only. Any other reproduction or redistribution is strictly prohibited. All rights reserved.
This content is provided for test preparation purposes only and does not imply an endorsement by Mometrix of any particular political, scientific, or religious point of view.

Answer Key and Explanations

1. C: In the first sentence in paragraph 2, it is stated that "Saturday was the day Adventure Land was opening." In paragraph 1, the narrator explains that she is excited and later states that Saturday is her friend's birthday, but the first reason given is that Adventure Land is opening.

2. D: The narrator provides many examples of her excitement throughout paragraph 3, such as that she could not sleep and was not listening to her mom because she was thinking about all of the fun things she was going to do.

3. A: The narrator begins the essay by stating that she was looking forward to Saturday, and the following paragraphs explain why. Although other elements are explained, the main focus is why Saturday is exciting.

4. B: Words like "vines" and "safari" bring about images that reflect the jungle. The narrator explained that the amusement park was decorated in the theme of the jungle and used these words to help create the image.

5. B: Paragraph 5 explains that Riley's mom wanted the children to stay with their buddies, and in paragraph 6, Riley's mom tells the children what to do if they get lost. If the children stayed with their buddy, there was less of a chance of someone getting lost.

6. D: In paragraph 12, the narrator states that since it was her friend's birthday, they were allowed to ride in the front seats.

7. A: The narrator mentions being lost several times throughout the essay, and the central conflict is when the children think someone is lost. The narrator explains that there are many people in the park to create an image that it would be easy to get lost, which would be bad.

8. C: Paragraphs 17-26 explain the conflict the children have when they think someone is lost. They become very worried and try to find George. The narrator mentions earlier that Riley's mother did not want anyone lost, and so the conflict is to find the lost friend.

9. B: Natalie was with George and the children assume that she was his buddy. In paragraph 6, Riley's mother states that if anyone gets lost, they should go to the food court. Since George is lost, the children assume he must have gone to the food court.

10. C: Bewildered means to become confused. Since the children were expecting George to be a person, they were confused to find a stuffed animal.

11. A: The conflict of the story is trying to find George, who is lost. The conflict is resolved when George is found.

15. B: Paragraph 2 explains all of the information that is in the prologue, and the author says that the prologue provides the plot of the play. The conflict is also explained in discussing the feud between the families.

16. A: Feud means disagreement, argument, or fight.

Copyright © Mometrix Media. You have been licensed one copy of this document for personal use only. Any other reproduction or redistribution is strictly prohibited. All rights reserved.
This content is provided for test preparation purposes only and does not imply an endorsement by Mometrix of any particular political, scientific, or religious point of view.

17. B: Paragraphs 6 and 7 explain that the author believes that even though they watch a play with the understanding that it will be tragic, they continue to watch it because they hope it will end happily.

20. D: In paragraph 4, the author explains that Juliet faked her death and that Romeo does not receive the message.

21. B: In paragraph 5, the author explains that it is interesting to explain at the beginning of the play that Romeo and Juliet die and that their deaths end their parents' feud.

22. C: In paragraph 2, the narrator explains that the prologue states that Romeo and Juliet take their lives and in doing so, end their parents' feud.

23. C: Personification is giving human traits to non-human objects. Wind, an object and not a person, cannot whisper.

24. D: A simile compares two things by using the words "like" or "as". The author compares the rain to rivers by using the word, "like".

25. B: "Mother" is a proper noun because it is referring to a unique name, rather than a common noun. "Mother" in the poem is used as a name, which is why it is capitalized.

26. A: Paragraph 1 discusses how Gibson was named and that he was born into music. Paragraph 2 discusses music within his parent's lives. Paragraph 3 discusses how he came to play instruments.

27. D: The story is third-person limited as it is not told in the first-person, by Gibson or any other character, and the narrator only knows the thoughts and feelings of one character, Gibson.

28. B: Paragraph 4 states that Gibson's family had just moved from Seattle, which explains that he is a new student in the school.

29. A: Paragraph 1 discusses music in Gibson's life and the fact that he was born into music through his family and even his name. He thinks that it was the music that chose him, and because of this, he "never really had a chance" to not have music be very involved in his life.

31. B: The narrator explains that Gibson wanted to stay in his seat and have no one look at him. He did not want the attention of the other children.

32. D: From the beginning of the essay, the narrator states that music was always a part of Gibson's life and helped shaped his interests. The essay moves into discussing Gibson at a new school, and eventually how his love of music helps him to be himself at school.

33. A: The conflict in the story is that as a new student, Gibson is teased by his fellow classmates. By showing his love of music as well as his talent, Gibson is himself and is liked by his classmates.

34. D: The main argument is stated in paragraph 4: "With the progression and extreme convenience of technology, printed books are going to soon become a thing of the past."

35. C: Paragraph 1 explains how stories have progressed, beginning with oral tradition and past the invention of the printing press. In context with the rest of the essay, this paragraph is important in explaining how stories progress and are provided within society.

Copyright © Mometrix Media. You have been licensed one copy of this document for personal use only. Any other reproduction or redistribution is strictly prohibited. All rights reserved.
This content is provided for test preparation purposes only and does not imply an endorsement by Mometrix of any particular political, scientific, or religious point of view.

36. B: Enduring means to put up with something unpleasant. Within the sentence, the phrase, "enduring a several hour flight," the word enduring, means to undergo.

37. A: In paragraph 1, it is stated that oral tradition was the main medium for storytelling before the invention of the printing press.

38. C: In paragraph 2, it is stated that reliance on books for information was changed with the invention of the Internet.

39. B: It is not a fact that "sliding a finger across the screen or pressing a button to move onto the next page is just as satisfying to the reader." Satisfaction is not something universal that can be proven for every reader. This statement is an opinion.

40. A: The author makes the argument in paragraph 5 that devices such as the iPad and Kindle are "therefore better than books because they have multiple uses."

41. D: In the beginning of the essay, the author explains how stories were passed through oral tradition. This was changed by the printing press, which is becoming less important with technology and the invention of the Internet and devices such as the iPad and Kindle.

42. C: A categorical claim is an arguable understanding of facts, rather than an absolute fact. The statement regarding the qualities of the iPad and Kindle is the only statement that is a fact.

44. C: The essay provides information on various aspects of the town of Aberystwyth, providing a portrait of the town as a whole.

45. A: Situated means to be placed in a certain location.

46. B: In an essay that is factual, proclaiming that the scenery is "gorgeous" or that a town is a "hidden luxury" is an opinion.

47. B: Paragraph 3 states that two main languages are traditionally spoken in Aberystwyth.

48. C: Paragraph 1 states, "A market town refers to European areas that have the right to have markets, which differentiates it from a city or village."

49. D: Paragraph 2 states, "Constitution Hill is a hill on the north end of Aberystwyth, which provides excellent views of Cardigan Bay and which is supported by the Aberystwyth Electric Cliff Railway."

Copyright © Mometrix Media. You have been licensed one copy of this document for personal use only. Any other reproduction or redistribution is strictly prohibited. All rights reserved.
This content is provided for test preparation purposes only and does not imply an endorsement by Mometrix of any particular political, scientific, or religious point of view.

Reading Practice Test #2

Questions 1 – 10 pertain to the following passage:

SUMMER'S HEAT

(1) I remember the day as if it were yesterday. It was Saturday afternoon and cloudless. The sun beat down upon my face, even through the chain link fenced dugout. It was so hot that I could feel my skin burning, and I was sweating, even though I wasn't on the field. I sat on the bench with a jug of water at my feet and a fistful of sunflower seeds. We were losing, three to one. I looked at our right fielder, Johnny, who was fanning his face with his glove as he was getting ready for the play.

(2) The ball was hit to the third basemen, and he got the last out of the inning at first base. The team ran into a huddle, and our coach told us to keep our eye on the ball. "Concentrate," he said.

(3) Philip hit the ball to the fence and was stopped on second base by the coaches. We were all shouting and very happy with his double. The next batter bunted the ball to the pitcher, and moved Philip to third base. Johnny then came to the plate and hit a double. Philip scored, and we were one run away from tying the game.

(4) "Max!" the coach shouted.

(5) I turned my head and was shocked to see that I wasn't imagining things. Coach was pointing right at me.

(6) "You're up," he said.

(7) I threw my sunflower seeds to the ground, stuffed my helmet onto my head, and grabbed my favorite bat. I took two practice swings and was ready for the pitcher.

(8) I hit two foul balls over the side fences. They were hard, and flew for a long time before ever hitting the ground. I was going to do it. I was going to get Johnny to home plate. I just needed one good pitch.

(9) The pitcher looked down at his feet and then stared into my eyes. I stared back. It was like there was no one else on the field. It was just us. He started his windup, and I dug my feet into the ground and adjusted my grip on the bat. The ball came in and I swung at hard as I could.

(10) I was confused. I didn't feel anything.

(11) "Strike three!" the umpire yelled behind me.

(12) I was out.

(13) Bradley came up after me and we ended up losing the game, three to two.

(14) The coaches told us we played a good game. They said that it was a team effort and that we should be proud of ourselves. My mom told me it was not my fault. "It was no one's fault," she said. "It is just a game."

Copyright © Mometrix Media. You have been licensed one copy of this document for personal use only. Any other reproduction or redistribution is strictly prohibited. All rights reserved.
This content is provided for test preparation purposes only and does not imply an endorsement by Mometrix of any particular political, scientific, or religious point of view.

(15) But it was not just a game to me. I felt like I had let everyone down and disappointed all of my teammates. It was the last game of the season, and we lost.

(16) I decided at that moment to spend my summer vacation training. I was going to do nothing but practice baseball. I spent two weeks outside, with just my baseball bat and a bucket of balls. I hit until it was dark and my mom forced me to come inside and eat dinner. When I asked her if we could install some lights into the backyard so that I could see and practice more, she looked at me with a very stern face and said the most horrible sentence.

(17) "No more baseball for the rest of the summer."

(18) My heart dropped. I felt sick to my stomach and filled with anger.

(19) "How can you do this to me?" I shouted back.

(20) "There is more to life than baseball," she said. "I want you to enjoy spending the summer playing with your friends."

(21) She then grounded me for the weekend for shouting at her.

(22) After a few days without baseball, I realized how fun it was to be a regular kid and spend time with my friends, swimming in the pool, fishing in the lake, and climbing trees. Once, someone suggested we play some baseball, and we gathered some of our friends together and played a game in the park. We didn't keep score, and had fun just playing. It was a great summer.

(23) When baseball season came around again, I played center field. My first time up to bat, I smiled. I was having fun. The pitch came and I swung hard. The ball landed on the other side of the fence, and I ran around the bases to cheers after hitting my first homerun.

1. What image is created in paragraph 1?

a. Saturday is boring
b. Baseball players are lazy
c. It is hot outside
d. The month of July

2. Why does the narrator include the detail that Johnny was "fanning his face with his glove"?

a. To demonstrate that Johnny is lazy
b. To explain why Max should be playing instead of Johnny
c. To show that Johnny is bored
d. To provide another image that it is hot outside

3. Why did Max's mom tell him no more baseball?

a. She wanted him to have fun and not worry about practice
b. She did not want to install lights
c. She was afraid he was going to get hurt
d. She did not want him to be a baseball player anymore

Copyright © Mometrix Media. You have been licensed one copy of this document for personal use only. Any other reproduction or redistribution is strictly prohibited. All rights reserved.
This content is provided for test preparation purposes only and does not imply an endorsement by Mometrix of any particular political, scientific, or religious point of view.

4. What is the point of view of the essay?

a. First-person omniscient
b. First-person limited
c. Third-person omniscient
d. Third-person limited

5. Why did Max think he was imagining things?

a. It was so hot outside
b. He could not believe his team was losing
c. The coach was calling his name to come into the game to bat
d. He was surprised to see that Philip scored

6. In paragraph 9, the author creates the mood of:

a. Tension
b. Anger
c. Comfort
d. Sadness

7. Why was Max confused after he swung in paragraph 10?

a. It was his first swing
b. He did not hit the ball
c. He hit the ball far
d. He thought he had another opportunity to hit

8. What does the word install mean in paragraph 16?

a. Break
b. Turn on
c. Put in
d. Make bigger

9. What is the main conflict of this essay?

a. Max balancing having fun with his love of baseball
b. Max striking out
c. Max's team losing the game
d. Max's mom forbidding baseball

10. How is the conflict resolved?

a. Max gets better at baseball
b. Max gets a new baseball team
c. Max's mom lets him practice more
d. Max realizing that baseball is a game and should be fun

Questions 11 – 18 pertain to the following passage:

Eating at the Theater

(1) Last Saturday night my family went to go see a movie, and I was introduced to an amazing movie theater, the Alamo Drafthouse Cinema. The Alamo Drafthouse Cinema is like no other movie theater experience. For one thing, no one under the age of eighteen is allowed into the theater without a parent or guardian, no matter the rating of the film. The most incredible part of the Alamo Drafthouse Cinema, and

Copyright © Mometrix Media. You have been licensed one copy of this document for personal use only. Any other reproduction or redistribution is strictly prohibited. All rights reserved.
This content is provided for test preparation purposes only and does not imply an endorsement by Mometrix of any particular political, scientific, or religious point of view.

what makes it so unique, is that you get to order an entire meal, get it delivered, and eat it all while watching the movie.

(2) The Alamo Drafthouse Cinema originated in Austin, Texas, and started out as a single screen theater. The unique concept caught a lot of attention and popularity, and soon, the theater was home to film premiers, and even hosted local and visiting filmmakers. In the years since its inception, the Alamo Drafthouse Cinema has grown into a larger franchise. There are currently five locations in Austin, and the theater has expanded into Houston, San Antonio, and Winchester, Virginia.

(3) When we first walked into the lobby, I noticed the decorations on the walls. They were very intricate and three-dimensional, and made me feel like I was a part of the theater, or maybe a part of the movie. When we were able to get inside of the theater, I was surprised to see that it looked like a normal movie theater expect for a large tabletop that extended across the length of every aisle of seats.

(4) I ordered a meal of chicken tenders and French fries, and my sister ordered a hamburger. We were not surprised to find that the food was delicious. Everything about the theater was great. The members of the staff inside of the lobby were very friendly, and our waiter was very nice. Throughout the movie, he walked as quickly as he could so that he would not disrupt the movie. My entire family had a wonderful time at the movies on Saturday, and we have all decided to go back again, to the Alamo Drafthouse Cinema.

11. Which of the following statements is an opinion?

a. The Alamo Drafthouse Cinema originated in Austin, Texas, and started out as a single screen theater.
b. For one thing, no one under the age of eighteen is allowed into the theater without a parent or guardian, no matter the rating of the film.
c. Everything about the theater was great.
d. In the years since its inception, the Alamo Drafthouse Cinema has grown into a larger franchise.

12. Why does the narrator say that the Alamo Drafthouse Cinema is "like no other movie theater experience"?

a. The movies are not shown at other theaters
b. The lobby is better
c. The food tastes better
d. No one under 18 can be admitted without a parent or guardian

13. What does the word intricate mean in paragraph 3?

a. Sturdy
b. Detailed
c. Flat
d. Expensive

Copyright © Mometrix Media. You have been licensed one copy of this document for personal use only. Any other reproduction or redistribution is strictly prohibited. All rights reserved.
This content is provided for test preparation purposes only and does not imply an endorsement by Mometrix of any particular political, scientific, or religious point of view.

14. Why did the narrator say that she felt a part of the theater?

a. The lobby had three-dimensional decorations
b. The large tabletop was familiar
c. The service was excellent
d. The narrator could order a meal

15. Why was the narrator not surprised that the food was delicious?

a. Because the narrator ordered normally good tasting food
b. Because the movie was really good
c. Because food tastes better when watching a movie
d. Because everything at the theater was good

16. The narrator said that the inside of the theater looked like a normal movie theater except:

a. There were three-dimensional decorations on the wall
b. There were no lights
c. There were round tables all around
d. There was a tabletop that extended across the aisle

17. In what order is this essay organized?

a. A review of the film and experience
b. An introduction, history of the theater, and description of experience
c. An introduction, description of the physical theater, and dislikes
d. A detailed explanation of the history of the theater

18. How many cities have at least one Alamo Drafthouse Cinema?

a. Four
b. Three
c. Five
d. One

Questions 19 – 29 pertain to the following passage:

The Royal Scenery

(1) To celebrate their fifteenth wedding anniversary, my parents decided to take our family on vacation to London. This was the first time that I had ever been out of the country, and I was very excited. While in London, we discovered some really cool places, but my favorite was The Regent's Park in the City of Westminster in central London.

(2) The Regent's Park, to which most people refer to as "Regent's Park," is one of the eight Royal Parks in Greater London. A Royal Park is land that was once owned by the royal monarchy, or crown, of the United Kingdom. A monarchy is a form of government where a monarch acts as the head of state. Currently, Queen Elizabeth II is the monarch of the United Kingdom.

(3) The parks were originally used as recreation for the royal family, but have been opened to the general public over the last two centuries. The largest of the Royal Parks in Central London are The Regent's Park, Hyde Park, St. James's Park, Green

Copyright © Mometrix Media. You have been licensed one copy of this document for personal use only. Any other reproduction or redistribution is strictly prohibited. All rights reserved.
This content is provided for test preparation purposes only and does not imply an endorsement by Mometrix of any particular political, scientific, or religious point of view.

Park, and Kensington Gardens, although the largest Royal Park in London is Richmond Park.

(4) Regent's Park is very big, and there are many attractions and things to do for both London citizens and travelers. Immediately, I was amazed with the beautiful scenery and the plethora of trees and ponds. It is also a very popular site for physical activities and exercise. There are several fields that are known as "sport pitches" that are used for soccer, cricket, rugby, and other sports. The park is lined with pedestrian trails, and there were many walkers and joggers.

(5) Regent's Park was my favorite park because it housed the London Zoo. In an attempt to create a close replica to the animals' natural environment, the animals were in the open, out of cages, in enclosed areas. My favorite attraction was the Galapagos Tortoises exhibit, as they were the largest tortoises I had ever seen.

(6) We all had a great time in London, and I loved seeing all of the great London attractions. It surprised me that with everything available to do in London, my favorite part of the city was a Royal Park.

19. What is the purpose for paragraph 1?

a. To talk about the narrator's parents' anniversary
b. To introduce why the family was in London
c. To explain what it was like to travel to London
d. To explain why the narrator liked central London

20. What does the word replica mean in paragraph 5?

a. Item
b. Family
c. Copy
d. Habitat

21. What is the largest Royal Park in London?

a. The Regent's Park
b. Hyde Park
c. Kensington Gardens
d. Richmond Park

22. What does the word plethora mean paragraph 4?

a. Excess
b. Ugliness
c. Few
d. Color

23. What reason did the narrator state for Regent's Park being her favorite?

a. It was the prettiest park
b. It was close to Hyde Park
c. It housed the London Zoo
d. It had fields for cricket

Copyright © Mometrix Media. You have been licensed one copy of this document for personal use only. Any other reproduction or redistribution is strictly prohibited. All rights reserved.
This content is provided for test preparation purposes only and does not imply an endorsement by Mometrix of any particular political, scientific, or religious point of view.

24. What was the original use for the Royal Parks?

a. To house Royal Zoos
b. It was where the monarch ruled
c. It was the site of the monarch's garden
d. Recreation for the royal family

25. What are "sport pitches"?

a. Pitchers for sport teams
b. Sport fields
c. Attractions in the zoo
d. Pedestrian trails

26. What was the narrator's favorite attraction at the zoo?

a. Galapagos Tortoises
b. The atrium
c. Butterfly Paradise
d. Reptile House

27. Why are some parks known as "Royal Parks"?

a. Queen Elizabeth II likes them
b. The parks are land originally owned by the monarchy
c. The parks are the biggest parks in London
d. It is where the head of state lives

28. Why was it surprising to the narrator that a park was her favorite part of the city?

a. Because parks are normally really boring
b. Because there is normally not a zoo at a park
c. Because the park is ugly
d. Because there are so many other fun attractions in London

29. What is the general purpose of this essay?

a. To talk about Regent's Park
b. To talk about Queen Elizabeth II
c. To talk about the narrator's trip to London
d. To talk about the London Zoo

Questions 30 – 38 pertain to the following passage:

The Little Big Surprise

(1) This cannot be happening to me, I thought. Not at my age. Not at their age! This was without a doubt, the worst possible thing that could be happening to me, and it was going to change all of our lives forever.

(2) It was a Sunday morning in late February. I had been studying all morning for a vocabulary test I had later in the week. I thought it was going to be my biggest problem for the week. I had no idea what was coming my way. My mom knocked on my door and asked me to come downstairs. We were going to be having a family meeting.

Copyright © Mometrix Media. You have been licensed one copy of this document for personal use only. Any other reproduction or redistribution is strictly prohibited. All rights reserved.
This content is provided for test preparation purposes only and does not imply an endorsement by Mometrix of any particular political, scientific, or religious point of view.

(3) Family meeting? I thought. It seemed really strange. We never had family meetings. Nothing was ever so formal. It had been just my mom, my dad, and me for twelve years, and whenever there was anything to be discussed, they just told me. But a family meeting? This was weird.

(4) I looked at my last flashcard and went downstairs. My parents were both sitting at the table and had very serious looks on their faces. At first, I thought I must have been in trouble, but I hadn't done anything wrong, at least that I knew. Then I saw a small smile come over my mom's face. She was really happy.

(5) I sat down. "What's going on?" I asked. "Is something wrong?"

(6) And then my mom said the most awful thing I could ever imagine.

(7) "You are going to have a new brother or sister!"

(8) I could not even process the information. Nothing made sense. They could not be having another baby! I was old! They were even older! I was in junior high, and I would be going to high school soon. People in high school didn't have baby brothers or sisters, did they? I was an only child! I was supposed to always be the only child!

(9) I immediately left the table and stormed into my bedroom. I went back to my flashcards and tried to forget everything that they had just said. I didn't want to think about things changing. I liked my life. I did not want everything to be changed and ruined.

(10) Over the next few months, I watched as my mother's stomach grew. It was amazing how quickly it all happened. Once it started, it seemed to grow more each week. My dad would laugh and say that the baby must be pretty big. It was interesting to think about a baby growing, but I did not want to think about anything.

(11) During the summer, my parents turned their office into a nursery. They painted the room a pale yellow color and bought a crib. Soon the room was filled with diapers, wipes, and baby powder. Everything smelled weird, like a baby.

(12) I tried not to think about how the house was looking different and that my mom was getting bigger every day. But then in the beginning of August, right before I was supposed to start school again, my mom said she had to go to the hospital. And my heart sank.

(13) "Is there something wrong?" I asked. "Are you okay? Is the baby okay?"

(14) My mom smiled at me. I thought that was pretty weird since she said she needed to be at the hospital.

(15) "The baby is fine," she said. "The baby is just ready to be born."

(16) My dad grabbed her overnight bad, and we raced to the car.

(17) A few hours later, my dad came out to see my grandparents and me in the waiting room. He had a big smile on his face and called out to me.

Copyright © Mometrix Media. You have been licensed one copy of this document for personal use only. Any other reproduction or redistribution is strictly prohibited. All rights reserved.
This content is provided for test preparation purposes only and does not imply an endorsement by Mometrix of any particular political, scientific, or religious point of view.

(18) "Do you want to meet your brother?" he said.

(19) A brother? I have a brother? I couldn't believe it. I walked into the room and saw my mom holding a baby. The nurses said he was a big baby, but he looked so little sitting in my mom's arms.

(20) "That's my brother," I said, and I could feel a huge smile spreading across my face. "I have a brother." It was amazing. I had someone to share my life and whom I could teach about the world.

(21) "His name is Gavin," my mom said. "Do you want to hold him?"

(22) I took my brother in my arms and smiled.

(23) "You're late," I said to him. "You should have been here years ago, but I'm glad you are here now."

30. What mood is created in paragraph 1?

a. Sadness
b. Anger
c. Suspense
d. Fear

31. Why did the narrator think the family meeting was weird?

a. Family meetings were usually on Saturdays
b. They had never had a family meeting before
c. They only had family meetings when the narrator was in trouble
d. Family meetings would not normally take place while the narrator was studying

32. What did the narrator think his biggest problem of the week was going to be?

a. A vocabulary test
b. A math test
c. A sports competition
d. The cold weather in February

33. What is the central conflict?

a. The narrator does not like babies
b. The narrator thinks his parents won't love him anymore
c. The narrator is afraid something is wrong with the baby
d. The narrator does not want his life to change

34. What does the word process mean in paragraph 8?

a. Handle
b. Understand
c. Maintain
d. Enjoy

Copyright © Mometrix Media. You have been licensed one copy of this document for personal use only. Any other reproduction or redistribution is strictly prohibited. All rights reserved.
This content is provided for test preparation purposes only and does not imply an endorsement by Mometrix of any particular political, scientific, or religious point of view.

35. What was a main reason the narrator used for why his parents could not have another baby?

a. His parents were old
b. They did not have room in the house
c. There would be more family meetings
d. The baby would get in too much trouble

36. In paragraph 10, the phrase "I did not want to think about anything" helps the reader to understand:

a. The narrator does not like to think
b. The narrator is confused
c. The narrator thinks a baby growing is weird
d. The narrator does not want his life to change

37. Why did the narrator's heart sink when his mom had to go to the hospital?

a. He knew the baby was coming
b. He was not ready yet
c. He was afraid there was something wrong with his mom or the baby
d. His dad was not home.

38. How is the narrator's internal conflict resolved?

a. He does well on the vocabulary test
b. His brother is born and he realizes he loves him
c. He thinks his life won't change that much
d. He started a new school year

Questions 39 – 42 pertain to the following passage:

What's Real About It?

(1) I suppose I don't understand why it is called reality television. It has been argued that reality television has been a part of television since the beginnings of television programming. Through game shows and daytime talk shows, real people, as in non-actors, have made appearances on television for the entertainment of others. A new genre of reality television that became the new phenomenon, however, was introduced in the year 2000, with shows such as "Survivor."

(2) The idea behind "Survivor" is like many in reality television. There are contestants, they are put in extreme situations, and in the end, someone wins a prize. The other main style of reality television involves cameras following someone around as they live their daily life.

(3) My confusion comes from the title of reality. Reality means the state of which things actually exist, but reality television does not display the state in which life actually exists. In real life, not many people will be deserted on a distant island or forced to live in a house with several strangers. Additionally, cameras do not follow people around on a normal day. People live their lives, and exist in a reality that is not meant for entertainment or for masses of people to watch.

(4) It is no surprise to discover that most audiences find it interesting to watch people who are not actors on television. There is something intriguing about fame

Copyright © Mometrix Media. You have been licensed one copy of this document for personal use only. Any other reproduction or redistribution is strictly prohibited. All rights reserved
This content is provided for test preparation purposes only and does not imply an endorsement by Mometrix of any particular political, scientific, or religious point of view.

for the average person. It is as if the viewer can relate more to the show that he or she is watching, because it is real people put in fake situations rather than fake people and characters acting in life-like situations. However, there cannot be anything called reality television that would be both an accurate description of life and provide necessary entertainment.

39. What is the main argument of this essay?

a. Reality television is not entertainment
b. Reality television uses actors
c. The basis of reality television is not reality
d. Most people do not enjoy reality television

40. Which of the following statements is not an opinion?

a. "Reality means the state of which things actually exist"
b. "There is something intriguing about fame for the average person"
c. "I suppose I don't understand why it is called reality television"
d. "It is as if the viewer can relate more to the show that he or she is watching"

41. How long does the author say that reality television has been a part of television?

a. Since 2000
b. Since the early 1950s
c. Within the last ten years
d. Since the beginning of television programming

42. Why does the author assume audiences like to watch reality television?

a. They enjoy watching real-life situations
b. Viewers can relate more to real people than actors
c. They wish they could be celebrities
d. They want to win prizes

Copyright © Mometrix Media. You have been licensed one copy of this document for personal use only. Any other reproduction or redistribution is strictly prohibited. All rights reserved.
This content is provided for test preparation purposes only and does not imply an endorsement by Mometrix of any particular political, scientific, or religious point of view.

Answer Key and Explanations

1. C: The author provides several images in paragraph 1, such as the day being cloudless, the sun beating down, skin burning, and sweating that create the image of that it is hot outside.

2. D: In paragraph 1, the author creates several images to display the overwhelming heat outside. Johnny fanning his face with his glove is another example.

3. A: Paragraph 16 explains that Max planned to spend the entire summer training for baseball. In paragraph 20, Max's mom explains that there is more to life than baseball and that she wants him to spend his summer having fun with his friends.

4. B: The story is told from Max's point of view, in the first person. The point of view is also limited because the audience does not receive any other character's thoughts and feelings.

5. C: It is explained in paragraph 1 that Max is sitting on the bench and is not playing in the game. In paragraph 5, Max explains that when he saw the coach pointing at him, he knew he was not imagining things.

6. A: Max and the pitcher are both in pressure situations. Max wants to hit the ball and help his team, and the pitcher wants to help his own team by not letting Max hit the ball. The mood is tense, as the author creates tension.

7. B: In paragraph 9, Max explains that he swung as hard as he could. In paragraph 10, Max says, "I didn't feel anything," and in paragraph 11, it is explained that Max struck out. He was confused because he did not hit the ball. He swung and he missed.

8. C: Install means to put in.

9. A: Max struggles throughout the essay to see that it was not anyone's fault that the team lost the baseball game. In believing that he let his team down, Max wants to practice baseball all summer and get better, but he is no longer having fun. His conflict is in having fun with baseball.

10. D: In paragraph 23, it is explained that Max smiled and was having fun when it was his turn to bat, and he ended up hitting a homerun.

11. C: To say, "everything about the theater was great," cannot be proven as fact. This is strictly an opinion that could differ with another person.

12. D: Paragraph 1 states, "The Alamo Drafthouse Cinema is like no other movie theater experience. For one thing, no one under the age of eighteen is allowed into the theater without a parent or guardian, no matter the rating of the film."

13. B: Intricate means extremely complicated or detailed.

14. A: In paragraph 3, the narrator states that the decorations in the lobby were "three-dimensional, and made me feel like I was a part of the theater, or maybe a part of the movie."

15. D: In paragraph 4, the narrator explains that, "Everything about the theater was great."

16. D: Paragraph 3 states, "I was surprised to see that it looked like a normal movie theater expect for a large tabletop that extended across the length of every aisle of seats."

Copyright © Mometrix Media. You have been licensed one copy of this document for personal use only. Any other reproduction or redistribution is strictly prohibited. All rights reserved.
This content is provided for test preparation purposes only and does not imply an endorsement by Mometrix of any particular political, scientific, or religious point of view.

17. B: The essay begins with an introduction as to why the narrator was at the theater, followed by a brief history of the theater to provide the reader with context, and ending with the narrator's own personal experience at the theater.

18. A: Austin, Houston, San Antonio, and Winchester all have at least one Alamo Drafthouse Cinema location.

19. B: The essay describes The Regent's Park in London, and the purpose of paragraph 1 is to introduce the essay and explain why the narrator was in London and discovered The Regent's Park.

20. C: Replica means an exact copy of something, especially on a smaller scale.

21. D: Paragraph 3 states that "the largest Royal Park in London is Richmond Park."

22. A: Plethora means an excess of something.

23. C: Paragraph 5 states, "Regent's Park was my favorite park because it housed the London Zoo."

24. D: Paragraph 3 states, "The parks were originally used as recreation for the royal family."

25. B: Paragraph 4 states, "There are several fields that are known as 'sport pitches' that are used for soccer, cricket, rugby, and other sports."

26. A: In paragraph 5, the narrator states, "My favorite attraction was the Galapagos Tortoises exhibit."

27. B: Paragraph 2 states, "A Royal Park is land that was once owned by the royal monarchy, or crown, of the United Kingdom."

28. D: In paragraph 6, the narrator states, "It surprised me that with everything available to do in London, my favorite part of the city was a Royal Park."

29. A: The majority of the essay is focused on The Regent's Park in central London. The attractions are discussed, as well as the history and purpose of the park.

30. C: The author creates a mood of suspense by not explaining what has happened to make the narrator feel like something was "the worst possible thing that could be happening to me."

31. B: Paragraph 3 states, "We never had family meetings." The narrator thinks that the meeting is strange because they had never had meetings before.

32. A: In paragraph 2, the narrator explains that he was studying for a vocabulary test he had later in the week. He then mentions that he thought it was going to be the biggest problem of the week.

33. D: Throughout the essay, the narrator explains that he likes his life and does not want things to change. He expresses that he is the only child and was supposed to always be an only child. In paragraph 9, he states, "I didn't want to think about things changing. I liked my life. I did not want everything to be changed and ruined."

34. B: When used as a verb, process means to gain acceptance or an understanding.

35. A: The narrator mentions in both paragraph 1 and paragraph 8 that he felt as though his parents were too old to have another baby and that he was too old to have a baby sibling.

Copyright © Mometrix Media. You have been licensed one copy of this document for personal use only. Any other reproduction or redistribution is strictly prohibited. All rights reserved.
This content is provided for test preparation purposes only and does not imply an endorsement by Mometrix of any particular political, scientific, or religious point of view.

36. D: The narrator mentions in paragraph 9, "I didn't want to think about things changing." In the next paragraph the narrator mentions that even though it was interesting to think about a baby growing, he still did not want to think about anything, meaning his life changing.

37. C: In paragraph 13, the narrator asks his mom if something is wrong and if she and the baby are okay.

38. B: In paragraph 20, the narrator states, "It was amazing. I had someone to share my life and whom I could teach about the world." The narrator comes to an understanding that even though his life is going to change, it is okay because he loves his brother and his new life will be good with his brother.

39. C: The author states in paragraph 3, "reality television does not display the state of which life actually exists." Throughout the essay, the narrator discusses the ways in which reality television does not reflect reality.

40. A: In this statement, the author is providing a factual definition of a word.

41. D: Paragraph 1 states, "It has been argued that reality television has been a part of television since the beginnings of television programming."

42. B: In paragraph 4, the author explains her assumptions that viewers relate more to real people than actors. "It is as if the viewer can relate more to the show that he or she is watching, because it is real people put in fake situations rather than fake people and characters acting in life-like situations."

Copyright © Mometrix Media. You have been licensed one copy of this document for personal use only. Any other reproduction or redistribution is strictly prohibited. All rights reserved.
This content is provided for test preparation purposes only and does not imply an endorsement by Mometrix of any particular political, scientific, or religious point of view.

How to Overcome Test Anxiety

Just the thought of taking a test is enough to make most people a little nervous. A test is an important event that can have a long-term impact on your future, so it's important to take it seriously and it's natural to feel anxious about performing well. But just because anxiety is normal, that doesn't mean that it's helpful in test taking, or that you should simply accept it as part of your life. Anxiety can have a variety of effects. These effects can be mild, like making you feel slightly nervous, or severe, like blocking your ability to focus or remember even a simple detail.

If you experience test anxiety—whether severe or mild—it's important to know how to beat it. To discover this, first you need to understand what causes test anxiety.

Causes of Test Anxiety

While we often think of anxiety as an uncontrollable emotional state, it can actually be caused by simple, practical things. One of the most common causes of test anxiety is that a person does not feel adequately prepared for their test. This feeling can be the result of many different issues such as poor study habits or lack of organization, but the most common culprit is time management. Starting to study too late, failing to organize your study time to cover all of the material, or being distracted while you study will mean that you're not well prepared for the test. This may lead to cramming the night before, which will cause you to be physically and mentally exhausted for the test. Poor time management also contributes to feelings of stress, fear, and hopelessness as you realize you are not well prepared but don't know what to do about it.

Other times, test anxiety is not related to your preparation for the test but comes from unresolved fear. This may be a past failure on a test, or poor performance on tests in general. It may come from comparing yourself to others who seem to be performing better or from the stress of living up to expectations. Anxiety may be driven by fears of the future—how failure on this test would affect your educational and career goals. These fears are often completely irrational, but they can still negatively impact your test performance.

Elements of Test Anxiety

As mentioned earlier, test anxiety is considered to be an emotional state, but it has physical and mental components as well. Sometimes you may not even realize that you are suffering from test anxiety until you notice the physical symptoms. These can include trembling hands, rapid heartbeat, sweating, nausea, and tense muscles. Extreme anxiety may lead to fainting or vomiting. Obviously, any of these symptoms can have a negative impact on testing. It is important to recognize them as soon as they begin to occur so that you can address the problem before it damages your performance.

The mental components of test anxiety include trouble focusing and inability to remember learned information. During a test, your mind is on high alert, which can help you recall information and stay focused for an extended period of time. However, anxiety interferes with your mind's natural processes, causing you to blank out, even on the questions you know well. The strain of testing during anxiety makes it difficult to stay focused, especially on a test that may take several hours. Extreme anxiety can take a huge mental toll, making it difficult not only to recall test information but even to understand the test questions or pull your thoughts together.

Copyright © Mometrix Media. You have been licensed one copy of this document for personal use only. Any other reproduction or redistribution is strictly prohibited. All rights reserved.
This content is provided for test preparation purposes only and does not imply an endorsement by Mometrix of any particular political, scientific, or religious point of view.

Effects of Test Anxiety

Test anxiety is like a disease—if left untreated, it will get progressively worse. Anxiety leads to poor performance, and this reinforces the feelings of fear and failure, which in turn lead to poor performances on subsequent tests. It can grow from a mild nervousness to a crippling condition. If allowed to progress, test anxiety can have a big impact on your schooling, and consequently on your future.

Test anxiety can spread to other parts of your life. Anxiety on tests can become anxiety in any stressful situation, and blanking on a test can turn into panicking in a job situation. But fortunately, you don't have to let anxiety rule your testing and determine your grades. There are a number of relatively simple steps you can take to move past anxiety and function normally on a test and in the rest of life.

Physical Steps for Beating Test Anxiety

While test anxiety is a serious problem, the good news is that it can be overcome. It doesn't have to control your ability to think and remember information. While it may take time, you can begin taking steps today to beat anxiety.

Just as your first hint that you may be struggling with anxiety comes from the physical symptoms, the first step to treating it is also physical. Rest is crucial for having a clear, strong mind. If you are tired, it is much easier to give in to anxiety. But if you establish good sleep habits, your body and mind will be ready to perform optimally, without the strain of exhaustion. Additionally, sleeping well helps you to retain information better, so you're more likely to recall the answers when you see the test questions.

Getting good sleep means more than going to bed on time. It's important to allow your brain time to relax. Take study breaks from time to time so it doesn't get overworked, and don't study right before bed. Take time to rest your mind before trying to rest your body, or you may find it difficult to fall asleep.

Along with sleep, other aspects of physical health are important in preparing for a test. Good nutrition is vital for good brain function. Sugary foods and drinks may give a burst of energy but this burst is followed by a crash, both physically and emotionally. Instead, fuel your body with protein and vitamin-rich foods.

Also, drink plenty of water. Dehydration can lead to headaches and exhaustion, especially if your brain is already under stress from the rigors of the test. Particularly if your test is a long one, drink water during the breaks. And if possible, take an energy-boosting snack to eat between sections.

Along with sleep and diet, a third important part of physical health is exercise. Maintaining a steady workout schedule is helpful, but even taking 5-minute study breaks to walk can help get your blood pumping faster and clear your head. Exercise also releases endorphins, which contribute to a positive feeling and can help combat test anxiety.

When you nurture your physical health, you are also contributing to your mental health. If your body is healthy, your mind is much more likely to be healthy as well. So take time to rest, nourish your body with healthy food and water, and get moving as much as possible. Taking these physical steps will make you stronger and more able to take the mental steps necessary to overcome test anxiety.

Copyright © Mometrix Media. You have been licensed one copy of this document for personal use only. Any other reproduction or redistribution is strictly prohibited. All rights reserved.
This content is provided for test preparation purposes only and does not imply an endorsement by Mometrix of any particular political, scientific, or religious point of view.

Mental Steps for Beating Test Anxiety

Working on the mental side of test anxiety can be more challenging, but as with the physical side, there are clear steps you can take to overcome it. As mentioned earlier, test anxiety often stems from lack of preparation, so the obvious solution is to prepare for the test. Effective studying may be the most important weapon you have for beating test anxiety, but you can and should employ several other mental tools to combat fear.

First, boost your confidence by reminding yourself of past success—tests or projects that you aced. If you're putting as much effort into preparing for this test as you did for those, there's no reason you should expect to fail here. Work hard to prepare; then trust your preparation.

Second, surround yourself with encouraging people. It can be helpful to find a study group, but be sure that the people you're around will encourage a positive attitude. If you spend time with others who are anxious or cynical, this will only contribute to your own anxiety. Look for others who are motivated to study hard from a desire to succeed, not from a fear of failure.

Third, reward yourself. A test is physically and mentally tiring, even without anxiety, and it can be helpful to have something to look forward to. Plan an activity following the test, regardless of the outcome, such as going to a movie or getting ice cream.

When you are taking the test, if you find yourself beginning to feel anxious, remind yourself that you know the material. Visualize successfully completing the test. Then take a few deep, relaxing breaths and return to it. Work through the questions carefully but with confidence, knowing that you are capable of succeeding.

Developing a healthy mental approach to test taking will also aid in other areas of life. Test anxiety affects more than just the actual test—it can be damaging to your mental health and even contribute to depression. It's important to beat test anxiety before it becomes a problem for more than testing.

Study Strategy

Being prepared for the test is necessary to combat anxiety, but what does being prepared look like? You may study for hours on end and still not feel prepared. What you need is a strategy for test prep. The next few pages outline our recommended steps to help you plan out and conquer the challenge of preparation.

Step 1: Scope Out the Test

Learn everything you can about the format (multiple choice, essay, etc.) and what will be on the test. Gather any study materials, course outlines, or sample exams that may be available. Not only will this help you to prepare, but knowing what to expect can help to alleviate test anxiety.

Step 2: Map Out the Material

Look through the textbook or study guide and make note of how many chapters or sections it has. Then divide these over the time you have. For example, if a book has 15 chapters and you have five days to study, you need to cover three chapters each day. Even better, if you have the time, leave an extra day at the end for overall review after you have gone through the material in depth.

If time is limited, you may need to prioritize the material. Look through it and make note of which sections you think you already have a good grasp on, and which need review. While you are studying, skim quickly through the familiar sections and take more time on the challenging parts.

Copyright © Mometrix Media. You have been licensed one copy of this document for personal use only. Any other reproduction or redistribution is strictly prohibited. All rights reserved.
This content is provided for test preparation purposes only and does not imply an endorsement by Mometrix of any particular political, scientific, or religious point of view.

Write out your plan so you don't get lost as you go. Having a written plan also helps you feel more in control of the study, so anxiety is less likely to arise from feeling overwhelmed at the amount to cover.

Step 3: Gather Your Tools

Decide what study method works best for you. Do you prefer to highlight in the book as you study and then go back over the highlighted portions? Or do you type out notes of the important information? Or is it helpful to make flashcards that you can carry with you? Assemble the pens, index cards, highlighters, post-it notes, and any other materials you may need so you won't be distracted by getting up to find things while you study.

If you're having a hard time retaining the information or organizing your notes, experiment with different methods. For example, try color-coding by subject with colored pens, highlighters, or post-it notes. If you learn better by hearing, try recording yourself reading your notes so you can listen while in the car, working out, or simply sitting at your desk. Ask a friend to quiz you from your flashcards, or try teaching someone the material to solidify it in your mind.

Step 4: Create Your Environment

It's important to avoid distractions while you study. This includes both the obvious distractions like visitors and the subtle distractions like an uncomfortable chair (or a too-comfortable couch that makes you want to fall asleep). Set up the best study environment possible: good lighting and a comfortable work area. If background music helps you focus, you may want to turn it on, but otherwise keep the room quiet. If you are using a computer to take notes, be sure you don't have any other windows open, especially applications like social media, games, or anything else that could distract you. Silence your phone and turn off notifications. Be sure to keep water close by so you stay hydrated while you study (but avoid unhealthy drinks and snacks).

Also, take into account the best time of day to study. Are you freshest first thing in the morning? Try to set aside some time then to work through the material. Is your mind clearer in the afternoon or evening? Schedule your study session then. Another method is to study at the same time of day that you will take the test, so that your brain gets used to working on the material at that time and will be ready to focus at test time.

Step 5: Study!

Once you have done all the study preparation, it's time to settle into the actual studying. Sit down, take a few moments to settle your mind so you can focus, and begin to follow your study plan. Don't give in to distractions or let yourself procrastinate. This is your time to prepare so you'll be ready to fearlessly approach the test. Make the most of the time and stay focused.

Of course, you don't want to burn out. If you study too long you may find that you're not retaining the information very well. Take regular study breaks. For example, taking five minutes out of every hour to walk briskly, breathing deeply and swinging your arms, can help your mind stay fresh.

As you get to the end of each chapter or section, it's a good idea to do a quick review. Remind yourself of what you learned and work on any difficult parts. When you feel that you've mastered the material, move on to the next part. At the end of your study session, briefly skim through your notes again.

But while review is helpful, cramming last minute is NOT. If at all possible, work ahead so that you won't need to fit all your study into the last day. Cramming overloads your brain with more information than it can process and retain, and your tired mind may struggle to recall even

Copyright © Mometrix Media. You have been licensed one copy of this document for personal use only. Any other reproduction or redistribution is strictly prohibited. All rights reserved.
This content is provided for test preparation purposes only and does not imply an endorsement by Mometrix of any particular political, scientific, or religious point of view.

previously learned information when it is overwhelmed with last-minute study. Also, the urgent nature of cramming and the stress placed on your brain contribute to anxiety. You'll be more likely to go to the test feeling unprepared and having trouble thinking clearly.

So don't cram, and don't stay up late before the test, even just to review your notes at a leisurely pace. Your brain needs rest more than it needs to go over the information again. In fact, plan to finish your studies by noon or early afternoon the day before the test. Give your brain the rest of the day to relax or focus on other things, and get a good night's sleep. Then you will be fresh for the test and better able to recall what you've studied.

Step 6: Take a Practice Test

Many courses offer sample tests, either online or in the study materials. This is an excellent resource to check whether you have mastered the material, as well as to prepare for the test format and environment.

Check the test format ahead of time: the number of questions, the type (multiple choice, free response, etc.), and the time limit. Then create a plan for working through them. For example, if you have 30 minutes to take a 60-question test, your limit is 30 seconds per question. Spend less time on the questions you know well so that you can take more time on the difficult ones.

If you have time to take several practice tests, take the first one open book, with no time limit. Work through the questions at your own pace and make sure you fully understand them. Gradually work up to taking a test under test conditions: sit at a desk with all study materials put away and set a timer. Pace yourself to make sure you finish the test with time to spare and go back to check your answers if you have time.

After each test, check your answers. On the questions you missed, be sure you understand why you missed them. Did you misread the question (tests can use tricky wording)? Did you forget the information? Or was it something you hadn't learned? Go back and study any shaky areas that the practice tests reveal.

Taking these tests not only helps with your grade, but also aids in combating test anxiety. If you're already used to the test conditions, you're less likely to worry about it, and working through tests until you're scoring well gives you a confidence boost. Go through the practice tests until you feel comfortable, and then you can go into the test knowing that you're ready for it.

Test Tips

On test day, you should be confident, knowing that you've prepared well and are ready to answer the questions. But aside from preparation, there are several test day strategies you can employ to maximize your performance.

First, as stated before, get a good night's sleep the night before the test (and for several nights before that, if possible). Go into the test with a fresh, alert mind rather than staying up late to study.

Try not to change too much about your normal routine on the day of the test. It's important to eat a nutritious breakfast, but if you normally don't eat breakfast at all, consider eating just a protein bar. If you're a coffee drinker, go ahead and have your normal coffee. Just make sure you time it so that the caffeine doesn't wear off right in the middle of your test. Avoid sugary beverages, and drink enough water to stay hydrated but not so much that you need a restroom break 10 minutes into the

Copyright © Mometrix Media. You have been licensed one copy of this document for personal use only. Any other reproduction or redistribution is strictly prohibited. All rights reserved.
This content is provided for test preparation purposes only and does not imply an endorsement by Mometrix of any particular political, scientific, or religious point of view.

test. If your test isn't first thing in the morning, consider going for a walk or doing a light workout before the test to get your blood flowing.

Allow yourself enough time to get ready, and leave for the test with plenty of time to spare so you won't have the anxiety of scrambling to arrive in time. Another reason to be early is to select a good seat. It's helpful to sit away from doors and windows, which can be distracting. Find a good seat, get out your supplies, and settle your mind before the test begins.

When the test begins, start by going over the instructions carefully, even if you already know what to expect. Make sure you avoid any careless mistakes by following the directions.

Then begin working through the questions, pacing yourself as you've practiced. If you're not sure on an answer, don't spend too much time on it, and don't let it shake your confidence. Either skip it and come back later, or eliminate as many wrong answers as possible and guess among the remaining ones. Don't dwell on these questions as you continue—put them out of your mind and focus on what lies ahead.

Be sure to read all of the answer choices, even if you're sure the first one is the right answer. Sometimes you'll find a better one if you keep reading. But don't second-guess yourself if you do immediately know the answer. Your gut instinct is usually right. Don't let test anxiety rob you of the information you know.

If you have time at the end of the test (and if the test format allows), go back and review your answers. Be cautious about changing any, since your first instinct tends to be correct, but make sure you didn't misread any of the questions or accidentally mark the wrong answer choice. Look over any you skipped and make an educated guess.

At the end, leave the test feeling confident. You've done your best, so don't waste time worrying about your performance or wishing you could change anything. Instead, celebrate the successful completion of this test. And finally, use this test to learn how to deal with anxiety even better next time.

Review Video: Test Anxiety
Visit mometrix.com/academy and enter code: 100340

Important Qualification

Not all anxiety is created equal. If your test anxiety is causing major issues in your life beyond the classroom or testing center, or if you are experiencing troubling physical symptoms related to your anxiety, it may be a sign of a serious physiological or psychological condition. If this sounds like your situation, we strongly encourage you to seek professional help.

Copyright © Mometrix Media. You have been licensed one copy of this document for personal use only. Any other reproduction or redistribution is strictly prohibited. All rights reserved.
This content is provided for test preparation purposes only and does not imply an endorsement by Mometrix of any particular political, scientific, or religious point of view.

Online Resources

Due to our efforts to try to keep this book to a manageable length, we've created a link that will give you access to all of your online resources:

mometrix.com/resources719/ssmcag7read

It's Your Moment, Let's Celebrate It!

Share your story @mometrixtestpreparation

Copyright © Mometrix Media. You have been licensed one copy of this document for personal use only. Any other reproduction or redistribution is strictly prohibited. All rights reserved.
This content is provided for test preparation purposes only and does not imply an endorsement by Mometrix of any particular political, scientific, or religious point of view.

DEAR FUTURE EXAM SUCCESS STORY

First of all, **THANK YOU** for purchasing Mometrix study materials!

Second, congratulations! You are one of the few determined test-takers who are committed to doing whatever it takes to excel on your exam. **You have come to the right place.** We developed these study materials with one goal in mind: to deliver you the information you need in a format that's concise and easy to use.

In addition to optimizing your guide for the content of the test, we've outlined our recommended steps for breaking down the preparation process into small, attainable goals so you can make sure you stay on track.

We've also analyzed the entire test-taking process, identifying the most common pitfalls and showing how you can overcome them and be ready for any curveball the test throws you.

Standardized testing is one of the biggest obstacles on your road to success, which only increases the importance of doing well in the high-pressure, high-stakes environment of test day. Your results on this test could have a significant impact on your future, and this guide provides the information and practical advice to help you achieve your full potential on test day.

Your success is our success

We would love to hear from you! If you would like to share the story of your exam success or if you have any questions or comments in regard to our products, please contact us at **800-673-8175** or **support@mometrix.com**.

Thanks again for your business and we wish you continued success!

Sincerely,
The Mometrix Test Preparation Team

Need more help? Check out our flashcards at:
http://mometrixflashcards.com/MTTC

Copyright © 2026 by Mometrix Media LLC. All rights reserved.
Written and edited by the Mometrix Exam Secrets Test Prep Team
Printed in the United States of America

TABLE OF CONTENTS

Introduction

Thank you for purchasing this resource! You have made the choice to prepare yourself for a test that could have a huge impact on your future, and this guide is designed to help you be fully ready for test day. Obviously, it's important to have a solid understanding of the test material, but you also need to be prepared for the unique environment and stressors of the test, so that you can perform to the best of your abilities.

For this purpose, the first section that appears in this guide is the **Secret Keys**. We've devoted countless hours to meticulously researching what works and what doesn't, and we've boiled down our findings to the five most impactful steps you can take to improve your performance on the test. We start at the beginning with study planning and move through the preparation process, all the way to the testing strategies that will help you get the most out of what you know when you're finally sitting in front of the test.

We recommend that you start preparing for your test as far in advance as possible. However, if you've bought this guide as a last-minute study resource and only have a few days before your test, we recommend that you skip over the first two Secret Keys since they address a long-term study plan.

If you struggle with **test anxiety**, we strongly encourage you to check out our recommendations for how you can overcome it. Test anxiety is a formidable foe, but it can be beaten, and we want to make sure you have the tools you need to defeat it.

Copyright © Mometrix Media. You have been licensed one copy of this document for personal use only. Any other reproduction or redistribution is strictly prohibited. All rights reserved.
This content is provided for test preparation purposes only and does not imply an endorsement by Mometrix of any particular political, scientific, or religious point of view.

Secret Key #1 – Plan Big, Study Small

There's a lot riding on your performance. If you want to ace this test, you're going to need to keep your skills sharp and the material fresh in your mind. You need a plan that lets you review everything you need to know while still fitting in your schedule. We'll break this strategy down into three categories.

Information Organization

Start with the information you already have: the official test outline. From this, you can make a complete list of all the concepts you need to cover before the test. Organize these concepts into groups that can be studied together, and create a list of any related vocabulary you need to learn so you can brush up on any difficult terms. You'll want to keep this vocabulary list handy once you actually start studying since you may need to add to it along the way.

Time Management

Once you have your set of study concepts, decide how to spread them out over the time you have left before the test. Break your study plan into small, clear goals so you have a manageable task for each day and know exactly what you're doing. Then just focus on one small step at a time. When you manage your time this way, you don't need to spend hours at a time studying. Studying a small block of content for a short period each day helps you retain information better and avoid stressing over how much you have left to do. You can relax knowing that you have a plan to cover everything in time. In order for this strategy to be effective though, you have to start studying early and stick to your schedule. Avoid the exhaustion and futility that comes from last-minute cramming!

Study Environment

The environment you study in has a big impact on your learning. Studying in a coffee shop, while probably more enjoyable, is not likely to be as fruitful as studying in a quiet room. It's important to keep distractions to a minimum. You're only planning to study for a short block of time, so make the most of it. Don't pause to check your phone or get up to find a snack. It's also important to **avoid multitasking**. Research has consistently shown that multitasking will make your studying dramatically less effective. Your study area should also be comfortable and well-lit so you don't have the distraction of straining your eyes or sitting on an uncomfortable chair.

The time of day you study is also important. You want to be rested and alert. Don't wait until just before bedtime. Study when you'll be most likely to comprehend and remember. Even better, if you know what time of day your test will be, set that time aside for study. That way your brain will be used to working on that subject at that specific time and you'll have a better chance of recalling information.

Finally, it can be helpful to team up with others who are studying for the same test. Your actual studying should be done in as isolated an environment as possible, but the work of organizing the information and setting up the study plan can be divided up. In between study sessions, you can discuss with your teammates the concepts that you're all studying and quiz each other on the details. Just be sure that your teammates are as serious about the test as you are. If you find that your study time is being replaced with social time, you might need to find a new team.

Copyright © Mometrix Media. You have been licensed one copy of this document for personal use only. Any other reproduction or redistribution is strictly prohibited. All rights reserved.
This content is provided for test preparation purposes only and does not imply an endorsement by Mometrix of any particular political, scientific, or religious point of view.

Secret Key #2 – Make Your Studying Count

You're devoting a lot of time and effort to preparing for this test, so you want to be absolutely certain it will pay off. This means doing more than just reading the content and hoping you can remember it on test day. It's important to make every minute of study count. There are two main areas you can focus on to make your studying count.

Retention

It doesn't matter how much time you study if you can't remember the material. You need to make sure you are retaining the concepts. To check your retention of the information you're learning, try recalling it at later times with minimal prompting. Try carrying around flashcards and glance at one or two from time to time or ask a friend who's also studying for the test to quiz you.

To enhance your retention, look for ways to put the information into practice so that you can apply it rather than simply recalling it. If you're using the information in practical ways, it will be much easier to remember. Similarly, it helps to solidify a concept in your mind if you're not only reading it to yourself but also explaining it to someone else. Ask a friend to let you teach them about a concept you're a little shaky on (or speak aloud to an imaginary audience if necessary). As you try to summarize, define, give examples, and answer your friend's questions, you'll understand the concepts better and they will stay with you longer. Finally, step back for a big picture view and ask yourself how each piece of information fits with the whole subject. When you link the different concepts together and see them working together as a whole, it's easier to remember the individual components.

Finally, practice showing your work on any multi-step problems, even if you're just studying. Writing out each step you take to solve a problem will help solidify the process in your mind, and you'll be more likely to remember it during the test.

Modality

Modality simply refers to the means or method by which you study. Choosing a study modality that fits your own individual learning style is crucial. No two people learn best in exactly the same way, so it's important to know your strengths and use them to your advantage.

For example, if you learn best by visualization, focus on visualizing a concept in your mind and draw an image or a diagram. Try color-coding your notes, illustrating them, or creating symbols that will trigger your mind to recall a learned concept. If you learn best by hearing or discussing information, find a study partner who learns the same way or read aloud to yourself. Think about how to put the information in your own words. Imagine that you are giving a lecture on the topic and record yourself so you can listen to it later.

For any learning style, flashcards can be helpful. Organize the information so you can take advantage of spare moments to review. Underline key words or phrases. Use different colors for different categories. Mnemonic devices (such as creating a short list in which every item starts with the same letter) can also help with retention. Find what works best for you and use it to store the information in your mind most effectively and easily.

Copyright © Mometrix Media. You have been licensed one copy of this document for personal use only. Any other reproduction or redistribution is strictly prohibited. All rights reserved.
This content is provided for test preparation purposes only and does not imply an endorsement by Mometrix of any particular political, scientific, or religious point of view.

Secret Key #3 – Practice the Right Way

Your success on test day depends not only on how many hours you put into preparing, but also on whether you prepared the right way. It's good to check along the way to see if your studying is paying off. One of the most effective ways to do this is by taking practice tests to evaluate your progress. Practice tests are useful because they show exactly where you need to improve. Every time you take a practice test, pay special attention to these three groups of questions:

- The questions you got wrong
- The questions you had to guess on, even if you guessed right
- The questions you found difficult or slow to work through

This will show you exactly what your weak areas are, and where you need to devote more study time. Ask yourself why each of these questions gave you trouble. Was it because you didn't understand the material? Was it because you didn't remember the vocabulary? Do you need more repetitions on this type of question to build speed and confidence? Dig into those questions and figure out how you can strengthen your weak areas as you go back to review the material.

Additionally, many practice tests have a section explaining the answer choices. It can be tempting to read the explanation and think that you now have a good understanding of the concept. However, an explanation likely only covers part of the question's broader context. Even if the explanation makes perfect sense, **go back and investigate** every concept related to the question until you're positive you have a thorough understanding.

As you go along, keep in mind that the practice test is just that: practice. Memorizing these questions and answers will not be very helpful on the actual test because it is unlikely to have any of the same exact questions. If you only know the right answers to the sample questions, you won't be prepared for the real thing. **Study the concepts** until you understand them fully, and then you'll be able to answer any question that shows up on the test.

It's important to wait on the practice tests until you're ready. If you take a test on your first day of study, you may be overwhelmed by the amount of material covered and how much you need to learn. Work up to it gradually.

On test day, you'll need to be prepared for answering questions, managing your time, and using the test-taking strategies you've learned. It's a lot to balance, like a mental marathon that will have a big impact on your future. Like training for a marathon, you'll need to start slowly and work your way up. When test day arrives, you'll be ready.

Start with the strategies you've read in the first two Secret Keys—plan your course and study in the way that works best for you. If you have time, consider using multiple study resources to get different approaches to the same concepts. It can be helpful to see difficult concepts from more than one angle. Then find a good source for practice tests. Many times, the test website will suggest potential study resources or provide sample tests.

Copyright © Mometrix Media. You have been licensed one copy of this document for personal use only. Any other reproduction or redistribution is strictly prohibited. All rights reserved.
This content is provided for test preparation purposes only and does not imply an endorsement by Mometrix of any particular political, scientific, or religious point of view.

Practice Test Strategy

If you're able to find at least three practice tests, we recommend this strategy:

Untimed and Open-Book Practice

Take the first test with no time constraints and with your notes and study guide handy. Take your time and focus on applying the strategies you've learned.

Timed and Open-Book Practice

Take the second practice test open-book as well, but set a timer and practice pacing yourself to finish in time.

Timed and Closed-Book Practice

Take any other practice tests as if it were test day. Set a timer and put away your study materials. Sit at a table or desk in a quiet room, imagine yourself at the testing center, and answer questions as quickly and accurately as possible.

Keep repeating timed and closed-book tests on a regular basis until you run out of practice tests or it's time for the actual test. Your mind will be ready for the schedule and stress of test day, and you'll be able to focus on recalling the material you've learned.

Copyright © Mometrix Media. You have been licensed one copy of this document for personal use only. Any other reproduction or redistribution is strictly prohibited. All rights reserved.
This content is provided for test preparation purposes only and does not imply an endorsement by Mometrix of any particular political, scientific, or religious point of view.

Secret Key #4 – Pace Yourself

Once you're fully prepared for the material on the test, your biggest challenge on test day will be managing your time. Just knowing that the clock is ticking can make you panic even if you have plenty of time left. Work on pacing yourself so you can build confidence against the time constraints of the exam. Pacing is a difficult skill to master, especially in a high-pressure environment, so **practice is vital**.

Set time expectations for your pace based on how much time is available. For example, if a section has 60 questions and the time limit is 30 minutes, you know you have to average 30 seconds or less per question in order to answer them all. Although 30 seconds is the hard limit, set 25 seconds per question as your goal, so you reserve extra time to spend on harder questions. When you budget extra time for the harder questions, you no longer have any reason to stress when those questions take longer to answer.

Don't let this time expectation distract you from working through the test at a calm, steady pace, but keep it in mind so you don't spend too much time on any one question. Recognize that taking extra time on one question you don't understand may keep you from answering two that you do understand later in the test. If your time limit for a question is up and you're still not sure of the answer, mark it and move on, and come back to it later if the time and the test format allow. If the testing format doesn't allow you to return to earlier questions, just make an educated guess; then put it out of your mind and move on.

On the easier questions, be careful not to rush. It may seem wise to hurry through them so you have more time for the challenging ones, but it's not worth missing one if you know the concept and just didn't take the time to read the question fully. Work efficiently but make sure you understand the question and have looked at all of the answer choices, since more than one may seem right at first.

Even if you're paying attention to the time, you may find yourself a little behind at some point. You should speed up to get back on track, but do so wisely. Don't panic; just take a few seconds less on each question until you're caught up. Don't guess without thinking, but do look through the answer choices and eliminate any you know are wrong. If you can get down to two choices, it is often worthwhile to guess from those. Once you've chosen an answer, move on and don't dwell on any that you skipped or had to hurry through. If a question was taking too long, chances are it was one of the harder ones, so you weren't as likely to get it right anyway.

On the other hand, if you find yourself getting ahead of schedule, it may be beneficial to slow down a little. The more quickly you work, the more likely you are to make a careless mistake that will affect your score. You've budgeted time for each question, so don't be afraid to spend that time. Practice an efficient but careful pace to get the most out of the time you have.

Copyright © Mometrix Media. You have been licensed one copy of this document for personal use only. Any other reproduction or redistribution is strictly prohibited. All rights reserved.
This content is provided for test preparation purposes only and does not imply an endorsement by Mometrix of any particular political, scientific, or religious point of view.

Secret Key #5 – Have a Plan for Guessing

When you're taking the test, you may find yourself stuck on a question. Some of the answer choices seem better than others, but you don't see the one answer choice that is obviously correct. What do you do?

The scenario described above is very common, yet most test takers have not effectively prepared for it. Developing and practicing a plan for guessing may be one of the single most effective uses of your time as you get ready for the exam.

In developing your plan for guessing, there are three questions to address:

- When should you start the guessing process?
- How should you narrow down the choices?
- Which answer should you choose?

When to Start the Guessing Process

Unless your plan for guessing is to select C every time (which, despite its merits, is not what we recommend), you need to leave yourself enough time to apply your answer elimination strategies. Since you have a limited amount of time for each question, that means that if you're going to give yourself the best shot at guessing correctly, you have to decide quickly whether or not you will guess.

Of course, the best-case scenario is that you don't have to guess at all, so first, see if you can answer the question based on your knowledge of the subject and basic reasoning skills. Focus on the key words in the question and try to jog your memory of related topics. Give yourself a chance to bring the knowledge to mind, but once you realize that you don't have (or you can't access) the knowledge you need to answer the question, it's time to start the guessing process.

It's almost always better to start the guessing process too early than too late. It only takes a few seconds to remember something and answer the question from knowledge. Carefully eliminating wrong answer choices takes longer. Plus, going through the process of eliminating answer choices can actually help jog your memory.

Summary: Start the guessing process as soon as you decide that you can't answer the question based on your knowledge.

Copyright © Mometrix Media. You have been licensed one copy of this document for personal use only. Any other reproduction or redistribution is strictly prohibited. All rights reserved.
This content is provided for test preparation purposes only and does not imply an endorsement by Mometrix of any particular political, scientific, or religious point of view.

How to Narrow Down the Choices

The next chapter in this book (**Test-Taking Strategies**) includes a wide range of strategies for how to approach questions and how to look for answer choices to eliminate. You will definitely want to read those carefully, practice them, and figure out which ones work best for you. Here though, we're going to address a mindset rather than a particular strategy.

Your odds of guessing an answer correctly depend on how many options you are choosing from.

Number of options left	5	4	3	2	1
Odds of guessing correctly	20%	25%	33%	50%	100%

You can see from this chart just how valuable it is to be able to eliminate incorrect answers and make an educated guess, but there are two things that many test takers do that cause them to miss out on the benefits of guessing:

- Accidentally eliminating the correct answer
- Selecting an answer based on an impression

We'll look at the first one here, and the second one in the next section.

To avoid accidentally eliminating the correct answer, we recommend a thought exercise called **the $5 challenge**. In this challenge, you only eliminate an answer choice from contention if you are willing to bet $5 on it being wrong. Why $5? Five dollars is a small but not insignificant amount of money. It's an amount you could afford to lose but wouldn't want to throw away. And while losing $5 once might not hurt too much, doing it twenty times will set you back $100. In the same way, each small decision you make—eliminating a choice here, guessing on a question there—won't by itself impact your score very much, but when you put them all together, they can make a big difference. By holding each answer choice elimination decision to a higher standard, you can reduce the risk of accidentally eliminating the correct answer.

The $5 challenge can also be applied in a positive sense: If you are willing to bet $5 that an answer choice *is* correct, go ahead and mark it as correct.

Summary: Only eliminate an answer choice if you are willing to bet $5 that it is wrong.

Copyright © Mometrix Media. You have been licensed one copy of this document for personal use only. Any other reproduction or redistribution is strictly prohibited. All rights reserved.
This content is provided for test preparation purposes only and does not imply an endorsement by Mometrix of any particular political, scientific, or religious point of view.

Which Answer to Choose

You're taking the test. You've run into a hard question and decided you'll have to guess. You've eliminated all the answer choices you're willing to bet $5 on. Now you have to pick an answer. Why do we even need to talk about this? Why can't you just pick whichever one you feel like when the time comes?

The answer to these questions is that if you don't come into the test with a plan, you'll rely on your impression to select an answer choice, and if you do that, you risk falling into a trap. The test writers know that everyone who takes their test will be guessing on some of the questions, so they intentionally write wrong answer choices to seem plausible. You still have to pick an answer though, and if the wrong answer choices are designed to look right, how can you ever be sure that you're not falling for their trap? The best solution we've found to this dilemma is to take the decision out of your hands entirely. Here is the process we recommend:

Once you've eliminated any choices that you are confident (willing to bet $5) are wrong, select the first remaining choice as your answer.

Whether you choose to select the first remaining choice, the second, or the last, the important thing is that you use some preselected standard. Using this approach guarantees that you will not be enticed into selecting an answer choice that looks right, because you are not basing your decision on how the answer choices look.

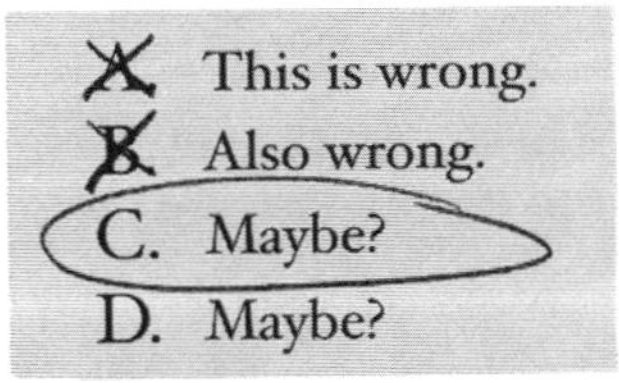

This is not meant to make you question your knowledge. Instead, it is to help you recognize the difference between your knowledge and your impressions. There's a huge difference between thinking an answer is right because of what you know, and thinking an answer is right because it looks or sounds like it should be right.

Summary: To ensure that your selection is appropriately random, make a predetermined selection from among all answer choices you have not eliminated.

Copyright © Mometrix Media. You have been licensed one copy of this document for personal use only. Any other reproduction or redistribution is strictly prohibited. All rights reserved.
This content is provided for test preparation purposes only and does not imply an endorsement by Mometrix of any particular political, scientific, or religious point of view.

Test-Taking Strategies

This section contains a list of test-taking strategies that you may find helpful as you work through the test. By taking what you know and applying logical thought, you can maximize your chances of answering any question correctly!

It is very important to realize that every question is different and every person is different: no single strategy will work on every question, and no single strategy will work for every person. That's why we've included all of them here, so you can try them out and determine which ones work best for different types of questions and which ones work best for you.

Question Strategies

⊘ Read Carefully

Read the question and the answer choices carefully. Don't miss the question because you misread the terms. You have plenty of time to read each question thoroughly and make sure you understand what is being asked. Yet a happy medium must be attained, so don't waste too much time. You must read carefully and efficiently.

⊘ Contextual Clues

Look for contextual clues. If the question includes a word you are not familiar with, look at the immediate context for some indication of what the word might mean. Contextual clues can often give you all the information you need to decipher the meaning of an unfamiliar word. Even if you can't determine the meaning, you may be able to narrow down the possibilities enough to make a solid guess at the answer to the question.

⊘ Prefixes

If you're having trouble with a word in the question or answer choices, try dissecting it. Take advantage of every clue that the word might include. Prefixes can be a huge help. Usually, they allow you to determine a basic meaning. *Pre-* means before, *post-* means after, *pro-* is positive, *de-* is negative. From prefixes, you can get an idea of the general meaning of the word and try to put it into context.

⊘ Hedge Words

Watch out for critical hedge words, such as *likely, may, can, often, almost, mostly, usually, generally, rarely*, and *sometimes*. Question writers insert these hedge phrases to cover every possibility. Often an answer choice will be wrong simply because it leaves no room for exception. Be on guard for answer choices that have definitive words such as *exactly* and *always*.

⊘ Switchback Words

Stay alert for *switchbacks*. These are the words and phrases frequently used to alert you to shifts in thought. The most common switchback words are *but, although*, and *however*. Others include *nevertheless, on the other hand, even though, while, in spite of, despite*, and *regardless of*. Switchback words are important to catch because they can change the direction of the question or an answer choice.

Copyright © Mometrix Media. You have been licensed one copy of this document for personal use only. Any other reproduction or redistribution is strictly prohibited. All rights reserved.
This content is provided for test preparation purposes only and does not imply an endorsement by Mometrix of any particular political, scientific, or religious point of view.

✓ Face Value

When in doubt, use common sense. Accept the situation in the problem at face value. Don't read too much into it. These problems will not require you to make wild assumptions. If you have to go beyond creativity and warp time or space in order to have an answer choice fit the question, then you should move on and consider the other answer choices. These are normal problems rooted in reality. The applicable relationship or explanation may not be readily apparent, but it is there for you to figure out. Use your common sense to interpret anything that isn't clear.

Answer Choice Strategies

✓ Answer Selection

The most thorough way to pick an answer choice is to identify and eliminate wrong answers until only one is left, then confirm it is the correct answer. Sometimes an answer choice may immediately seem right, but be careful. The test writers will usually put more than one reasonable answer choice on each question, so take a second to read all of them and make sure that the other choices are not equally obvious. As long as you have time left, it is better to read every answer choice than to pick the first one that looks right without checking the others.

✓ Answer Choice Families

An answer choice family consists of two (in rare cases, three) answer choices that are very similar in construction and cannot all be true at the same time. If you see two answer choices that are direct opposites or parallels, one of them is usually the correct answer. For instance, if one answer choice says that quantity *x* increases and another either says that quantity *x* decreases (opposite) or says that quantity *y* increases (parallel), then those answer choices would fall into the same family. An answer choice that doesn't match the construction of the answer choice family is more likely to be incorrect. Most questions will not have answer choice families, but when they do appear, you should be prepared to recognize them.

✓ Eliminate Answers

Eliminate answer choices as soon as you realize they are wrong, but make sure you consider all possibilities. If you are eliminating answer choices and realize that the last one you are left with is also wrong, don't panic. Start over and consider each choice again. There may be something you missed the first time that you will realize on the second pass.

✓ Avoid Fact Traps

Don't be distracted by an answer choice that is factually true but doesn't answer the question. You are looking for the choice that answers the question. Stay focused on what the question is asking for so you don't accidentally pick an answer that is true but incorrect. Always go back to the question and make sure the answer choice you've selected actually answers the question and is not merely a true statement.

✓ Extreme Statements

In general, you should avoid answers that put forth extreme actions as standard practice or proclaim controversial ideas as established fact. An answer choice that states the "process should be used in certain situations, if…" is much more likely to be correct than one that states the "process should be discontinued completely." The first is a calm rational statement and doesn't even make a definitive, uncompromising stance, using a hedge word *if* to provide wiggle room, whereas the second choice is far more extreme.

Copyright © Mometrix Media. You have been licensed one copy of this document for personal use only. Any other reproduction or redistribution is strictly prohibited. All rights reserved.
This content is provided for test preparation purposes only and does not imply an endorsement by Mometrix of any particular political, scientific, or religious point of view.

✓ Benchmark

As you read through the answer choices and you come across one that seems to answer the question well, mentally select that answer choice. This is not your final answer, but it's the one that will help you evaluate the other answer choices. The one that you selected is your benchmark or standard for judging each of the other answer choices. Every other answer choice must be compared to your benchmark. That choice is correct until proven otherwise by another answer choice beating it. If you find a better answer, then that one becomes your new benchmark. Once you've decided that no other choice answers the question as well as your benchmark, you have your final answer.

✓ Predict the Answer

Before you even start looking at the answer choices, it is often best to try to predict the answer. When you come up with the answer on your own, it is easier to avoid distractions and traps because you will know exactly what to look for. The right answer choice is unlikely to be word-for-word what you came up with, but it should be a close match. Even if you are confident that you have the right answer, you should still take the time to read each option before moving on.

General Strategies

✓ Tough Questions

If you are stumped on a problem or it appears too hard or too difficult, don't waste time. Move on! Remember though, if you can quickly check for obviously incorrect answer choices, your chances of guessing correctly are greatly improved. Before you completely give up, at least try to knock out a couple of possible answers. Eliminate what you can and then guess at the remaining answer choices before moving on.

✓ Check Your Work

Since you will probably not know every term listed and the answer to every question, it is important that you get credit for the ones that you do know. Don't miss any questions through careless mistakes. If at all possible, try to take a second to look back over your answer selection and make sure you've selected the correct answer choice and haven't made a costly careless mistake (such as marking an answer choice that you didn't mean to mark). This quick double check should more than pay for itself in caught mistakes for the time it costs.

✓ Pace Yourself

It's easy to be overwhelmed when you're looking at a page full of questions; your mind is confused and full of random thoughts, and the clock is ticking down faster than you would like. Calm down and maintain the pace that you have set for yourself. Especially as you get down to the last few minutes of the test, don't let the small numbers on the clock make you panic. As long as you are on track by monitoring your pace, you are guaranteed to have time for each question.

✓ Don't Rush

It is very easy to make errors when you are in a hurry. Maintaining a fast pace in answering questions is pointless if it makes you miss questions that you would have gotten right otherwise. Test writers like to include distracting information and wrong answers that seem right. Taking a little extra time to avoid careless mistakes can make all the difference in your test score. Find a pace that allows you to be confident in the answers that you select.

Copyright © Mometrix Media. You have been licensed one copy of this document for personal use only. Any other reproduction or redistribution is strictly prohibited. All rights reserved.
This content is provided for test preparation purposes only and does not imply an endorsement by Mometrix of any particular political, scientific, or religious point of view.

⊘ Keep Moving

Panicking will not help you pass the test, so do your best to stay calm and keep moving. Taking deep breaths and going through the answer elimination steps you practiced can help to break through a stress barrier and keep your pace.

Final Notes

The combination of a solid foundation of content knowledge and the confidence that comes from practicing your plan for applying that knowledge is the key to maximizing your performance on test day. As your foundation of content knowledge is built up and strengthened, you'll find that the strategies included in this chapter become more and more effective in helping you quickly sift through the distractions and traps of the test to isolate the correct answer.

Now that you're preparing to move forward into the test content chapters of this book, be sure to keep your goal in mind. As you read, think about how you will be able to apply this information on the test. If you've already seen sample questions for the test and you have an idea of the question format and style, try to come up with questions of your own that you can answer based on what you're reading. This will give you valuable practice applying your knowledge in the same ways you can expect to on test day.

Good luck and good studying!

Copyright © Mometrix Media. You have been licensed one copy of this document for personal use only. Any other reproduction or redistribution is strictly prohibited. All rights reserved.
This content is provided for test preparation purposes only and does not imply an endorsement by Mometrix of any particular political, scientific, or religious point of view.

Copyright © Mometrix Media. You have been licensed one copy of this document for personal use only. Any other reproduction or redistribution is strictly prohibited. All rights reserved.
This content is provided for test preparation purposes only and does not imply an endorsement by Mometrix of any particular political, scientific, or religious point of view.

Understanding Students with Autism Spectrum Disorder

Typical Cognitive Development in Infancy According to Piaget's Theory

Piaget defined four stages of cognitive development. He called the first stage sensorimotor to characterize infants' cognitive processes: they perceive sensory information from their surrounding environments and respond to these by engaging in motor activities, e.g., rooting, suckling, looking, listening, reaching, and grasping. Piaget divided the sensorimotor stage into six substages: Reflexes, from 0–1 month; Primary Circular Reactions from 1–4 months wherein infants finds accidental actions like thumb-sucking pleasurable and then intentionally repeats them; Secondary Circular Reactions from 4–8 months when infants intentionally repeat actions to evoke environmental effects; Coordination of Reactions from 8–12 months, featuring obviously intentional actions, comprehension of cause and effect, and combining schemas (concepts); Tertiary Circular Reactions from 12–18 months, when children experiment with trial-and-error; and Early Representational Thought from 18–24 months, when children begin representing things or events with symbols. A significant sensorimotor development is Object Permanence, i.e., realizing things still exist when out of sight.

Piaget called his second stage of cognitive development, between the ages of 2–7 years, Preoperational, because children have not yet developed the ability to perform mental operations, i.e., mentally manipulating information, and do not understand concrete logic. Piaget called children in this stage egocentric, i.e., they cannot assume another's perspective. For example, Preoperational children can select a picture matching a three-dimensional scene they just saw, but cannot select a picture matching what someone else would see from a different physical location/position. They do not understand what Piaget termed conservation, the concept that quantities remain constant regardless of shape or appearance. For example, children judge the same amount of liquid differently by its appearance in differently shaped containers (short wide versus tall narrow), even when seeing it poured from one to the other. Piaget identified additional characteristics of Preoperational thinking as animism (attributing human qualities to inanimate objects) and magical thinking (attributing external events to one's internal thoughts).

Around ages 7–11 years, children are in what Piaget termed the Concrete Operations stage. A salient feature of this stage is that children develop the ability to think logically and conduct mental operations with regard to concrete objects. However, they still have trouble comprehending hypothetical and abstract concepts. A significant ability developing during this stage is the understanding of reversibility, i.e., that actions can be reversed. Whereas the younger Preoperational child watching someone pour liquid from a short, wide container to a tall, narrow one believes the taller container has more liquid, the Concrete Operations child sees the amount is the same despite different container shapes. Reversibility aids this insight. Children in Concrete Operations also understand sequences between mental categories, e.g., their pet is a poodle, a poodle is a dog, and a dog is an animal. The introduction of formal school subjects, especially math, is no coincidence with the age range of this stage because children in Concrete Operations are first able to do simple arithmetic computations.

Piaget termed his final stage of cognitive development, from around age 12 into adulthood, as Formal Operations. This reflects the individual's ability to understand and manipulate completely abstract concepts without needing to refer to concrete objects. This stage also features the development of logic, the addition of deductive reasoning to the inductive reasoning children

Copyright © Mometrix Media. You have been licensed one copy of this document for personal use only. Any other reproduction or redistribution is strictly prohibited. All rights reserved.
This content is provided for test preparation purposes only and does not imply an endorsement by Mometrix of any particular political, scientific, or religious point of view.

develop in the previous stage of Concrete Operations, and systematic planning. Children/teens/adults can now consider hypothetical situations; apply general principles to predict specific events (deductive reasoning) as well as make generalizations from multiple specific details (inductive reasoning, which typically develops during Concrete Operations); and plan organized, systematic approaches to problem-solving. They are more fully able to consider another's viewpoint and feelings, and can understand abstract concepts like liberty, justice, democracy, truth, and beauty.

Delays in Cognitive Development That Represent Atypical Development

Whether caused by neurological deficits or damage, deprivation or other environmental factors, or a combination, some children do not develop cognitive skills typically. They may develop them much later than others or not at all. They may also demonstrate differences in the quantity and quality of their cognitive skills. Children with cognitive developmental delays, for example, can have significant difficulty with learning colors, shapes, and similar basic concepts. They often have trouble learning more advanced concepts, such as counting numbers, reading printed language, and writing language. In addition, children with delayed and/or deficient cognitive development can demonstrate a failure to generalize things they learn to other situations or contexts. Moreover, when children have problems with adjusting to new situations and changes in their environments, this can be a sign of delayed or deficient cognitive development.

Characteristics of Atypical Social and Emotional Development in Children

When children experience developmental delays that are manifested in the social and emotional domain, one characteristic is being too trusting of others, which allows others to take advantage of them. This is often associated with intellectual disability or intellectual disabilities. Another characteristic of some children with atypical social and emotional development is not reading or understanding others' nonverbal cues indicating emotional states or social conventions, and/or linguistic cues during interpersonal interactions, preventing them from responding appropriately. This is commonly associated with autism spectrum disorders. Autistic children also may show excellent verbal skills in monologues, but be unable to initiate and maintain conversations and have difficulty with turn-taking. Some children fail to develop the ability to consider others' viewpoints at typical ages, remaining egocentric; this interferes with social interaction. This is common to various conditions, including intellectual disability, autism, and behavior disorders. Children with ADHD tend to have difficulties with impulse control, emotional self-regulation, and sustaining attention, interfering with social interactions as much as with academic performance.

Signs of Atypical Development in the Area of Gross Motor Skills

Motor development follows a hierarchical pattern. In other words, for example, if a child cannot stand, s/he cannot walk, and if s/he cannot walk, s/he cannot run. When a baby is between 3 and 12 months old, some signs of atypical gross motor skills development include that the child does not open his/her hands during the normal age range; that the child has trouble holding his/her head up; the child cannot sit up without support, and/or the child has difficulty sitting up even with support; and the child does not begin to pull up on furniture or stand up during this age range. Between 12 and 36 months, signs of delayed/atypical development include problems with walking and/or running; with ascending or descending stairs; with rolling, catching, and throwing a ball; and with jumping and hopping. Children with atypical motor development may demonstrate higher or lower muscle tone than normal and problems with motor planning, motor coordination, balance, and proprioception.

Copyright © Mometrix Media. You have been licensed one copy of this document for personal use only. Any other reproduction or redistribution is strictly prohibited. All rights reserved.
This content is provided for test preparation purposes only and does not imply an endorsement by Mometrix of any particular political, scientific, or religious point of view.

Fine Motor Skills for Young Children

Young children need fine motor skills to play with toys, eat meals, turn lights on/off, and hold crayons, paintbrushes, spoons, etc. During evaluations, many children perform poorly on certain tasks, from delays not in cognitive development but in fine motor development. Oral/motor skills, like the control of jaw, lip, mouth, and tongue movements for eating and speaking, are included in fine motor skills. While occupational therapists work with other fine motor skills, speech-language pathologists and occupational therapists may both work to remediate oral/motor skill deficits. If a baby has trouble orally grasping the nipple or bottle to nurse, this can indicate delayed fine motor development. Babies whose hands are in fists more often than open may have fine motor delays. A baby having problems manually bringing toys to his/her mouth and/or mouthing them can have atypical fine motor development. Difficulty holding small objects with a pincer grasp or with a thumb and a forefinger is another sign of delayed fine motor development.

Early Language Development and Its Relationship to Other Developmental Domains

The development of language skills is critical to the development of cognitive, emotional, and social skills. These are all interrelated, so problems in any one area usually cause problems/delays in others. Receptive language is the ability to understand spoken and written language. Receptive language develops before expressive language: children must understand what they hear before they learn to speak, and to read and comprehend written language before they learn to write. Hence a child's receptive vocabulary typically exceeds his/her expressive vocabulary: s/he can understand more words than s/he can use. Nonverbal receptive language includes understanding others' facial expressions. Verbal receptive language includes understanding what others say; understanding qualitative concepts like big/little and tall/short and quantitative concepts like a lot, a little, all, none, etc.; understanding and following simple directions; listening to stories; understanding and following complex/multiple directions to do a series of things; and understanding others' questions. Written receptive language includes identifying upper- and lowercase letters and numbers, and also reading and comprehending simple and complex sentences and paragraphs.

Receptive, Expressive, and Pragmatic Language

Receptive language is comprehending language we hear and read. Expressive language is our production of spoken and written language. Pragmatic language is our using receptive and expressive language to facilitate social interactions. Expressive and pragmatic language depend upon receptive language, which precedes them. If a baby is not imitating others' vocal sounds or behaviors or responding to hearing his/her name called and/or seems not to be listening to others' speech by the age of 12 months, this can indicate delayed/deficient receptive language development. By three years, if a child does not follow instructions and/or does not learn to speak normally, this can indicate receptive language delay. When children frequently ask others to repeat and/or have trouble answering questions by five years old, they may have receptive language delays. By seven years, signs of receptive language deficits include having trouble understanding stories told/read aloud; avoiding participating in social activities; and having trouble processing or making sense of verbal information. Having trouble reading sentences by nine years old is another sign.

Expressive Language Development

Expressive language is that language we produce in order to communicate with others, whether through spoken or written words, vocal sounds, facial expressions, physical gestures, and/or body language. Babies and children develop expressive language gradually and in a cumulative sequence.

Copyright © Mometrix Media. You have been licensed one copy of this document for personal use only. Any other reproduction or redistribution is strictly prohibited. All rights reserved.
This content is provided for test preparation purposes only and does not imply an endorsement by Mometrix of any particular political, scientific, or religious point of view.

Nonverbal expressive language consists of all of that expressive communication that does not involve the use of words. For example, when a baby cries, that is a form of nonverbal expressive language. Smiling also communicates pleasure, recognition, and/or affection toward others. Laughing expresses amusement or delight. Frowning expresses displeasure, sadness, or anger. When infants and toddlers learn to wave "bye-bye," they are using nonverbal expressive language. When babies and young children point at things, they nonverbally communicate a variety of messages—like "I want that"; "Look at that"; "What is that?"; "I see that." When young children throw objects, whether to express anger, protest something, or get an adult to retrieve it as a game, this is also nonverbal expressive language.

Vocal and Spoken Verbal Expressive Language

Verbal expressive language can be spoken or written. In infants, early forms of verbalization also include vocalizations. For example, babies "coo" by repeating prolonged vowel sounds; "grunt" or make guttural sounds expressing satisfaction/contentedness; and soon begin to babble by repeating consonant-vowel combinations like "babababa," "dadadada," etc. Babies also imitate adults' vocal sounds and facial expressions. Their first words are often parent names like "Mama" and "Dada," which coincide closely with babbling sounds. As their speech develops, they echo/repeat others' utterances. In the holophrastic stage, toddlers use single words to express phrase concepts, like "up" to mean "Pick me up" or "Look at the bird up there." They combine pointing with nouns to identify people, animals, and things, like "baby," "doggie," or "car." They soon learn to use the socially conventional utterances "thank you" and "please." Toddlers then learn to combine two words to express phrase concepts, like "Daddy go" or "Mommy shoe," which can also convey a variety of meanings.

Once they can speak using more than one-word expressions, young children begin to ask questions and answer others' questions. They progress to correctly using words expressing qualitative concepts, including opposites like big and little, tall and short, etc.; and quantitative concepts, including opposite and relative quantities like all, none, a lot, or a little. As their expressive language skills develop, they reflect children's receptive understanding of the concepts underlying the words. The toddler's basic "She walk" phrase gives way to the more advanced present progressive verb tense "She is walking" in preschoolers. Children begin to use pronouns like "I" and "you," rather than using no pronouns or only "me" or "Mommy." They then develop possessive pronouns like "mine" and "my" [+ object]. They start including prepositions like on, in, over, and under. They use past tenses, both regular and irregular ("gave") and future constructions like "will/is going to" [+verb]. They progress from two-word to three- and four-word phrases, and then full sentences with subject, auxiliary verb, verb, and object.

Activities That Preschool and Young School-Age Children Learn to Do That Reflect Written Expressive Language Skills Development

Children learn to speak before they learn to write, though there is also some overlap in their developing spoken and written expressive language skills. These both also depend on the development of the receptive language skills of listening and reading comprehension. Young children first learn to trace letters, then they copy them, and then they write them. They follow the same progression with tracing, copying, and writing numbers. They copy examples of simple words, like "Mom," and then do the same with more complex words like "truck." Once they have copied words and can remember letters, they progress to writing the letters in sequence to spell written words (d-a-d-d-y). Thereafter, they learn to write consecutive words that form sentences, such as "I love my kitty." Eventually, school-age children can write connected sentences that form paragraphs, like "I love my kitty. One day my friends will come over. I will show my kitty to my friends."

Copyright © Mometrix Media. You have been licensed one copy of this document for personal use only. Any other reproduction or redistribution is strictly prohibited. All rights reserved.
This content is provided for test preparation purposes only and does not imply an endorsement by Mometrix of any particular political, scientific, or religious point of view.

Signs That Babies and Young Children Are Demonstrating Atypical Development or Delays in Their Use of Spoken Expressive Language

Babies normally babble at a few to several months. An infant's not babbling by eight months is a sign of delayed/atypical spoken language development. A child not uttering any words by 18 months is not developing expressive language normally. Children over two years using only single words show atypical development. After four years, speaking mainly in "baby talk" is atypical. Echolalia (continually repeating what others say) is normal in younger children, but beyond three years is atypical. Talking to oneself aloud is typical of toddlers, but children continuing this practice extensively past three years show delayed development. Children older than three years who do not take conversational turns but talk "in circles" are not developing typically. Children over four years who have trouble expressing their needs and wants show atypical development. Answering open-ended questions ("What did you do at Jimmy's?") with single words indicates a delay in a six-year-old. Overgeneralizing, i.e., naming many objects with one word like calling all vehicles cars, is another sign of delayed expressive language development.

Nonverbal and Behavioral Signs of Delayed Expressive Language Development

Babies who make no, or very little, eye contact with others by 12 months of age are not developing typically. Another sign indicating a need for evaluation is not pointing at things by this age. Children who demonstrate few or no skills at taking turns by a year old can have expressive language delays. Little or no demonstration of joint attention, i.e., attending to the same thing as his/her parent, is another sign of developmental delay. So is a lack of joint action, i.e., engaging in the same activity as the parent. Children who consistently hit others or have temper tantrums when they cannot communicate a message to others show signs of delayed expressive language. Crying, yelling, and similar shows of frustration when trying to communicate also indicate developmental delays. In addition, young children with such delays may rarely if ever initiate conversations with others, and may not want to engage in activities with others.

Physical and Motor Development of Children with down Syndrome

Children with Down syndrome show overall slower development in physiology and motor skills. They grow more slowly in physical size and also ultimately attain smaller full statures than typically developing children. They tend to have lower/weaker muscle tone, or hypotonia. They commonly start walking significantly later than other children. Even once they learn to walk, they may not develop physical coordination, balance, and proprioception as soon or ever as well as other children. The oral-motor skills components of motor development are also slower to develop in those with Down syndrome, compounded by having large, thick, often protruding tongues, which can interfere with eating skills and clear speech. Additional physiological stigmata of Down syndrome include small hands and feet; short, stubby fingers; short, thick necks; small heads, flattened in back; small noses; and Asian-appearing eyes with epicanthal folds. Down syndrome children are more likely to have celiac disease (gluten intolerance), gastroesophageal reflux, hypothyroidism, hearing and vision problems, and to develop senile dementias earlier than normally.

Language Development of Students with Autism Spectrum Disorders

An estimated one-half of those on the autism spectrum never develop verbal language skills. The other half range from echolalia as their only speech production to perfectly functional, high-level speech, and everything in between. Some autistic students display advanced vocabularies and fluent speech in long monologues about topics interesting them, often including the highly specialized and/or technical, but are unable to initiate or maintain two-way conversations with others. These individuals have difficulty with turn-taking and the give-and-take of verbal

Copyright © Mometrix Media. You have been licensed one copy of this document for personal use only. Any other reproduction or redistribution is strictly prohibited. All rights reserved.
This content is provided for test preparation purposes only and does not imply an endorsement by Mometrix of any particular political, scientific, or religious point of view.

interactions. Some high-functioning autistic persons can conduct normal conversations with others, but their speech patterns may sound a bit singsong, odd, or quirky. Many autistic students have difficulty understanding emotional overtones in others' speech, such as sarcasm or humor. Additionally, they often cannot understand nonverbal cues like facial expressions, gestures, and body language indicating emotions or social customs, though many can learn this through explicit training.

Social and Emotional Development of Students on the Autism Spectrum

Emotional and social differences can be observed in autistic people from early childhood, when many of them avoid eye contact with others and resist physical contact with parents, like flinging themselves backward from being hugged/held or going rigid in their bodies when held. Many also engage in repetitive, stereotypic self-stimulating behaviors like rocking. Students with autism experience the same internal emotions as others, but may not express these normally. Moreover, they often have great difficulty noticing or understanding the emotions of others and their expression of them. As a result, their behavior in social situations can appear rather strange, especially from high-functioning autistic individuals with above-average intelligence. For example, as autism expert John Gerdtz once related, "It's really strange when you're talking with someone who has a PhD in mathematics, and he suddenly turns and walks away right in the middle of the conversation." Autistic individuals frequently fail to follow social conventions because they do not understand them.

Behavioral Differences Observed in Individuals on the Autism Spectrum

One area of behavioral difference among the autistic is language: some people with autism spectrum disorders (ASDs) have few or no verbal skills; others have limited speech and language; others have more functional, but odd-sounding speech and language; and still others have highly functioning verbal skills. Some are able to speak extensively on favorite topics but cannot start or continue social conversations. Another area is social and emotional: those with ASDs have difficulty observing, interpreting, and using socially accepted behaviors indicating emotions. A common autistic deficit is tolerating interruptions, changes, or transitions in activities. Autistic people frequently display narrowly limited interests and activities, and rigid thinking and behavior. The lower functioning often engage in repetitive behaviors; the higher functioning can focus intensely on a single activity for long periods, but not shift or divide their attention. Some autistic individuals react to sudden changes, or sensory input they find painful due to hypersensitivity, with panic reactions including screaming, self-injurious behavior, and/or withdrawal into rocking, counting, or other repetitive self-soothing actions.

Similarities and Differences Between Deaf and Hearing Students

Although a major difference in deaf students is that they learn language through visual rather than auditory modalities, they also have many similarities to hearing students. They have the same need to communicate and interact socially with others. Unfortunately, the majority of hearing people do not know sign language; and while many deaf people can visually read speech, many others who sign exclusively and adhere to deaf culture function best within the signing deaf community and are at significant disadvantages in hearing milieus. While deaf students often do not understand humor based on word play or sound, they do appreciate humor, and the deaf culture has its own inside jokes. Deaf students have equal interests in competing in sports and academics as hearing students do. They feel the same emotions as others. While they hug each other more and spend longer times on good-byes, their social interactions still fulfill the same needs for belonging, connection, and communication.

Copyright © Mometrix Media. You have been licensed one copy of this document for personal use only. Any other reproduction or redistribution is strictly prohibited. All rights reserved.
This content is provided for test preparation purposes only and does not imply an endorsement by Mometrix of any particular political, scientific, or religious point of view.

Hearing children are surrounded by speech sounds from birth, and they absorb a great deal of their knowledge and understanding of language and speech through this immersion. However, deaf children do not benefit from sensory input in the auditory mode. Those whose parents use sign language and/or speech reading learn to comprehend and produce language through the visual modality instead. This is a major difference, because the main basis for communication among the majority of the population is auditory; and written language, with its relationship to spoken language, has the same auditory basis. Instead of auditory cues like tone of voice, grammatical inflections (like verb tense or plural endings), or intonations like the rising end of a question, deaf students rely exclusively on visual cues like facial expressions, gestures, and body language; and in ASL (American Sign Language), built-in signs conveying grammatical information.

Similarities and Differences Between Blind and Sighted Students

Although the totally blind cannot read printed text, blind students still often want to read and enjoy it. Some read available Braille texts by touch. Others listen to books on tape and/or use text-to-speech computer software, greatly expanding their options of available texts. Though blind students may not understand visual humor like sight gags, they still appreciate humor. Students not blind from birth have additional frames of reference for understanding visual expressions and comparisons. For example, Helen Keller, who became deaf-blind at 19 months, reportedly was told she had blue eyes and asked, "Are they like wee skies?" Without hearing or sight, Keller had to learn tactile finger-spelling to communicate, yet her accomplishments made her famous. A woman who became blind around nine years old found hilarious a coworker's description of another employee bundled up in a fur coat and hat with only her nose protruding. Blind people have the same social, communication, and emotional needs; they just need supplementary auditory information/verbal descriptions of what they cannot see.

Blind students with normal hearing do not miss out on the auditory medium wherein children learn to understand and use speech and language as deaf students do. However, while they can learn spoken language normally, they cannot learn to read and write visually as other children can. They must learn Braille and have access to Braille publications to read and/or listen to books on tape. Today they have the added advantage of computer text-to-speech software. Another significant difference is that blind students cannot learn their way around schools and other large, complex buildings simply through the experience of navigating them a few times. Sighted individuals often take this for granted. Blind students usually need help from Orientation and Mobility specialists to learn how to get around in indoor and outdoor settings. Without the benefit of the multitude of visual information others have, it can be very confusing not to know just which way to go, but even where one is and in what position relative to one's surroundings (orientation).

Similarities and Differences Between Physically Disabled Students and Others

Physically normal students, and sometimes even educators, may not realize that even navigating through a school building—a seemingly simple everyday activity they take for granted—is not the same for the physically disabled. For example, buildings with traditional construction frequently include doorways too narrow for wheelchairs, solid obstacles impossible or difficult to move around, or stairs and grades not safely traversed using crutches. Federal legislation protecting the rights of the disabled has now mandated that all new constructions be accessible to them; however, this does not address old/existing buildings that often cannot be retrofitted. Also, physically disabled students have the same needs and desires to compete, win, and play as others, which should not be discounted. For example, wheelchair basketball and races are popular alternatives. In some schools, students in wheelchairs are also included in regular sports teams and games.

Copyright © Mometrix Media. You have been licensed one copy of this document for personal use only. Any other reproduction or redistribution is strictly prohibited. All rights reserved.
This content is provided for test preparation purposes only and does not imply an endorsement by Mometrix of any particular political, scientific, or religious point of view.

Fundamental Needs for Students with Disabilities as They Grow Up, in Terms of Understanding, Communication, and Disclosure of Disability

Young people with disabilities will benefit by learning to understand themselves more fully; to understand their disabilities more completely; and to explain their disabilities more effectively to others. They will often need help from experts to make decisions whether to disclose their disability to others and to become more prepared for such disclosure. Even more importantly, young people with disabilities need to gain a better comprehension of how their opportunities in social, educational, and employment contexts can often be enhanced by disclosing their disabilities in certain situations. Where appropriate, disclosure of disability can give them access to services and accommodations they would not be entitled to if they were not disabled. Experts have prepared informational publications to support them in this issue. For example, the National Collaborative on Workforce and Disability for Youth (NCWD-Y) has published *The 411 on Disability Disclosure: A Workbook for Youth with Disabilities* to help youth and parents make informed decisions about disclosure and its various impacts.

Aspects of the Family's Role Relative to Their Children with Disabilities

Families play a critical role by frequently serving as their disabled child's first case manager. In this capacity, they are the most consistent and know the most about their child's abilities and needs. Families help coordinate the services disabled children need. They help them explore career possibilities and interests. They supply housing, transportation, adaptive equipment, and other necessities. When young people with disabilities progress from high school to college or employment and community living, their families support the transitions they must make. Families can help their children achieve greater understanding of themselves and their disabilities. However, many families do not realize how crucial such self-knowledge is, and many assume the schools teach this when they seldom do. Also, when educators and families avoid directly discussing disabilities and focus instead on abilities and strengths, children can grow up not realizing their disability's impact and the accommodations to facilitate their success. Students who avoid identification as disabled for fear of labeling and stigma are frequently unprepared for self-advocacy.

Emotional and Caregiving Impacts of Disabilities on Families

Caring for a disabled child or family member, particularly one with more severe disabilities, is a daily stressor that can exhaust caregivers and all family members emotionally and physically. Emotional stress includes anxiety, anger, guilt, and insecurity—about the disability's cause, other family members' needs, whether caregivers are doing enough, the future, etc. Families grieve the disabled member's functional losses, initially and recurrently. A member's disability frequently causes major changes in family life. Members, especially females, may discard or alter jobs and/or career plans for caregiving duties. Some members feel too involved in care while others feel left out, and within-family relationships change. Different loyalties and/or alliances develop within the family. Past research has found that while disability tended to increase marital tension, it did not necessarily increase divorce rates.

Financial and Service Challenges of Disability on Family Systems

The challenges and demands on family systems are compounded when a member has a disability, and such challenges are typically long-term. Regardless of the type of family, the age of the disabled member, and the type of disability, many of the family demands are the same. For example, obtaining appropriate health services, social services, and educational services of sufficient quality often entail significant economic burdens, as do modifying the home to accommodate a disability and procuring adaptive equipment, medications, and special diets. Although families may qualify

Copyright © Mometrix Media. You have been licensed one copy of this document for personal use only. Any other reproduction or redistribution is strictly prohibited. All rights reserved.
This content is provided for test preparation purposes only and does not imply an endorsement by Mometrix of any particular political, scientific, or religious point of view.

for public funding, e.g., from Medicaid, Social Security SSI, or private health insurance, additional challenges are not only to discover which programs and services their child is eligible for, but moreover to interact with various bureaucracies to confirm such eligibility—frequently on a repeated basis. Another major problem is service coordination among providers, like doctors, teachers, counselors, physical and occupational therapists, social workers, and dietitians. Frequently providers are not informed of one another's actions and may give contradictory information.

When a family member has a disability, it can deplete the family's resources in terms of money, time, and energy far out of proportion to other demands. This often detracts from meeting other needs of the family and its other members. The family members find they must change their lifestyle, for example, spending less money, time, and energy on leisure activities and staying at home more. Families may abandon their plans and dreams for the future because they no longer have enough of these resources to pursue them. Community members may exclude the disabled member and family; avoid them; and/or denigrate them with looks or comments. Though federal legislation mandates inclusion, many communities do not have the resources, facilities, and programs to enable full inclusion. Many families state they feel burdened not by the disabled member, but by rejection, judgment, stigmatization of the member and family, and other negative behaviors and attitudes—from not only strangers, but also service providers, friends, and relatives.

Sources of Variation in the Impact of Disabilities on Families

Research shows the functioning and health of family members can be compromised by disability's additional demands. This includes elevated risks of behavioral and psychological symptoms in other family members. But despite this greater risk, studies also find that the majority of children and adults in families with a disabled member do not demonstrate such behavioral or psychological problems. This is attributed to the family members' adaptive abilities: they find and apply various coping skills to address the additional stresses caused in their life by the disability. Even though having a disabled member can cause families to experience grief, fatigue, depletion of resources, and other stressors, many families have also reported experiencing greater family closeness, acceptance of other people, new friendships, deepened spiritual faith, greater self-efficacy and sense of competence, more respect for life, and becoming stronger as a family. Thus, both negative and positive consequences are associated with having a family member with a disability.

Psychosocial Effects on Families of Various Aspects of Disabilities

Families are affected differentially by the degree of a member's disability: its type, i.e., whether it is a motor, sensory, or cognitive disability; how visible the disability is; how much pain or other symptoms are involved; the disabled member's life expectancy or prognosis; how much treatment and/or care is required; and whether the disability is progressive, constant, or relapsing in nature. Some experts believe these characteristics have more influence on a chronic condition's psychosocial impact than the diagnosis itself. Constant disabilities, e.g., spinal cord injuries, necessitate major initial family restructuring, plus long-term endurance and persistence. While the family can plan for a known future, they can still become exhausted, especially if community resources are lacking. Progressive disabilities, e.g., dementia or degenerative arthritis, cause grief over continuous losses, uncertainty about living arrangements and degrees of dependency, and increasing demands in caretaking. Relapsing disabilities, e.g., cancer or epilepsy, require less continual care but more ability to shift suddenly from normal to crisis mode and rapidly activate resources.

Copyright © Mometrix Media. You have been licensed one copy of this document for personal use only. Any other reproduction or redistribution is strictly prohibited. All rights reserved.
This content is provided for test preparation purposes only and does not imply an endorsement by Mometrix of any particular political, scientific, or religious point of view.

Impacts of Children's Cognitive or Intellectual Disabilities on Their Families

Research studies have shown that families appear to have more difficulty coping with cognitive or intellectual disabilities. Mental impairments can limit the disabled member's ability to assume responsible roles or to live independently, and/or increase the demands on families to be more vigilant to protect the disabled member. In cases of severe or profound intellectual disability, families may experience additional stress caused by boundary ambiguity—i.e., the disparity between the disabled member's physical and psychological presence makes his or her membership in the family unclear to the other members, as the disabled member is present as a part of the family in some ways, but in other ways is absent or only partially present. The ambiguity of this situation causes families more stress, as it can be more difficult for them to plan the roles of the other family members when they do not know what they can expect.

Interaction of Medical Advances with Some Disabling Physical Conditions

When the life expectancy of a disabled member is unclear, the family finds it harder to plan its members' future roles in life; to know future care costs; or, when the member needs help with daily living activities, to decide on optimal living arrangements. For example, individuals with Down syndrome often have congenital heart defects and died younger in the past, but with improved medical care, they now live longer. And between 1970 and 1991, the survival of American children with cystic fibrosis increased by 700 percent, from a median life expectancy of eight years to twenty-six years. This opens up new questions about marriage, procreation, and other difficult family choices. Ethical problems are also presented when medical advances can extend the lives of those with serious medical conditions. Considerations include weighing benefits versus costs, when and/or why to intervene and how aggressively. Family members may disagree about these. Moreover, courts and/or hospitals may prohibit chosen family actions. Such cases provoke much controversy (witness the 1998–2005 case of Terri Schiavo).

Considerations for Families with Disabled Children/Members Related to Differences in the Degree, Extent, or Severity of Functional Impairment

A person's functional status is the extent to which s/he can perform activities of daily living (ADLs) like self-feeding, toileting, or walking. The severity of impairment in these activities caused by a disability can be assessed. The human help, support, and equipment an individual will require is inversely related to his/her functional status, and families are typically the main providers of such assistance. Providing it can constitute a burden for them, compromising their physical and mental health. For instance, research has found that parents and particularly mothers whose disabled children have lower functional status have more symptoms of depression. Another factor to consider is that when disabled children and their parents both grow older, and/or when grandparents are caregivers, their ability to provide the same amounts and durations of care can become more limited due to the physical stresses of caregiving, which may be unmanageable for many elderly persons.

Differences in the Impacts of Disabilities on Families According to the Age of Disability Onset and the Age of the Parents at Onset or Diagnosis

In contrast to disabilities manifested in late adulthood, which are more predictable and less disruptive psychologically to families, disabilities occurring earlier in life are perceived as less normal, affect development more, and require making more adjustments for longer times. Congenital disabilities shape the identity and life of a child, so the child and family are not required to adjust to a sudden loss of function. An example is the difference between a child born with spina bifida versus a normal adolescent who sustains an injury and suddenly becomes paraplegic. Parental age at onset is also a factor in family response to disability. Adolescent parents still have

Copyright © Mometrix Media. You have been licensed one copy of this document for personal use only. Any other reproduction or redistribution is strictly prohibited. All rights reserved.
This content is provided for test preparation purposes only and does not imply an endorsement by Mometrix of any particular political, scientific, or religious point of view.

salient developmental needs themselves; plus, they usually have fewer resources and less maturity for coping with the additional demands of their child's disability. Older parents have greater risks of bearing children with Down syndrome and other disabilities, lesser endurance for caregiving, and more fears about who will care for their child after their deaths.

Interrelationship of Disability and Child Development

Because childhood development is sequential, the mastery of skills at each level or stage depends upon the successful completion of the previous stage. Therefore, the earlier in a child's life the onset of a disabling condition is, the more it interrupts the child's developmental progress. Accomplishing developmental tasks is complicated in many ways for children with disabilities. This influences what family roles the child can adopt and consequently affects the family. If an infant's disability prevents the infant from responding to parental efforts at nurturing, this impedes the development of bonding, secure attachment, and trust, undermining parenting competence. Toddlers must actively explore their social environments to develop self-control and autonomy. But sensory, motor, or cognitive disabilities can hamper such exploration. Parents may be overprotective for fear of additional damage or injury, and/or, due to guilt or sympathy, overindulgent. Others' negative feedback about the child's disability can reinforce these parental behaviors, additionally limiting the child's development of self-control and autonomy.

Challenges of Disabilities When Children with Disabilities Begin to Attend School

As Freud, Erikson, Piaget, and others have observed, when children begin school, their social and emotional focus shifts from the parent-child relationship to developing social relationships outside of the home with peers, children of other ages, and adults other than parents. The focus of child development consequently shifts from mainly personal skills and parental attachment to social competencies and interpersonal skills. In spite of government mandates of special education and inclusion, schools still vary significantly in their effectiveness with these. Insufficient funding for special education programs; inadequate training of school staff for accommodating instruction to special needs; and frequently, negative attitudes regarding disabilities in school personnel and other children, constitute some of the obstacles faced by children with disabilities and their parents. Because of the variance among schools in this respect, some families realize great resources in school programs, while others realize great additional challenges in trying to advocate for their disabled children's educational rights with schools and other service providers.

Challenges of Adolescent Development to Teens with Disabilities

As especially elucidated by Erikson, adolescents have the developmental tasks of developing their individual identities, separating from their childhood relationships with parents, and becoming more independent. Having a disability makes these tasks more challenging for a teenager. While normally developing adolescents often engage in risk-taking, e.g., experimenting with alcohol and tobacco, as part of this process, teens with disabilities may refuse prescribed medications, diets, or other disability-related treatments as their form of the risk-taking part of the developmental process. The natural adolescent development of sexuality also involves additional complications for disabled teens, as they often experience anxieties and fears about their desirability, performance, and future potential for marriage and reproduction. The complications they encounter can include being exploited sexually by others for the cognitively disabled, risk of contracting sexually transmitted diseases, and possible higher risks of pregnancy for girls with disabilities.

Stimulants Like Amphetamines Are Often Prescribed to Children with ADHD

Many adults do not understand why a child who is already hyperactive would be prescribed a stimulant drug, thinking this would only make them even more so. However, stimulants like

Copyright © Mometrix Media. You have been licensed one copy of this document for personal use only. Any other reproduction or redistribution is strictly prohibited. All rights reserved.
This content is provided for test preparation purposes only and does not imply an endorsement by Mometrix of any particular political, scientific, or religious point of view.

amphetamines often have the effect of helping children with ADHD to focus their attention better for longer time periods. This compares to the effects of caffeine and controlled amphetamine doses in helping normal but tired adults concentrate better. Serious amphetamine side effects include rapid, uneven, or pounding heartbeat; burning or pain with urination; increased talkativeness; other unaccustomed behaviors; extremes of depression or elation; muscular twitches/motor tics; physical tremors; hallucinations; and dangerous elevations in blood pressure, with symptoms like buzzing in the ears, severe headaches, shortness of breath, cardiac arrhythmias, chest pain, confusion, anxiety, seizures, and others. Less serious side effects include blurred vision, dizziness, weakness, moderate headaches, irritability, restlessness, agitation, insomnia, dry mouth, bad taste in the mouth, constipation, diarrhea, stomachache, nausea, vomiting, fever, loss of appetite, weight loss, hair loss, loss of libido, and others.

Depakote (Divalproex Sodium)

Depakote is an anticonvulsive prescribed to control seizures. It can sometimes cause pancreatitis or liver damage. If so, symptoms include jaundice, low-grade fever, pale/clay-colored stools, dark-colored urine, loss of appetite, upper stomach pain, nausea, and vomiting. Emergency medical attention should be pursued if the child has these symptoms. Additional serious side effects include agitation, anxiety, depression, hostility, mental or physical hyperactivity, restlessness, suicidal or self-injurious ideations, confusion, fainting, weakness, bruising easily, urine in the blood, body aches, swollen glands, other flu-like symptoms, decreased urination, excessive sleepiness, incoordination, nystagmus, double vision, painful skin, burning eyes, rashes with blisters and peeling, and other symptoms. Allergic reactions to Depakote cause symptoms of breathing difficulty, hives, and/or swelling of the throat, tongue, lips, or face. Less serious side effects include mild sleepiness, mild weakness, upset stomach, constipation, diarrhea, tremors, changes in vision, hair loss, an unpleasant/unusual taste in the mouth, and others. Educators should always know students are taking seizure medications. They should not first assume behavior or mental disorders or sleep deprivation.

Pulmozyme (Dornase Alfa)

A doctor may prescribe Pulmozyme to a patient who has cystic fibrosis. This condition causes thick mucus secretions in the lungs, interfering with normal breathing. Excessive DNA in the pulmonary secretions causes these symptoms. Pulmozyme is a synthesized protein that breaks down this extra DNA. It makes the lung secretions thinner and thus less likely to obstruct breathing, and also decreases the patient's risk of respiratory tract infections. Pulmozyme is given in solution via inhalation from a nebulizer. Allergic reactions to Pulmozyme cause symptoms like breathing difficulty, swelling of the face, lips, or tongue, hives, swelling/closing of the throat, chest pain, and/or fever. Emergency medical attention or immediate physician contact are indicated for these, which are the primary serious side effects. Less serious Pulmozyme side effects include changes in the voice; a sore throat; laryngitis; rashes; conjunctivitis, or red, irritated, or inflamed eyes; nasal congestion and/or discharge; and other symptoms, for which a doctor should be consulted.

Childhood Anxiety Disorders

According to psychiatrists, children with anxiety are often prescribed the wrong medications when practitioners fail to understand the children's experiences and lack knowledge of evidence-based anxiety treatments. Anxious children have attentional difficulties, not from attention deficits but worries. They are often misdiagnosed as having ADHD and prescribed stimulants. These improve concentration, but not mood; they can even increase anxiety and the insomnia it causes. Alpha-two agonists, e.g., clonidine or guanfacine, lower arousal levels and can calm children, but do not treat their anxiety. Some practitioners even prescribe antipsychotics, also inappropriate for anxiety disorders. Serotonin-specific reuptake inhibitor (SSRI) antidepressants are most effective in

Copyright © Mometrix Media. You have been licensed one copy of this document for personal use only. Any other reproduction or redistribution is strictly prohibited. All rights reserved.
This content is provided for test preparation purposes only and does not imply an endorsement by Mometrix of any particular political, scientific, or religious point of view.

research studies and patient treatments by experienced psychiatric physicians. These can improve children's anxiety relatively fast, e.g., beginning in a week or two, and are most effective in conjunction with cognitive-behavior therapy. Benzodiazepines (Valium, Librium, Dalmane, Halcion, Xanax, Ativan, etc.), used as anti-seizure treatments, sleep aids, and muscle relaxants as well as anxiolytics, also provide short-term help for extreme anxiety, but not long-term help like SSRIs.

Childhood Schizophrenia

While the symptoms of childhood schizophrenia can differ from adult symptoms, the same antipsychotic medications are prescribed to children as adults (though in different dosages), in conjunction with psychotherapy. A few of these drugs include Haldol, Thorazine, Stelazine, Mellaril, Risperdal, Loxitane, Moban, and lithium, which is also often prescribed for bipolar disorder. Antipsychotics in the phenothiazine class, such as Thorazine, Stelazine, and Mellaril, have significant risks of side effects like tardive dyskinesia, which refers to repetitive, involuntary movements that can be irreversible even upon discontinuing treatment; dystonias, like involuntary tongue thrusts, muscular rigidity, etc.; and extrapyramidal syndrome, involving muscle spasms, which are usually reversible on discontinuing treatment but may need other treatments to resolve when they are serious or interfere with breathing. Another side effect is pseudoparkinsonism, which mimics the symptoms of Parkinson disease including "pill-rolling" finger tremors, "mask-like" flat facial appearance, a shuffling gait, and muscular rigidity. A very serious side effect is neuroleptic malignant syndrome. Thorazine and other phenothiazines can also themselves cause psychiatric side effects.

Gabapentin

Although gabapentin is prescribed to adults for the nerve pain of shingles and for Restless Legs Syndrome, it is prescribed to children primarily for seizure disorders. For epilepsy, it is prescribed alone or with other medications to children at least 12 years old as well as adults, and with other medications to children aged 3–12 years for partial seizures. Caution is advised with patients having liver disease, kidney disease, or heart disease. Gabapentin can cause suicidal or self-injurious ideations in some patients. It can also cause depression, anxiety, changes in mood or behavior, agitation, hostility, restlessness, or physical or mental hyperactivity. Serious gabapentin side effects include increased instead of decreased seizures; fever, body aches, swollen glands, flu-like symptoms; bleeding or bruising easily; skin rashes; severe tingling, numbness, or pain; muscular weakness; chest pain, heart arrhythmia, shortness of breath; rapid weight gain, edema/swelling; less/no urination; confusion; nausea, vomiting; worsened/new coughing; difficulty breathing; nystagmus; and upper stomach pain, loss of appetite, dark urine, and jaundice (signs of liver damage).

Gabapentin is prescribed to children to control seizures. It is also prescribed to adults for Restless Legs Syndrome and for nerve pain secondary to shingles. It may be prescribed to some children for whom other anti-seizure medications have not been effective. Some less serious side effects of gabapentin include sleepiness, dizziness, weakness, fatigue; constipation, diarrhea, nausea; blurred vision; headaches; swelling of the breasts; dryness of the mouth; and loss of coordination or balance. In children particularly, gabapentin is more likely to cause problems with memory, changes in behavior, difficulty concentrating, and restless, aggressive, or hostile behavior. If parents or caregivers observe any of these side effects in children who are taking gabapentin, they should always contact the prescribing physician. Educators should always ensure they are informed when students are taking seizure medications, especially younger children less likely to know/understand or volunteer this information. They should not automatically assume a child has an attention deficit or behavior disorder instead. They should also realize this is probably the reason if a student seems sleepy.

Copyright © Mometrix Media. You have been licensed one copy of this document for personal use only. Any other reproduction or redistribution is strictly prohibited. All rights reserved.
This content is provided for test preparation purposes only and does not imply an endorsement by Mometrix of any particular political, scientific, or religious point of view.

Spina Bifida

Spina bifida is a neural tube defect: the neural tube that will become the baby's brain, spinal cord, and enclosing tissues does not close completely. Of its several types, spina bifida occulta frequently needs no treatment. Spina bifida meningocele requires surgery to replace the meninges back into the spinal column and close the vertebral opening. Spina bifida myelomeningocele needs surgery within 24 to 48 hours of birth to lessen infection risk and protect the spinal cord from further trauma. Surgeons sometimes install a shunt in the infant's brain during surgery to control hydrocephalus, a buildup of fluid in the brain. Fetal surgery, before week 26 of gestation, reduces children's needs for brain shunts, crutches/walkers/braces, etc., but is risky for mothers and highly elevates premature birth risk. Despite early surgery, children with myelomeningocele often have lower-body paralysis and bladder and bowel problems. Treatment includes exercises preparing for later assisted walking. Myelomeningocele complications include tethered spinal cord from postoperative scar tissue, inhibiting growth. Surgery can restore some function and mitigate the extent of disability

Muscular Dystrophy

Muscular dystrophy, a genetic condition, makes muscle fibers unusually vulnerable to damage, causing progressive weakness. Symptoms include breathing/swallowing difficulties and limb contractures. Some forms affect the heart and other organs. Among at least seven forms of MD, the Duchenne type comprises roughly half of all cases and is most common in boys. Children learning to walk may fall often; have trouble getting up, running, and jumping; waddle when walking; and have enlarged calf muscles. They also often have learning disabilities. With no cure, treatment focuses on decreasing/preventing spinal and joint deformities and enabling mobility as long as possible. Prednisone and other corticosteroids can slow progression of some forms of MD and enhance muscular strength, but also weaken bones, elevating fracture risks, with long-term use. Surgeries can loosen contracted joints, correct spinal scoliosis to ease breathing, and install pacemakers for MD-related heart conditions. Range-of-motion exercises improve flexibility. Braces support weak muscles, stretch muscles and tendons, and preserve flexibility, slowing contracture progression Some patients need C-PAP sleep apnea devices or ventilators.

Cystic Fibrosis

Children who inherit cystic fibrosis have a genetic defect that makes normally thin, slippery secretory juices become thick and sticky. These fluids, which normally lubricate the tissues, when thickened obstruct passageways, ducts, and tubes, particularly in the lungs and pancreas. CF has no cure, and treatment involves complex management. However, improved detection and intervention have decreased complications and ameliorated symptoms, allowing children to live longer. Treatment focuses on loosening and eliminating mucus from the lungs; preventing and controlling lung infections; preventing and treating intestinal obstructions; and supplying sufficient nutrition. This includes antibiotics; mucus-thinning medications; bronchodilators to keep airways open; pancreatic enzymes to improve nutrient absorption; chest clapping by hand or mechanical device, inflatable vibrating vests, and breathing masks/tubes; breathing exercises and strategies; nutritional counseling; energy-conserving techniques; counseling, and/or support groups. Additional procedures include oxygen therapy to prevent pulmonary hypertension, endoscopy and lavage to suction mucus, surgical nasal polyp removal, feeding tubes for supplemental nutrition, surgical removal of bowel obstructions, and lung transplants.

Cerebral Palsy

Damage or deficient development in the brain before birth usually causes cerebral palsy, which affects muscle tone, posture, and movement. It can include spasticity causing muscular rigidity and

Copyright © Mometrix Media. You have been licensed one copy of this document for personal use only. Any other reproduction or redistribution is strictly prohibited. All rights reserved.
This content is provided for test preparation purposes only and does not imply an endorsement by Mometrix of any particular political, scientific, or religious point of view.

incoordination, athetosis causing involuntary movements and exaggerated reflexes, or both. Its effects can range from an unsteady gait or slight limp to complete loss of walking and speech, and every degree in between these. Botox can help isolated spasticity, and muscle relaxants can help generalized spasticity. CP patients benefit from physical therapy to improve motor development, mobility, strength, balance, and flexibility. Splints or braces can stretch stiff muscles, prevent contractures, and help some children walk. Occupational therapists provide adaptive equipment and alternate strategies to help children participate independently in daily routines and activities. Speech-language therapists help children speak clearly, use sign language or communication boards/devices, and improve eating/swallowing muscle use. Orthopedic surgery for severe deformities or contractures can reposition bones or joints; lengthen contracted tendons and muscles to reduce pain and increase mobility; and sometimes sever extremely spastic muscles.

Historical Emergence of the Identification of Autism Spectrum Disorders

Autism spectrum disorders were not recognized as disorders per se, or given a name, until the middle of the 20th century. In 1943, at the Johns Hopkins Hospital, Dr. Leo Kanner studied eleven children with common behavior patterns. He originated the term "early infantile autism" to describe their disorders. Concurrently, Dr. Hans Asperger, an Austrian pediatrician, identified a milder version of the disorder, which was named Asperger syndrome, after him. An alternative name for autism spectrum disorders which has evolved is pervasive developmental disorders. Today, the APA's Diagnostic and Statistical Manual of Mental Disorders (DSM-5) includes five types of autism spectrum disorders (ASDs) or pervasive developmental disorders (PDDs). All of these disorders have general characteristics of impairment in communication skills, impairment in social interactions, and stereotypic, repetitive patterns of behaviors. These characteristics vary in severity by individual. Some children are identified with ASD by eighteen months of age, many by three years old.

Symptoms of Autism Spectrum Disorders and How Parents Observe These

Some babies eventually diagnosed with ASDs appear to be different from birth. For example, they may not respond to other people in the usual ways by making direct eye contact, smiling, cooing, etc. Or they may tend to focus their attention completely on one object for long periods of time, which is not normal in infants. Other babies seem normal at birth and appear to be developing normally in their earliest years; then their behaviors suddenly change. Toddlers who have been babbling may become silent; those who interacted socially may become withdrawn or cease to respond to others' social advances; and some children may develop self-injurious behaviors. Parents are typically the first adults to observe different behaviors in newborns and behavioral changes in young children. Researchers have found that though parents may not know the specific nature or extent of the problem, they are usually accurate in noticing abnormal development.

Recent Estimated Prevalence Rates of Autistic Disorders in the United States

The Centers for Disease Control (CDC)'s 2007 report represents the most recent government survey on autism rates in the United States; it is based on data obtained in 2000 and 2002 from the health and school records of eight year old children in 14 communities throughout the country. The report shows a substantial increase over rates in the 1980s and early 1990s. There is much controversy over whether these changes reflect an actual increase in the incidence of autistic disorders. Contributing factors include an increase in awareness of autistic disorders on the part of professionals and by the public, leading to more cases being diagnosed. Changes made to the official criteria for diagnoses are leading to children being diagnosed with ASDs instead of with other disorders (e.g. intellectual disabilities, emotional or behavioral disorders) or some who may not have been diagnosed at all. The CDC estimates 2-6 per 1,000 children 3-10 years old have ASDs.

Copyright © Mometrix Media. You have been licensed one copy of this document for personal use only. Any other reproduction or redistribution is strictly prohibited. All rights reserved.
This content is provided for test preparation purposes only and does not imply an endorsement by Mometrix of any particular political, scientific, or religious point of view.

Comparative Risk of Autistic Spectrum Disorders (ASDs) in Children by Gender

The Centers for Disease Control and Prevention (CDC) and National Institute of Mental Health (NIMH) estimate that the risk of ASDs is 3 to 4 times higher for boys than for girls. The CDC estimates that 2-6 per 1,000, or 1 in 500-1 in 150 of children aged 3-10 years have ASDs. This is a comparatively lower rate than that of intellectual disabilities, which is estimated to affect 9.7 per 1,000 children of these ages. However, the estimated rate of ASDs is higher than estimated rates of cerebral palsy, at 2.8 per 1,000; of hearing loss, at 1.1 per 1,000; and of visual impairment, at 0.9 per 1,000. The five types of ASDs defined are Autistic Disorder; Asperger syndrome, which has milder symptoms; Pervasive Developmental Disorder Not Otherwise Specified (PDD-NOS), which does not fit other categories; Rett syndrome, which is fairly rare; and Childhood Disintegrative Disorder, which is very rare.

Rett Syndrome and Childhood Disintegrative Disorder

Rett syndrome is a rather rare form of ASD, affecting one out of 10,000-15,000 children who are nearly all female. This can be attributed to the discovery of an associated genetic mutation, which scientists sponsored by the National Institute of Child Health and Human Development isolated. They hope to use this information to design screenings for earlier identification to facilitate earlier intervention, and possibly to delay/halt is progression. Babies with Rett syndrome develop normally at first; symptoms emerge around 6-18 months old. Developed skills—talking/babbling, social interaction, hand/foot control—are lost as the child regresses. Childhood Disintegrative Disorder is very rare, affecting more males. Fewer than two per 100,000 children having ASDs are estimated to have CDD. Average onset age is 3-4 years, differentiating it from Rett syndrome. Symptoms, more severe than in classical autism, include loss of motor, language, social skills, bowel and bladder control; seizures and intellectual disabilities.

Signs Which Can Indicate Autistic Disorders

Some signs that parents can be aware of which might indicate a autistic disorder include: If a baby does not babble, point at things or people, or make meaningful gestures by one year of age; if a child does not speak at least one word by the age of 16 months; if the child does not put two words together by the age of two years; if the child does not respond to hearing his or her name; or if a child with normal early development loses linguistic or social skills previously demonstrated. Some additional signs that can indicate autistic disorders are avoiding eye contact, poor or inconsistent eye contact; not appearing to know how to play with toys; preoccupation with rigidly aligning toys in rows; being overly attached to a certain toy/object; not smiling at others, even parents, family members, or other familiar people; or seeming hearing-impaired at times.

Social Symptoms

Many children with ASDs do not interact with other people, seeming to prefer being alone. Some avoid eye contact. They may resist, pull away, or passively tolerate it when their parents hug or cuddle them rather than reciprocating. They tend not to go to parents for comfort. They are likely to respond atypically to their parents' demonstrations of love and anger. It seems from research findings that children with ASDs are attached to their parents, but do not show it normally, so parents have difficulty perceiving it. Many parents misconstrue their autistic child's behavior as rejection. Autistic children have trouble understanding social cues. They perceive a mother's saying "Come here" the same way whether she is inviting a hug or is angry. They also often lack the understanding that others may have different points of view. Hence they cannot see things from another person's perspective, so they cannot anticipate others' behaviors.

Copyright © Mometrix Media. You have been licensed one copy of this document for personal use only. Any other reproduction or redistribution is strictly prohibited. All rights reserved.
This content is provided for test preparation purposes only and does not imply an endorsement by Mometrix of any particular political, scientific, or religious point of view.

Differences in Communication

Some children with ASDs are nonverbal for life. Some autistic infants coo and babble at first but then stop. Some autistic children have delayed language development, not speaking until middle childhood (e.g. ages 5-9). Some autistic children speak single words but not phrases, while some repeat the same phrase over and over. Some who can speak words cannot form meaningful sentences. Some display echolalia, repeating whatever others say. Some children only echo others, never producing original utterances; others can communicate verbally and also display echolalia. Some speak well and have big vocabularies, but speak in monologues—just as they concentrate intensely on one activity or subject for long times—as they have difficulty understanding the social, interactional aspect of taking turns in conversation. Receptively, they usually do not understand tones of voice or facial expressions, so they fail to perceive sarcasm, jokes, and other non-literal meanings.

Children with ASDs, who are verbal, are still likely to speak in odd ways. The facial expressions, gestures, and body language they display are not typically congruent with what they say, what they mean, or how they feel. Their tones of voice also do not reflect what they feel. They may speak in a flat, monotone voice like a robot, use a high-pitched voice, or have a sing-song delivery instead of the normal prosody (intonations and rhythms) heard in normal speech. Some autistic children who have good language and speech development will speak like "little adults," as they do not catch on to the "kid speak" expressions used by their peers due to their deficits in understanding social behaviors and contexts. Children with ASDs who are nonverbal or have limited verbal and gestural expression, unable to get what they need or want in those ways, may just grab things or scream.

Repetitive Stereotypic Behaviors and Behavioral Rigidity

Many ASD children rock back and forth, flap their hands or arms, make other repeated hand movements, walk on their toes, or abruptly freeze in place. They often line toys up precisely, not using them for pretend play, getting very upset if anything is moved. Intensely focused attention on one object/activity/subject is another manifestation of repetitive behavior. Students may become obsessed with learning everything about, for example, lighthouses, vacuum cleaners, or train schedules. Scientific subjects, numbers, and symbols are frequent objects of preoccupation. ASD children require perfectly consistent schedules and environments. They become extremely upset at the smallest deviation in the time of any daily activity or the location of any object. Some scientists hypothesize that rigid order provides stability in a confusing world. Another hypothesis is that repetitive, self-stimulating behaviors replace external stimuli the child shuts out as being painful and, for needed stimulation, substitutes things he can control.

Sensory Problems

ASD children's perceptions of sensory information are inaccurate, creating confusion for them rather than learning from their senses via accurate perceptions. Many ordinary sensations can be painful to ASD children. A slightly scratchy label or fabric in clothing can feel like sandpaper; lights can seem so bright, or sounds so loud, that they hurt. They may also have extreme reactions to certain smells or tastes. Particular types of sounds can cause distress, such as a sudden thunderstorm, the sound of a telephone ringing, a vacuum cleaner's noise, or even the sound of waves lapping at the shore. Additionally, ASD brains seem unable to balance sensory input: some children with ASD will not feel pain or extremely cold temperatures; some have no pain response to accidentally smashing their heads into walls or breaking a limb. While some will not react to serious injuries, yet they will scream at being touched lightly.

Copyright © Mometrix Media. You have been licensed one copy of this document for personal use only. Any other reproduction or redistribution is strictly prohibited. All rights reserved.
This content is provided for test preparation purposes only and does not imply an endorsement by Mometrix of any particular political, scientific, or religious point of view.

Students with Autism Spectrum Disorders with and Without Co-Existing Intellectual Disabilities

Some students with ASDs have intellectual disabilities and some do not. Some autism researchers estimate the proportions as roughly 50/50 (Gerdtz, 1994). While the causes of ASDs are not known, it is generally agreed that the symptoms of ASDs are related to neurological damage or defects. Thus it is not uncommon for perhaps half of ASD students to have co-existing intellectual disabilities. Non-autistic students with mild intellectual disabilities can have fairly uniform test or subscale IQ scores across all domains, i.e. all their cognitive functions show the same levels, whereas ASD students are more likely to vary widely across domains. An ASD student might score much higher, for example, in visual skills than in language skills. ASD individuals with above-average IQs can demonstrate striking discrepancies, such as between intellectual and social development; for example, you could be discussing higher mathematics with such an individual when he suddenly walks away in mid-conversation.

Incidence of Seizures

According to the National Institute of Mental Health (NIMH), 25% of or one out of four children with autism spectrum disorders develops a seizure disorder. Some children with ASDs develop seizures in early childhood; others start having them during adolescence, perhaps triggered by pubertal changes. Seizures are caused by abnormal electrical activity in the brain. Because ASDs are attributed to neurological differences, it is logical that in some cases, neurological damage or deficits can include seizures as well as autism, just as the damage or deficits cause intellectual disabilities and autism in some children. High fevers and sleep deprivation are sometimes factors implicated in seizures. An electroencephalogram (EEG), which records the brain's electrical currents, can verify the existence of seizures. Anticonvulsant medications are prescribed to treat most seizure disorders. Dosage must be carefully adjusted; however, this can be difficult. Common side-effects of seizure medications include drowsiness, dizziness, nausea, and blurred vision.

Tuberous Sclerosis

Tuberous sclerosis is a rare genetic disorder causing benign tumors, which can exert pressure in the brain, causing neurological and behavioral problems. 1%-4% of those with ASD have tuberous sclerosis. Fragile X syndrome is a genetic mutation wherein part of the X chromosome is pinched/"fragile." A male's Y chromosome does not transmit the defect, so fathers with the mutation only pass it to daughters. Mothers with the Fragile X gene pass it to both sexes. All the children of a mother with one Fragile X chromosome and one normal X chromosome, and a father with no mutation have 50/50 chances of inheriting the syndrome. According to recent (2003) statistics, 5% of individuals with ASDs have Fragile X syndrome; 10%-15% of individuals with Fragile X syndrome have some autistic symptoms. When one child has ASD and Fragile X syndrome, boys born to the same parents have a 50% probability of Fragile X.

Diagnostic Process

Some infants evidence some symptoms of autism spectrum disorders when they are only a few months old. Others have symptoms first emerging during the early childhood years. Many parents and professionals have expressed concerns about labeling a young child as having an ASD, as this influences their treatment, educational placement, and subsequent development. However, mental health professionals also point out the importance of early diagnosis and early intervention. These conflicting considerations must be balanced. Long-term research finds that intensive interventions with ASD children during preschool years, in optimum educational placements for at least two years, produce better results. Clinicians diagnose ASD based on behavioral observations. Diagnostic criteria require that the child had problems in at least one of the three areas of communication,

Copyright © Mometrix Media. You have been licensed one copy of this document for personal use only. Any other reproduction or redistribution is strictly prohibited. All rights reserved.
This content is provided for test preparation purposes only and does not imply an endorsement by Mometrix of any particular political, scientific, or religious point of view.

socialization, or restricted behavior before age 3. Developmental screening during well-baby checkups constitutes the first stage of the process; comprehensive evaluation by a multidisciplinary team is the second.

All children should have developmental screenings during well-baby or well-child checkups by their pediatricians. If the doctor or the parents observe any signs of possible ASD, the child should first undergo screening using an approved screening instrument. The screening does not determine diagnosis, but indicates whether referral for comprehensive evaluation is needed. The comprehensive evaluation is often conducted by a multidisciplinary team, which can include a psychiatrist, psychologist, neurologist, speech-language pathologist, or other professionals qualified to diagnose ASDs. Evaluation should include neurological and genetic testing since these factors are involved, and ASDs are often accompanied by additional neurological or genetic problems. It should also include in-depth testing of cognitive and language development. A complete audiological evaluation is needed to rule in/rule out hearing loss. Children who put everything in their mouths during prolonged oral-motor stages need lead screening; most ASD children are found to have elevated blood lead levels.

The Autism Diagnosis Interview-Revised (ADI-R) consists of a structured interview with over 100 items to give to a child's parent or caregiver. It covers four general areas: the child's communication; higher social interaction; repetitive behaviors; and symptoms at age of onset. The Autism Diagnostic Observation Schedule (ADOS-G) is an observational measure used by the clinician to elicit social and communicative behaviors frequently abnormal, delayed, or missing in ASD children. The Childhood Autism Rating Scale (CARS) is administered with children aged 2+. Examiners combine parental information with direct observations. The CARS has ratings for the behavioral areas of body movements, adaptation to change, listening response, verbal communication, and relationship to people. The clinician rates the child's behavior in terms of deviance from norms of typical behaviors for children the same age. The team evaluates the child's individual strengths and weaknesses, makes a formal diagnosis, and explains evaluation findings to the parents.

Screening Babies and Young Children for Autistic Symptoms

A pediatric "well-baby/well-child" checkups should include a developmental screening. Parents should request this if their pediatrician does not routinely do it. Parents can review their baby albums/books, photographs, and family videos to recall when their child achieved developmental milestones and when the first observed symptomatic behaviors. Screening instruments include the Checklist of Autism in Toddlers (CHAT), a modified version (M-CHAT), the Screening Tool for Autism in Two-Year-Olds (STAT), and the Social Communication Questionnaire (SCQ) for children aged 4+. Some instruments use only parent responses; others combine parent questionnaires with direct observation of the child. Pointing and pretend play are key screening items to identify ASDs before age 2. Screening instruments are not for making an individual diagnosis of ASD; they are for determining the need to refer a child for further testing for possible ASD diagnosis. The instruments named here may not identify high-functioning autistics or children with Asperger syndrome.

Screening Instruments for Asperger Syndrome and High-Functioning Autism

A good many children with autism spectrum disorders have milder symptoms and higher levels of functioning. Children with Asperger syndrome, for example, typically have milder deficits in functioning than in "classical" autism. Other children ultimately diagnosed with autistic disorders, with high levels of intelligence and of some functional skills, are deemed "high-functioning." Screening instruments for autism, e.g. the CHAT, M-CHAT, STAT, and SCQ will often not identify these children as having ASDs. The Autism Spectrum Screening Questionnaire (ASSQ), the

Copyright © Mometrix Media. You have been licensed one copy of this document for personal use only. Any other reproduction or redistribution is strictly prohibited. All rights reserved.
This content is provided for test preparation purposes only and does not imply an endorsement by Mometrix of any particular political, scientific, or religious point of view.

Australian Scale for Asperger's Syndrome, and the Childhood Asperger Syndrome Test (CAST) are designed to identify school-aged children with Asperger syndrome or high-functioning autism and are found to be reliable. These instruments are intended for children without significant language delays who have social and behavioral deficits. Positive screenings should be followed by comprehensive evaluation. Even with passed screening, if the pediatrician subsequently detects signs of possible ASD, further testing is needed.

Treatments

Two main generalizations that the majority of professionals agree to are (1) the importance of early intervention; and (2) that most ASD children benefit from specialized programs that are highly structured. Specifically, experts find that there is no one treatment program that is best for all ASD children. Due to individual differences, each child's needs are different and different treatments may apply. The Autism Society of America recommends parents ask professionals the following about any possible treatment: Whether the treatment can cause any kind of harm to the child; if the treatment fails, how it will affect the child and the family; whether the treatment has been validated by scientific research; whether the treatment specifies assessment procedures; and how the treatment will be integrated into the child's existing educational program. They caution parents against becoming so enamored of a program that they overlook curricula teaching functional, social, and vocational skills.

A good treatment program for autism spectrum disorders should first identify a child's individual interests. The activities offered in the program should then address and build upon those interests. Any treatment program for ASDs should provide a highly predictable schedule, as individuals with ASDs cannot tolerate anything irregular or unexpected. They require consistency, order, and structure. The treatment program should not only provide very structured activities; it should, moreover, have ways of actively engaging a child's attention to and participation in them. A child's desirable behaviors should consistently receive positive reinforcement throughout the treatment. Research and experience have revealed that a major influence on program success is the involvement of parents. Teachers, therapists, and parents collaborate to determine which behaviors should be changed and which skills should be taught. Parents are children's first teachers, so more treatment programs are now training children's parents to continue the treatment in the home.

Applied Behavior Analysis (ABA) and Therapeutic and Educational Intervention

Many treatment methods exist for ASDs. Applied behavior analysis (ABA) has widespread popularity as an effective method for ASDs and other disorders. Clinical psychologist, autism expert, and one of the founders of ABA, Dr. (Ole) Ivar Lovaas led research at UCLA, advising intensive, 1:1 teacher-child interaction 40 hours weekly. This formed a foundation for researchers and educators to design effective early interventions for ASD children. ABA is based on B. F. Skinner's principles of operant conditioning, behavior modification, and behavior analysis to eliminate, reduce, or modify undesirable, maladaptive behaviors and increase, shape, and teach more adaptive, functional, desirable behaviors. The systematic nature of behaviorism and ABA affords a good fit with the rigidity and need for consistency of ASD individuals. A Surgeon General's Report (1999) stated: "Thirty years of research demonstrated the efficacy of applied behavioral methods in reducing inappropriate behavior and in increasing communication, learning, and appropriate social behavior."

Early Intervention Programs

For ASD children younger than 3 years old, early intervention programs typically are delivered in the home or at child-care centers. Early skills in social interaction and communication are taught in effective early intervention programs. Interventions focus on addressing specific deficiencies in

Copyright © Mometrix Media. You have been licensed one copy of this document for personal use only. Any other reproduction or redistribution is strictly prohibited. All rights reserved.
This content is provided for test preparation purposes only and does not imply an endorsement by Mometrix of any particular political, scientific, or religious point of view.

learning; language; attention; motivation; imitation; compliance; and the initiation of interactions. Behavioral techniques, communication therapy, occupational therapy, physical therapy, and social play interventions are used. Teachers often start the day with physical activities to promote development of body awareness and coordination. Typical motor skill development activities include painting, stringing beads, and assembling puzzles. Learning by doing is emphasized. For example, teachers model using language to make requests during snack times, and encourage children's social interaction. Behavior therapists, students, and parents, all extensively trained, work directly with the children and assist the teachers. The behavioral technique of positive reinforcement is a key component of such effective early intervention programs.

Characteristics of Public School Education

While children under 3 years old with ASDs are eligible for early intervention programs, children over 3 years old with ASDs typically receive the free, public education guaranteed to them by Federal law. They law requires them to receive special education services and an individualized education plan (IEP). Elementary school children may be in a separate class for ASD students, or may be integrated into regular classes for part or all of the school day. In inclusion programs at many public schools, the child is in a regular classroom most of the day, attending special education classes at specified times, wherein making friends and behavior in social situations should be taught. Assistance with delayed skills, plus growth in strength areas, should be afforded in elementary grades. Curricula should be adapted to individual student needs. High-functioning ASD students who can manage academic tasks can still use help organizing work and avoiding distractions.

Instructional Needs of Students During Adolescence in Middle and High School Grades

While functional communication and social skills are emphasized with ASD students in elementary grades, practical needs for life are included in middle and high school instruction. Important areas for older students include learning to participate in recreational activities, learning to use public transportation, learning skills needed for community living, and gaining work experience. The changes of adolescence cause stress and confusion for all teenagers, including those with autism. Some behaviors improve in adolescence; some escalate. Typical autistic behaviors or aggression sometimes increase in response to teen stress. Social sensitivity accompanying adolescence can magnify the differences of ASD students. As other teens are preoccupied with appearance, popularity, dating, and grades, ASD teens may come to realize that they do not have friends, dates, or career plans like their peers. This can be depressing for some students, but some respond with increased motivation to learn new behaviors and improve their social skills.

Medications and Antidepressants

Because children with ASDs may respond differently to medications than those with normal development, medications should be prescribed by doctors having experience with ASD children and be carefully monitored. Many prescriptions for ASDs are "off-label," i.e. for a purpose or age group other than those approved by the FDA but chosen by doctors as appropriate for certain ASD children. Serotonin-selective reuptake inhibitors (SSRIs) are antidepressants popularly prescribed for anxiety, depression, or obsessive-compulsive disorder (OCD) symptoms. They are also found to reduce the frequency of ritualistic, repetitive behaviors common to both OCD and ASD, and to improve eye contact and social interaction in ASD patients. Among SSRIs, Prozac® (fluoxetine) is FDA-approved for OCD and depression in children aged 7 up; for OCD, Luvox® (fluvoxamine) in ages 8 up; Zoloft® (sertraline) in ages 6 up; and Anafranil® (clomipramine) for ages 10 up. Any of these drugs may be prescribed off-label for ASD symptoms.

Copyright © Mometrix Media. You have been licensed one copy of this document for personal use only. Any other reproduction or redistribution is strictly prohibited. All rights reserved.
This content is provided for test preparation purposes only and does not imply an endorsement by Mometrix of any particular political, scientific, or religious point of view.

Prescription of Medications for Severe Behavior Problems

When ASD children exhibit severe behavior problems, doctors have prescribed anti-psychotic medications normally used to control symptoms of mental illnesses, such as hallucinations, delusions, etc. Anti-psychotics inhibit the activation of the neurotransmitter dopamine. The neurological involvement of ASDs can explain why severe behavior problems in ASD children are also often alleviated by anti-psychotic drugs. Among older, traditional/"typical" anti-psychotics, Haldol® (haloperidol) has been found effective in a number of research studies for treating serious ASD behavior problems. It is known for decreasing aggression in schizophrenia, other psychoses, and in ASD children. However, Haldol® can have significant adverse side-effects like sedation, muscular stiffness; and tardive dyskinesia (involuntary movements), which can become permanent. Newer "atypical" anti-psychotics are being tested with ASD children. Risperdal® (risperidone) has been found effective and well-tolerated for treating severe autistic behavior problems. Common side-effects are sedation, increased appetite and weight gain. Longitudinal studies are needed to determine long-term side-effects.

Neuroimaging Techniques Allowing Scientists to Identify Brain Structures

Computerized tomography (CT) and positron emission tomography (PET) scans, single-photon emission computed tomography (SPECT), and magnetic resonance imaging (MRI) now permit researchers to conduct comparative research of normal and ASD brain tissue. Post-mortem and MRI studies have implicated the cerebellum, cerebral cortex, corpus callosum, limbic system, basal ganglia, and brain stem in autistic spectrum disorders. Research is also ongoing into neurotransmitters, the brain's chemical messengers, and the parts they may play in ASDs. Neurotransmitters being studied include dopamine, serotonin, and epinephrine. Research findings also suggest a strong involvement of genetic factors in the etiologies of ASDs. Twin studies and family studies suggest underlying genetic predispositions to ASD. The Autism Genetic Resource Exchange is conducting 2-hour in-home screenings of several hundred families having more than one member diagnosed with ASD and collecting tissue samples from them. Scientists working on this project seek to isolate the most significant genes involved in ASD.

Functional Behavior Analysis of Maladaptive Behaviors

The principle upon which functional behavior analysis is based is that all behaviors serve some kind of function or purpose. Children lacking required communication skills or coping skills will communicate through their behavior instead. Professionals need to determine what unmet need a child has; and what need the child's specific maladaptive behavior meets. To substitute a more adaptive behavior, they must first discover the reasons for the behavior. To do this, they must be able to answer the following questions: What is the child's intention by engaging in the maladaptive behavior? How effective has this behavior been heretofore; i.e., did the child regularly receive reinforcement (e.g. attention, including scolding) consequent to the behavior? Does the student have any other, more acceptable behaviors to meet the same need, or is the maladaptive behavior the only one? How can a replacement behavior be taught and reinforced so the child keeps using it?

Problem Behaviors That Are Specifically Due to Deficiencies Inherent in ASD

ASD children can have behavioral "meltdowns" for the same reasons as other children, but also for reasons caused by their disability. The need of ASD students for regularity and consistency is one such reason. ASD children also need predictability, or knowing what will happen next. Unexpected events frequently trigger problem behaviors. Sensory needs like noise, bright lights, and activity levels in classes can cause physical discomfort, hence agitation and maladaptive behaviors. Environmental needs like the size of the room or inaccessibility to materials also affect ASDs. Problems with spatial skills, mobility, or self-help skills are likely to result in frustration and result

Copyright © Mometrix Media. You have been licensed one copy of this document for personal use only. Any other reproduction or redistribution is strictly prohibited. All rights reserved.
This content is provided for test preparation purposes only and does not imply an endorsement by Mometrix of any particular political, scientific, or religious point of view.

in problem behaviors expressing that frustration. A student's relative coping skills, such as problem-solving ability or self-identification of sensory overload, are factors. The student's abilities to communicate feelings and needs verbally in an effective, expressive way, and to interpret the verbal and nonverbal language of others receptively, are affected by ASDs.

Functional Behavior Analysis (FBA)

A school team should meet to consider a functional behavior analysis (FBA) under such conditions as these: The student struggles with disruptive behaviors. The student exhibits indications of escalating anxiety. The student understands the assignments, but has trouble completing them due to other types of interference. The student is not meeting expectations. The student shows a dependency on ritualistic behaviors that interfere with doing school work. The student is having problems with sensory stimuli in the environment. The student is having trouble with social skills or interacting with other students. The student evidences resistance to authority figures or to expectations. The student is having problems being able to communicate effectively. The student's behavior shows sudden changes, for better or worse. The student is encountering any regular obstacles to succeeding in school or at home. The team should schedule planning times and assign participants and a coordinator for conducting a FBA.

Myles and Southwick (1999) find behavioral breakdowns occur in cyclic stages. They call the first stage "rumbling." It includes precursors/warning signs, which not everybody will understand or even notice, but which people who know the student well enough will observe and recognize. The second stage is "rage," the full-blown demonstration of the problem behavior. In addition to screaming, tantrums, aggression, and self-injurious behaviors, some ASD students will run away from the place/situation. While this signifies fear/escape rather than anger, the "rage" stage still applies despite its name, because the main characteristic is that one can no longer reason with the individual. The third stage is "recovery." While the student is trying to get over the outburst, if not managed appropriately, it can recur. Signs of each stage should be included in the FBA so supports can be furnished before, not after, the breakdown to prevent repeated cycling through the stages.

A single professional cannot conduct the FBA alone because it requires various perspectives obtained from different settings. Members should have observed the student's behavior for long time periods in diverse conditions and contexts. Teachers should be included—general and special education if the student works with both. In high school, teachers of subjects where the student succeeds and subjects where the student struggles should participate. Related service providers, such as the speech-language pathologist, occupational therapist, and psychologist should be included, along with any paraprofessional(s) working with the student. The parents should participate as they know their child best and will be affected by any program changes made for the student. The building administrator is needed to approve staff time, strategies, and changes to rules or routines. While not directly participating in planning, meetings, data gathering, etc., the student should be involved by giving his/her own perspective and other information.

The behaviors most troublesome to the student, not others, come first. Considering which behaviors would have the most positive effects on the student if changed is a good general rule. The team should consider whether the behavior: is dangerous to the student or others; is frequently or intensively disruptive; impedes peer acceptance/socialization; interferes with learning academic, social, or independence skills. Once a target behavior is established, the team should seek to answer if the behavior: has been a long-term problem with little/no improvement; entails aggression or property damage; is caused by the environment; is caused by a skill deficit, and if so, whether the student is able to learn the missing/deficient skill and apply it; what school staff and family's viewpoints are regarding when, where, and how the behavior happens; warning signs the student

Copyright © Mometrix Media. You have been licensed one copy of this document for personal use only. Any other reproduction or redistribution is strictly prohibited. All rights reserved.
This content is provided for test preparation purposes only and does not imply an endorsement by Mometrix of any particular political, scientific, or religious point of view.

displays; and whether improving the behavior would confer positive side-effects, e.g. better grades or peer acceptance.

Before beginning an intervention to change a maladaptive behavior, the behavior's current status must be established—how often it occurs and when, where, with whom, and under what conditions. It is impossible to measure the student's progress during intervention without a starting point. Team members must all agree to the same definition of a behavior. For example, one might define "talking out" as screaming while another might define it as quiet muttering. A more precise definition is needed so all members gathering data will measure the same thing. Recording methods should be sufficiently concrete to assure reliable information regardless of who is collecting data. Comments or anecdotes vary among individuals. Charts or checklists that each member can mark the same way are more reliable, less ambiguous, and more time-efficient as well. For example, X and O can be used for occurrence and non-occurrence of a behavior during specified time periods.

The school's functional behavior analysis team may use any or all of these sources. They can use formal and informal interviews conducted with school staff members, family members, and the student when this is appropriate. It is important to gather information from the student without drawing his or her attention to the target behavior, because this can change the student's behavior, resulting in inaccurate data. Sources also include direct observation and documentation of the student's behavior made by an objective third party; scatter plot charts of the behavior's occurrence over a period of time; Antecedent – Behavior – Consequence, ABC charts, or similar graphics; reviews of the student's past and present records; completed standardized Behavior Rating Scales; assessments of the student's motivation; assessments of the student's preferred reinforcements; and self-checks available for conducting functional behavior analyses and designing behavioral support plans. The team may also ask parents to collect behavioral data.

Elements to Be Addressed in a Behavioral Support Plan

A behavioral support plan for an ASD student with maladaptive behavior should consider: improving the student's skill deficit areas; promoting student motivation; minimizing adult control as a part of the behavior intervention plan; changing the antecedent conditions to the behavior; changing the consequences of the behavior; presenting practical, acceptable alternative choices for student responses and giving practice in using these; changing or adjusting curriculum requirements, teaching methods and strategies; changing the instructional setting, the class environment, or the physical characteristics of the location; and designing and carrying out a behavior intervention plan which the parents, staff, administration, and the student (as much as is possible) will accept and support. A good behavioral support plan will include such components as a behavior intervention plan (BIP); a crisis management plan; the environmental modifications necessary; instruction in needed skills; and strategies for maintaining the behavior changes effected through successful implementation of the BIP.

Factors That Affect the Measurement of a Maladaptive Behavior

When a school team has collected baseline data on the student's behavior, completed a functional behavior analysis, designed a behavior intervention plan and implemented it, they then must measure the student's subsequent behavior to compare with baseline and see if the intervention is helping. Any daily variations in the environment are reflected by variations in behavior, especially with ASD students, who need sameness and are upset by changes. Some factors include: stimulus overload; availability of teacher attention; task difficulty; comprehension of instructional demands; overcrowding; effectiveness of teaching; the student's motivation; effectiveness of support; timing and sequence of activities; fatigue or illness in the student. An ASD student may have understood

Copyright © Mometrix Media. You have been licensed one copy of this document for personal use only. Any other reproduction or redistribution is strictly prohibited. All rights reserved.
This content is provided for test preparation purposes only and does not imply an endorsement by Mometrix of any particular political, scientific, or religious point of view.

the curriculum during one unit or textbook chapter when baseline data were collected, but have difficulty with the next unit or chapter, partly because he does not understand the demands, which differ from the last unit/chapter and are hence unexpected/unpredictable.

Implementing and Measuring Behavior Intervention Plans

After behavioral interventions and supports have been implemented for a length of time judged reasonable for them to effect positive changes, the school team will need to collect new data measuring the same things measured by the baseline data they collected. They can then compare the new data with the baseline data. In doing this, they should focus on three areas: (1) whether the problem behavior has decreased, and if so, by how much; (2) whether the student's learning and use of replacement behaviors and alternative skills have increased, and if so, by how much; (3) if the target behavior has improved, what positive side effects have resulted, e.g. better grades, better peer acceptance, etc. If the BIP does not seem to be working, the team should work together on making minor "fine-tuning" adjustments; overhauling the whole plan; or asking for a professional consultation. Teams should schedule long-term collaboration time.

Avoiding Obstacles to Successful Behavioral Intervention Plans (BIPs)

In functional behavior analysis (FBA), the function should not be identified merely as "attention-seeking" or "escape." Seeking attention and escaping are motivated by another need. Ensuring thorough data collection and exploration before formulating a hypothesis can save time later. Documentation should include temporary behavioral influences, e.g. if the student was sick one day, took a hard test another day, and had a family member in the hospital another, to explain behavioral changes. All team members' views should be included for cohesive, cooperative teamwork. The FBA should not only describe problems but also student strengths, which should be used in developing supports and interventions, which must be usable and incorporated in natural school/community contexts. Reinforcing appropriate behavior is crucial and must be practicable for all. Teaching the student self-monitoring and self-evaluation should be included in the BIP for maintenance and self-reinforcement. The BIP must describe student warning signs of behavioral incidents.

Examples

Student Whose Teacher Unintentionally Increases His Occasional Maladaptive Behavior Through an Intervention Not Informed by a Functional Behavior Analysis (FBA)

Stephen is high-functioning and excels in math. He normally has good self-control. He hates the students in his math class. They are always giggling and whispering, which he finds unpredictable and distracting, but the teacher ignores them. He resents their copying his work and taking credit for it. From these tensions, he occasionally has an outburst. The teacher sends him to the office to finish his math. The office is a quiet, orderly, comfortable, and friendly place for Stephen. He can do his work more easily there and is more relaxed. After being sent to the office several times, Stephen's outbursts increase until he is engaging in various forms of disruptive behavior daily. With no analysis of the reasons for Stephen's behavior, the teacher thinks sending him to the office is punishment, and he will misbehave less to avoid repeating such embarrassment; however, it is really a reward for him.

Student Whose Behavioral Incidents Seem Inconsistent

Bobby, an ASD high school student with limited verbal expression, cannot explain his behavior. He is often removed from Ms. Scott's class for acting-out behavior. Gathering data, the team discovers he smiles at Ms. Scott and tries to comply with her directions, so it seems he does not dislike her; yet he retreats from her when she is nearby. His Homeroom teacher reports he acted out on

Copyright © Mometrix Media. You have been licensed one copy of this document for personal use only. Any other reproduction or redistribution is strictly prohibited. All rights reserved.
This content is provided for test preparation purposes only and does not imply an endorsement by Mometrix of any particular political, scientific, or religious point of view.

Teacher Appreciation Day, a very unusual behavior for him in Homeroom. Staff report incidents in the cafeteria on some days. The team compiles these pieces of data, brainstorming for a relationship. They realize Ms. Scott wears strong perfume; the Homeroom teacher received fresh flowers on Teacher Appreciation Day; and some days the cafeteria has strong odors of food or cleaning products. Testing their odor hypothesis, Ms. Scott eliminates her perfume and other smells from the room. Bobby stops avoiding her and acting out.

Copyright © Mometrix Media. You have been licensed one copy of this document for personal use only. Any other reproduction or redistribution is strictly prohibited. All rights reserved.
This content is provided for test preparation purposes only and does not imply an endorsement by Mometrix of any particular political, scientific, or religious point of view.

Assessing Students with Autism Spectrum Disorder and Developing Individualized Programs

Reliability and Validity

Reliability is consistency of an assessment instrument's data across repeated administrations. For example, reliable test scores are similar when the same test-taker is given the test two/three times at two-week intervals. Internal consistency reliability is consistency of test items with one another by measuring the same quantity/construct. Inter-rater consistency is reliability among individuals scoring the same test. Intra-rater consistency is an individual's consistency in rating responses to various test items. Validity is whether a test measures what it claims/intends to measure. Content validity means a test includes items representing the complete range of possible items. Construct validity means a test's scores measure the construct they are meant to measure, like intelligence. Criterion validity means a test's scores effectively measure a construct according to established criteria. Concurrent validity, a type of criterion validity, means a test measures the criterion and the construct at the same time. Predictive validity, another type of criterion validity, means test scores effectively predict future outcomes, as when aptitude tests predict future subject grades.

Standard Deviation, Standard Score, and Scaled Score

Standard deviation measures variability within a set of numbers. In interpreting assessment results, it measures how much scores among a group of test-takers vary around the mean/average. For example, a bell curve shows a normal distribution of test scores: the high center represents the majority of scores closest to the mean, while the lower sides represent standard deviations above and below it. SD is calculated by obtaining the square root of the sum of deviations of each score and the mean, and dividing this figure by the number of scores in the group. The standard score, or z score, represents the amount whereby an individual score deviates from the mean, measured in SDs. For example, a common SD unit for IQ tests is 15 where the mean is 100. A scaled score is obtained by converting a group of test scores to a scale/distribution with a designated mean and SD. For example, the US Medical Licensing Examination (USMLE) has a mean of 200 and a SD of 20.

Domain and Item Response Theory

In educational assessment, the term "domain" is the identified scope of expected learning to be assessed. Tests typically present students with samples of assessment tasks. The results of these tests are then interpreted to generalize the performance on the full range of possible assessment tasks that would measure the domain of intended learning. Item Response Theory (IRT) posits that performance on a test item is attributed to three influences: the item itself; the test-taker; and the interaction between the two. In education, when large groups of test-takers are given many test items to produce large data sets, raters can use formulae to separate influences on test items from the test-takers' true ability, skills, or knowledge. However, the kind of assessment that is normally conducted within a given educational program does not afford enough data to calculate parameters according to Item Response Theory that would be stable enough to be meaningful.

Mean, Median, and Mode

The mean is the average of a group of numbers, e.g., scores within a group of students taking the same test. Among six students, if one scores 50%; one 60%; one 70%; one 80%; one 90%; and one 100%, the sum of scores = 450; divided by 6 (students/scores) yields an average/mean of 75%. The

Copyright © Mometrix Media. You have been licensed one copy of this document for personal use only. Any other reproduction or redistribution is strictly prohibited. All rights reserved.
This content is provided for test preparation purposes only and does not imply an endorsement by Mometrix of any particular political, scientific, or religious point of view.

median is the center-most score in a group. For example, if the range of student scores on a test is 65%, 75%, 80%, 85%, and 95%, then 80% = the middle/median. When there is an even number of scores, the median is the average of the two most central scores. For example, with four scores of 50%, 60%, 70%, and 80%, 60% and 70% are averaged for a median of 65%. The mode is the most frequent score in a set. If in a group of students, one scored 100% on a test; one, 95%; two, 90%; three, 85%; four, 80%; three, 75%; two, 70%; and one, 65%, the mode = 80%.

Positive Skew and Negative Skew

When the majority of a group of numbers, such as test scores, is concentrated toward the high end of the range/distribution with the minority "tail" of scores near the low end, this group of numbers is said to be positively skewed. When the majority of scores is bunched near the lower end of the distribution, with a minority "tail" near the higher end, the set of scores is negatively skewed. A normal curve is called a bell curve because it resembles the shape of a bell, with the largest number of scores collected around the center mean or average score and the numbers of scores descending as they move away from the center and mean. Parametric statistics assume a normal distribution. However, in typical educational assessments, the data obtained as scores on testing instruments are not usually found to be distributed normally.

Standard Error of Measurement (SEM) and Standard Error of the Mean

If an individual student took a lot of tests that were similar in size or length (i.e., the number of items on each test), the assessors can estimate how much that student's scores will vary. This estimate is called the Standard Error of Measurement (SEM). The SEM is calculated using the reliability coefficient that is established for a given test and the Standard Deviation (SD) that has been established for the group of scores that the student achieved. When a group of students takes a test, the assessors can estimate how much the mean or average score of that group would vary if they selected many samples with the same sizes and then calculated the means or averages of their scores. This estimate of variance around the mean of a group's test scores is called the Standard Error of the Mean.

Confidence Interval

Statisticians use the Confidence Interval to express the range wherein a "true" or "real" score is situated. The purpose is to acknowledge and address the fact that the measurement of a student's performance contains "noise," i.e., interfering/confounding variables that influence the measure of pure ability/achievement, akin to static in a radio, phone, or other sound signal. Giving a Confidence Interval shows the probability that a student's true score is within the range defined by that interval. For example, a student might take a test and receive a score of 80%. If that student took several other, similar tests, most likely the student's scores would not all be exactly 80%; they would be similar, but vary. The assessors might give a Confidence Interval of + 2 Standard Deviations, 95% of the time. Computing Confidence Intervals does not use Standard Scores (z scores), but literal scores to show the upper and lower limits of the range of likely scores.

Generalizability, Compensatory Grading, Noncompensatory Grading, and a Cut Score

Generalizability is related to reliability, i.e., the consistency of test scores over repeated administrations; but it moreover refers to the specific features of a certain test administration. It means the results on one test can be generalized to apply to other tests with similar formats, content, and operations. Generalizability can also refer to whether a test's results can be generalized from an individual or group to the larger population. Compensatory grading is the practice of balancing out lower performance in one area or subject with higher performance in another. Noncompensatory grading does not permit such balancing, but requires a similar standard

Copyright © Mometrix Media. You have been licensed one copy of this document for personal use only. Any other reproduction or redistribution is strictly prohibited. All rights reserved.
This content is provided for test preparation purposes only and does not imply an endorsement by Mometrix of any particular political, scientific, or religious point of view.

of achievement in each area or subject. A cut score is a predetermined number used to divide categories of data or results from a test instrument. For example, a cut score can divide the categories of passing and failing scores. It can also divide the category of passing scores from a category of "honors" or "excellent" or "superior" scores.

Educators use a cut score to determine which scores are passing and which are failing. They set a particular number as the cut score; all scores above it are passing and all scores below the cut score are failing. Using methods developed for multiple-choice tests allows them to adjust for various factors, e.g., the difficulty of a certain test or assessing student population with special needs, rather than arbitrarily assigning the same cut score to all tests. One such method for establishing a cut score is the Nedelsky method: the assessor(s) identify a "borderline" group of students, i.e., those who do not always pass or fail, but tend to score on the borderline of passing/failing. The assessor(s) estimate how many of these "borderline" students will probably answer a given test item correctly. A common number for this group is 10 students. The sum of the percentages of students estimated to respond correctly to each test item is rounded to an integer, yielding the cut score.

Angoff Method

To determine which scores on a given test are passing or failing, educators can use several established methods. In the Angoff method, one or more assessors select a group of "borderline" students (i.e., those not always passing or failing but with equal chances of either) and estimate which choice(s) in a multiple-choice test item these students could eliminate as an incorrect answer and what percent of the choices left these students would guess as correct. For example, if they might eliminate one choice of five as wrong, their probability of guessing the right choice from the four choices left is 25% (1/4). The assessors add up the percentages for all of the test items and round the sum to an integer, which would be the cut score for that test. In the modified Angoff procedure, the assessors also estimate how many of the students would fail the test, and if they deem it necessary, they modify their estimations to produce a number of failures they find more reasonable.

Ebel Method

Rather than arbitrarily setting the same pass/fail cut score for all tests, several methods exist for determining an appropriate cut score for a particular instrument. The Ebel method considers the importance and difficulty level of each test item in establishing a cut score for a test. First the testers divide all test items into six categories: High, Medium, and Low importance; and High, Medium, and Low difficulty. Then, after selecting a group of "borderline" students who do not always pass or fail tests but are about equally likely to do either, they estimate how many of these students would probably get each item correct in each of these six categories. They add up their estimated percentages for each test item and round the sum to an integer, which is the cut score. The assessors can also then modify their estimations based on data they may obtain from a student class or group's actual test results.

Hofstee Method

Several methods have been developed to set a cut score, the score above which all scores are passing and below which all scores are failing, for a particular test with a multiple-choice format. The Hofstee method is also called the compromise method. It addresses the difference between norm-referenced and criterion-referenced tests, i.e., tests that compare individual student scores to the average scores of a normative sample of students found representative of the larger population versus tests that compare student scores to a pre-established criterion of achievement. Educators estimate an acceptable number of students who would fail the test and the largest number of test

Copyright © Mometrix Media. You have been licensed one copy of this document for personal use only. Any other reproduction or redistribution is strictly prohibited. All rights reserved.
This content is provided for test preparation purposes only and does not imply an endorsement by Mometrix of any particular political, scientific, or religious point of view.

items a student who fails the test would answer correctly. They then plot the answers to this number of items plus two more on the cumulative score distribution. This allows them to determine how many items students could miss and how many failed test items would affect the number of students who could fail.

Norm-Referenced Tests and Criterion-Referenced or Domain-Referenced Tests

In reference to testing large groups, like the entire student body of a school, district, or state, the high-stakes standardized tests given are typically norm-referenced tests; that is, they compare students' scores to a normative sample of students deemed representative of the general population. Criterion-referenced tests may or may not be standardized and compare student scores to a predetermined set of criteria for acceptable performance. In the context of educational programs, norm-referenced tests seek to determine the highest or lowest achievement rather than the absolute score achieved. For example, educators might determine the 10 highest student scores on a certain test to reinforce with "best in group" awards. In this context, measures of mastery learning are examples of criterion-referenced or domain-referenced testing. Educators establish a minimum performance level score that equates to passing. Student scores are compared against this score, so the students in a given class could all pass or all fail the test.

Formative Assessments Versus Summative Assessments

Formative assessments are given during a lesson, unit, course, or program. Their purpose is to give the teachers and students an idea of how well each student is learning what the teacher has planned and expected for them to learn. The teacher uses the results of formative assessments to explain to each student his/her strengths and weaknesses, and how s/he can build on the strengths and improve the weaknesses, and to report student progress to parents, administrators, and others. Summative assessments are given after a lesson, unit, course, or program has been completed. Their purpose is to determine whether the student has passed the segment of instruction. This determines whether they need to repeat the instruction or can move on to successive segments. Summative assessments apply to lessons or units within a class, to courses in a subject, to promotion from one grade level to the next, and to graduation.

Item Analysis

Item analysis is often used to evaluate test items that use multiple-choice formats to show the quality of the test item and of the test overall. Item analysis has an implicit orientation of being norm-referenced rather than criterion- or domain-referenced. That is, it evaluates test items using performance within the group of test-takers rather than an externally preset criterion for expected achievement. Characteristics analyzed in test items include how many high-scoring students got an item correct; how many low-scoring students got the item correct; the test item's discrimination index for separating high- and low-scoring test-takers; the test item's difficulty index; how many test-takers chose each of the answer choices on each test item; the quality of the correct answer choices; and the reliability of the test, i.e., how consistent its results are across separate administrations to the same test-takers.

"Discrimination Index" and "Difficulty Index"

The discrimination index is a measure of how well a specific test item can separate students who generally score high on the test from students who generally score low on it. Educators obtain a point biserial correlation between high total scores and low total scores with correct or incorrect item responses. Typically, they use total test scores to select the top 27% and bottom 27% of test-takers to magnify the variation between high and low test performance. When analyzing standardized, norm-referenced tests, the preferred discrimination index is .50. The difficulty index

Copyright © Mometrix Media. You have been licensed one copy of this document for personal use only. Any other reproduction or redistribution is strictly prohibited. All rights reserved.
This content is provided for test preparation purposes only and does not imply an endorsement by Mometrix of any particular political, scientific, or religious point of view.

is a simple measure of how difficult a test item is considered. It is obtained by calculating the percentage of all students taking a test who answered a certain test item correctly.

Sensitivity and Specificity

Sensitivity refers to how well a test identifies every member of a defined group. The more sensitive a test is, the more likely it can include some individuals who should not be in that group. Specificity refers to how well a test identifies only those members of a defined group. The more specific a test is, the more likely it will omit some individuals who should be included in that group. Among many KR formulas used to estimate statistically a test's reliability or consistency, the KR20 is one that assumes that the relative difficulty of items on a test, and the correlations among those items, are basically equal. The KR20 formula deducts the variances of all individual test items from the total test's variance, which produces an estimate of the test's internal consistency reliability. When a test has items of dissimilar difficulty, the Horst's modification can be used to correct for this by estimating the maximal variance possible within a given range of item difficulties for that test.

Variations in Test Administration

Exclusive of actual test items, in some states the test administration instructions may be clarified or simplified. Other than item responses, students may be allowed to highlight or make other marks in their test booklets. Students may be tested in small groups rather than whole class settings. Test administrators may give students additional time within the testing day to complete a test. Individual students may be tested separately with direct examiner supervision. Students with visual impairments may use visual magnifiers for test text, and hearing-impaired students may use audio amplification. Individual study carrels/enclosures may be used as noise buffers for hearing-impaired or distractible students. Special lighting, acoustics, special furniture, or adaptive furnishings may be allowed. Masking or colored overlays may be used to sustain student visual attention. American Sign Language (ASL) or Manually Coded English (MCE) may also be used to give test instructions (but not test items) to deaf, hard-of-hearing, or nonverbal students.

Accommodations That May Be Allowed in Some US States for Modified Assessments of Students with Special Needs on Standardized Tests

Some states allow students to mark their test responses in their test booklets, and then the school personnel transfer these onto the standardized answer form used by other students to be electronically scored. For students with vision, hearing, manual, or motor impairments, they may dictate their responses to multiple-choice test items aloud or in American Sign Language (ASL) or Manually Coded English (MCE) to a designed scribe who writes, types, or fills in bubbles, circles choices, or otherwise marks the student's answers on a form. For essay questions, some students may be permitted to use word processing software programs, with the spell-check and grammar-check features disabled. Other students may be allowed to dictate their essay answers orally to a voice recorder or scribe, or manually in sign language to an interpreter/scribe, or using speech-to-text computer software. In these cases, students supply all writing conventions of spelling and grammar in their dictation. Assistive devices that allow independent student work may be used.

For blind or visually impaired students or those with visual processing deficits, testers may provide Braille transcriptions of the printed test; large-print versions of the test; or, if the student needs larger type than the fonts used in large-print versions, test items may be enlarged. Students who require additional time and/or shorter testing durations (e.g., those with cognitive impairments, attention deficits, or behavior disorders) may be allowed to take a test normally administered in one sitting over more than one day and/or take supervised breaks during one test section. Medication effects and fluctuating attention and/or performance levels can be addressed by administering tests at the optimal time of day for the student. Examiners may test some students in

Copyright © Mometrix Media. You have been licensed one copy of this document for personal use only. Any other reproduction or redistribution is strictly prohibited. All rights reserved.
This content is provided for test preparation purposes only and does not imply an endorsement by Mometrix of any particular political, scientific, or religious point of view.

homes or hospitals. Test items and answer choices may be presented in sign language, audio recordings, or read aloud. On math and science tests, like in fifth grade, some students may be allowed to use calculators and/or concrete math manipulatives.

Variations Some US States Allow in Administering Standardized Tests Using Modified Assessment Procedures for Students Who Are English Language Learners (ELL) or Learning English as a Second Language (ESL)

Students whose native language is not English are allowed some variations by the US states to participate in standardized testing in the English language on a more equable footing with native English speakers. For example, they may hear the printed test instructions translated into their native language and read aloud. They may be allowed to ask questions in their native language to clarify test instructions. ESL/ELL students may be granted additional, supervised breaks during a testing day or test portion, providing they complete the portion within the testing day. (Standardized tests typically display a "STOP" sign to indicate the ends of test portions.) Students learning English may be allowed to take tests separately in groups with other ELL/ESL students, under supervision by school personnel cleared for test security, particularly if their regular instruction and/or testing have included similar flexibility. ELL/ESL students taking math and science tests may be permitted access to word lists or glossaries translated from English to their native language, excluding formulae or definitions.

Adaptions to Assessments for Special-Needs Students

General testing adaptations include using these oral directions interchangeably: "Find," "Show me," "Point to," and "Give me." Testers should place stimulus cards and manipulatives however the student is best able to perceive these. Concrete materials should be set on surfaces with boundary edges so they cannot roll away or fall down when students use them. Testers should arrange the test environment to eliminate or reduce distractions for students more susceptible to these. For visually impaired students, testers may enlarge stimulus cards as needed. They may replace visual stimuli with Braille, beeping objects or other auditory stimuli, or textured materials if the student is accustomed to using these regularly. Testing teachers can cut out the outlines of shapes or figures from stimulus cards. They may substitute spoken cues like "Tell me" instead of "Show me." As necessary, they may describe the content of pictorial stimuli. They should let students handle concrete objects as is needed. Students who wear corrective glasses should always wear these during assessments.

Teachers can allow students to use augmentative communication devices for receiving and responding to test stimuli. For students who use American Sign Language (ASL) or manually coded English, teachers should use these languages or have an interpreter use them instead of spoken instructions or stimuli whenever appropriate. Nonverbal students should be allowed to give test responses using vocalizations, gestures, or movements instead of speech. Some students may draw pictures instead of writing. (This can also apply to students with dyslexia.) As is appropriate, teachers may accept eye gazes as responses instead of speech or gesture. Students who wear hearing aids must wear them during assessments; teachers should check that they work first. Students with sensorimotor impairments should be given longer times to initiate responses. Teachers should accept changes in facial expressions or muscle tone as observed behaviors. Teachers should stabilize and position students to afford the most controlled possible motions. Teachers should also let students direct others to perform physical tasks.

Technological Development of Portfolio Assessments into ePortfolios

Just as physical portfolios show a student's work and creative products accumulated over time, ePortfolios store documents and photos of products and can be shared with others; but given the

Copyright © Mometrix Media. You have been licensed one copy of this document for personal use only. Any other reproduction or redistribution is strictly prohibited. All rights reserved.
This content is provided for test preparation purposes only and does not imply an endorsement by Mometrix of any particular political, scientific, or religious point of view.

advent of social networks, they benefit from additional advantages of immediate communication and reinforcement. Digital archives can portray a student's life, from birth through early childhood family learning via scrapbooks, and through formal schooling and into employment and professional development. In portfolios, key processes include collecting products for the digital archive; selecting those demonstrating certain standards or goals by creating hyperlinks for others, which leads to reflecting or metacognition, helping the student construct meaning from the works s/he selected, aided by new storytelling models generated by technology; directing or goal-setting; presenting ePortfolios; and getting feedback on them. Social networking includes processes of connecting with others; listening to or reading posts; responding by commenting on posts; and sharing via linking or tagging. Key processes technology enables include archiving; linking and thinking; digital storytelling; collaborating; and publishing.

Students can be internally motivated (self-directed by inner goals) or externally motivated by outer rewards. The ePortfolios enabled by technology can support students' internal motivation and autonomy by establishing online environments wherein others feel good about participating, keeping systems relatively open, and giving users freedom to participate. Social networks support student autonomy by giving them choices and voices in the content they post and view; opportunities to share and give feedback; and far greater immediacy in all of their interactions. Students can experience academic and personal mastery through social networking, which affords the motivational factors of what Csikszentmihályi called "flow" (energized, positive, task-aligned, spontaneous, single-minded, focused, immersed, joyful, deep, and total engagement in an activity); the ability to showcase their achievements; and the benefits of enhanced self-insight and self-awareness. Via choice and personalization, students find their passions and voices. Constructing ePortfolios also helps students develop senses of purpose by engaging in something beyond themselves, understanding the relevance of what they learn, and seeing the "big picture."

SCREENING

Screening is the important first step of the assessment process mandated by federal laws. All newborns should be screened for developmental disabilities, and children should continue to be screened through early childhood, preschool, and school years. While more obvious disabilities like spina bifida, cerebral palsy, Down syndrome, autism, multiple disabilities, or severe sensory impairment are detected early, others like learning disabilities, ADHD, and some behavior disorders often go unidentified until school. Public schools typically conduct periodic screenings of large student groups from grades K–3. Very low standardized achievement test scores can lead to referral for formal evaluation—only with written parental consent—to identify possible disabilities. Also, students' parents, teachers, and other school staff may identify students with suspected disabilities, as when they evidence behavioral or academic difficulties in classrooms. Some students are not identified with disabilities until higher grades, due to ineffective screening, referral, assessment, and/or identification procedures; to disabilities acquired later through injury, illness, etc.; or to problems not apparent until school demands surpass student coping skills.

While school screenings are vital and the process of identifying students with disabilities has a basic structure, there are no uniform or standardized sets of checklists, procedures, or testing instruments to identify disabilities in most students. The kinds of referral processes and tests utilized vary, both across and within states. According to educational experts, two main problems with screening procedures are over-identification and under-identification of disabilities. Research studies have shown that students have been over-identified with learning disabilities, while students with behavior disorders are under-identified, especially compliant students who are not aggressive or disruptive but have problems like social isolation, depression, or school phobia. Educators have been improving screening procedures to resolve these problems. For example,

Copyright © Mometrix Media. You have been licensed one copy of this document for personal use only. Any other reproduction or redistribution is strictly prohibited. All rights reserved.
This content is provided for test preparation purposes only and does not imply an endorsement by Mometrix of any particular political, scientific, or religious point of view.

Walker et al (1990) created the Systematic Screening for Behavioral Disorders with three steps: first, teachers rank students according to designated criteria; then select the three highest ranked students and complete checklists to quantify their observations about them; and school psychologists/counselors observe identified students prior to any formal evaluation referrals.

Prereferral Interventions

Prereferral interventions are a frequent practice intended to better the process of identifying students with disabilities by decreasing referrals to special education services and give regular education teachers more assistance and advice. Rather than first referring a student for evaluation to diagnose a possible disability, teachers initially try to address behavior or learning problems in the classroom through modifications. Only if modifications are found inadequate to the student's difficulties, and the teacher believes special services may be required, does s/he initiate the referral process. Most states in the US require or recommend prereferral intervention in some form. One approach uses Teacher Assistance Teams (TATs). TATs usually comprise four members: the referring teacher and three other teachers. These teams provide teachers with a forum to meet, discuss, and brainstorm ideas to instruct students and/or manage them. Another approach is collaborative consultation. Specialists like speech-language pathologists work directly with referring teachers in planning, implementing, and evaluating instruction for students identified in regular education classrooms.

IDEA and IEP

After screenings and prereferral interventions have been completed and a student is referred for formal evaluation or evaluation is requested, professionals must evaluate all developmental/learning areas related to the disability suspected. Test results are applied to decisions regarding eligibility for special education and related services, and an appropriate educational program. If parents disagree with evaluation results, they have the right under the IDEA to arrange an Independent Educational Evaluation (IEE) and to request payment for this evaluation by the school system. Once evaluation results have been collected and reported, parents meet with teachers and other qualified professionals to review them. They decide together whether the student meets the IDEA definition of a "child with a disability." Parents are entitled under the law to request a hearing challenging the eligibility decision if they disagree. If the child is found eligible for special education and related services, an IEP team must meet within 30 calendar days of eligibility determination to write an IEP.

Under the federal IDEA law, each US state is held responsible for locating, identifying, and evaluating all children in that state as having disabilities and in need of special education and related services. To carry out this mandate, the states engage in Child Find processes. This is one way that children are identified with disabilities. The state's Child Find system may ask a child's parents for permission to evaluate the child, or parents can contact the Child Find system themselves and request evaluation of their child. Another way children are identified is by referral. A teacher or other school professional suspecting a student might have a disability may request, in writing or orally, the student's evaluation. Parents must give consent before the evaluation can be made. The law also stipulates that a requested evaluation be within a reasonable time after receiving parental consent. Parents who suspect disability in their child may also request that the school evaluate the child.

First IEP Meeting

After a student is determined eligible for special education and related services according to the IDEA, the school must schedule the first meeting to write an Individualized Education Program (IEP) for the student. The IDEA mandates that ALL students that receive special education and

Copyright © Mometrix Media. You have been licensed one copy of this document for personal use only. Any other reproduction or redistribution is strictly prohibited. All rights reserved.
This content is provided for test preparation purposes only and does not imply an endorsement by Mometrix of any particular political, scientific, or religious point of view.

related services must have an IEP written for them. By this law, the school system must contact the parents and all others who are to participate in the IEP process. They must inform the parents early enough to ensure they are able to arrange to attend the meeting. They must schedule the meeting at a place and time with which the parents and the school agree. They must inform the parents of the purpose of this meeting and its location, date, and time. They must also inform the parents who else will be attending the meeting. The school staff is also to inform the parents that they may invite any other people to the IEP meeting who have special expertise or knowledge about their child.

In the first IEP meeting for a student, the IEP team includes the student, the parents, the student's teacher(s), specialists, other school personnel who interact with the student; outside consultants if invited; and any others with knowledge about the student, invited by the parents. If a group other than this IEP team decides placement for the student, the parents must also be included in that group. Parents must give consent before initial provision of special education and related services. With this consent, services must commence as soon as possible following the first IEP meeting. When parents disagree with the content of the IEP and/or their child's placement, they can discuss this with other IEP team members and work toward solutions. If the parents still disagree, they may request mediation or the school can offer mediation services. Parents also have the right to file complaints with the state education agency and to request a due process hearing. Mediation must be made available at this hearing.

Implementing an IEP

Once the IEP team has met and developed an IEP for a student and the parents agree with it, the school must give them a copy of the IEP. Each teacher and service provider working with the student can access the student's IEP and must know his/her specific duties in implementing the IEP. The school must ensure that the IEP is implemented as it is written, including providing all accommodations, modifications, and supports to the student as specified in the IEP document. As outlined in the IEP, the school must measure the student's progress toward yearly IEP goals. The school regularly informs the parents of their child's progress and whether it is sufficient for meeting the annual goals. Progress reports must be provided at least as frequently as those reporting nondisabled students' progress. IEPs are reviewed at least annually—more if the parents or the school request it. The IEP is revised if needed. Parents must be invited to review meetings, can suggest changes, and agree/disagree with IEP goals and/or placement.

Legal Requirements for the Reevaluation of the Special Education Student in the IEP Process

All students receiving special education and related services are required by law to have an Individualized Education Plan (IEP). It is developed by the IEP team, which includes the student, parents, teachers, other school employees, other professionals, and any others invited by parents or schools who have contributions relevant to the student and his/her education. The student has received a formal evaluation to determine eligibility. The IEP is reviewed at least annually or more often if the school or parents request it and is revised as needed. Additionally, the student must be reevaluated at least every three years. Educators often call such reevaluation a "triennial." Reevaluation is made to determine whether the student still meets the IDEA definition of a "child with a disability" or not, and to reexamine the educational needs of the student. The three-year interval is a minimum, though: if circumstances indicate it, and/or if the parents or teachers request a new evaluation, the student must be reevaluated sooner than after three years.

Copyright © Mometrix Media. You have been licensed one copy of this document for personal use only. Any other reproduction or redistribution is strictly prohibited. All rights reserved.
This content is provided for test preparation purposes only and does not imply an endorsement by Mometrix of any particular political, scientific, or religious point of view.

Information a Student's IEP Legally Must Include About Current Performance, Annual Goals, and Special Education and Related Services

The IDEA requires the IEP to state the student's "present levels of educational performance," i.e. the student's current progress in school. Results of evaluations made to determine eligibility for special services; classroom tests and in-class and homework assignments; and observations contributed by parents, teachers, related service providers, and other school personnel provide the information for the statement of the student's current school performance. This statement includes the impacts of the student's disability on his/her progress and engagement in the school's general education curriculum. Annual goals are those the student can reasonably attain within a school year. These are subdivided into short-term objectives, or benchmarks. Goals can be academic, behavioral, social, or physical. Goals must be measurable to show if the student has met them. The IEP must name all special education and related services to be provided to or on behalf of the student, including supplementary services and aids; changes to the program; and training, professional development, or other provisions supporting school staff in providing services to the student.

Legally Required Information in an IEP Related to the Student's Participation with Nondisabled Students; Participation in Statewide and District-Wide Testing; and Dates and Locations of Services

All students identified with disabilities and eligible for special education and related services must have IEPs (Individualized Education Programs). The IEP must include an explanation of the degree, if any, to which the student will NOT be participating with nondisabled students in regular classrooms and other school activities. Regarding statewide and district-wide standardized achievement tests regularly given by school systems to students at certain age or grade levels, the IEP must identify which modifications in test administration the student will need. Moreover, if any such test is deemed inappropriate for a particular student, the student's IEP must explain why and state what alternative testing will be substituted. The student's IEP must also state when the student's special education and related services will start, how often services will be provided, in what locations services will be given, and the duration of the services.

Legal Requirements to Be Included in the IEP Regarding a Student's Needs for Transition Services, What Transition Services Are Needed, the Student's Reaching the Age of Majority, and Progress Measurement

While a student reaches the age of 14—or sooner when applicable—the student's IEP must include in its pertinent sections which courses the student must take to attain his/her postschool goals. Every IEP following this must also contain a statement of the student's needs in transition services. Transition may be to postsecondary education; job training; and/or community living. When the student is 16 years old—or before if appropriate—the IEP must define which transition services the student will need as preparation for exiting the current school program/system. At least one year before the student reaches the age of majority, his/her IEP must state the student has been informed of any rights that will transfer from parents/caregivers to him/her. This only applies in states where rights are transferred when minor children reach majority age. Law requires the IEP to state how the school will measure the student's educational progress and how it will inform the student's parents of their child's progress.

Content That May Be Included in Students' IEPs in Addition to What Is Always Required

While the IDEA federally mandates certain content in students' IEPs, individual states and school systems have much flexibility regarding what other information they require. Since federal law dictates that school districts document their compliance with federal requirements, some states and school systems choose to add information in their students' IEPs that serves to document their

Copyright © Mometrix Media. You have been licensed one copy of this document for personal use only. Any other reproduction or redistribution is strictly prohibited. All rights reserved.
This content is provided for test preparation purposes only and does not imply an endorsement by Mometrix of any particular political, scientific, or religious point of view.

compliance with both federal and state laws. In general, some examples of additional elements IEPs can contain that document this compliance include: documentation that the school held the meeting(s) for writing, reviewing, and revising when necessary the student's IEP on a timely basis; documentation that the school furnished the student's parents with a copy of their legally mandated procedural safeguards and rights; documentation that the school has placed the student in the least restrictive environment possible where s/he can experience adequate learning and progress; and documentation that the school received parental consent to provide their child with evaluations, special education, and related services.

Ways That the Regular Education Teacher Contributes as a Member of a Special Education Student's IEP Team

If a special education student participates in regular education at all (which is increasingly the case these days), at least one of the student's regular education teachers must be included in the IEP team. This teacher can inform other team members about the regular classroom's general curriculum, and also what kinds of services, changes in the educational program, and/or aids would help the student to learn and succeed best. S/he can also suggest strategies for managing classroom behavior if this is an issue. The regular education teacher can also talk with the rest of the team about which supports the school staff will need to help the student progress toward annual IEP goals, engage in regular curriculum and succeed in it, participate in extracurricular activities, and be included in instruction with both nondisabled and disabled peers. Such school staff supports can include additional training, professional development, etc., not only for teachers but also administrators, cafeteria staff, bus drivers, and all others providing services to students with disabilities..

Contributions of the IEP Team Member Who Can Interpret the Student's Evaluation Results and of the IEP Team Member Who Represents the School System

The IEP team member who can interpret evaluation results can not only explain to other members what test results signify, e.g., the type of disability and deficit areas, but moreover how to design instruction appropriate to the student and characteristics identified by evaluation results. Skillfully interpreting test results informs the team how the student is currently faring in school and helps them pinpoint areas of particular student needs. This member's role is not only understanding and explaining test results, but furthermore explaining the instructional implications of those results and helping plan accordingly suitable instruction. The school system representative contributes extensive knowledge about teaching students with disabilities and about the special education services available in the school system. This member can discuss the school resources the student and educators will need. It is also important for this individual to have the authority for committing school system resources, and the ability for assuring all services specified in the IEP are actually provided to the student and staff.

Key Members of the IEP Team

Members of a student's IEP team are not limited to, but include: the student; the parents; the special education teacher(s); specialist(s) or other service provider(s); the regular education teacher(s); someone able to interpret evaluation results; a representative of the school system; a representative of a transition services agency; and others having special expertise/knowledge about the student. (Sometimes an individual member fulfills more than one of these functions.) Parents are important team members for knowledge of their child, including his/her strengths and needs and their ideas about how to improve his/her education. Parents can contribute insights about their child's learning style and processes, what academic and life areas are of particular interest to their child, and other things only parents know about their children. Parents can

Copyright © Mometrix Media. You have been licensed one copy of this document for personal use only. Any other reproduction or redistribution is strictly prohibited. All rights reserved.
This content is provided for test preparation purposes only and does not imply an endorsement by Mometrix of any particular political, scientific, or religious point of view.

consider other team members' recommendations about areas to focus on in school and can share their own suggestions. Additionally, parents can report to the school whether their child is applying skills s/he has learned in school, at home, and in other settings outside school.

Ways in Which the Special Education Teacher Participates in the IEP Team

Informed by her/his training and experience in special education, the special education teacher contributes to the IEP team by discussing various topics. These include how to make adaptations and modifications to the general education curriculum that will enable the student to learn in the regular education setting; which supplementary services and aids the student is likely to require for succeeding in regular classrooms and other places; techniques for modification of assessments that enables the student to better demonstrate what s/he has learned; and additional elements of individualizing the instruction according to the unique needs of the student. Special educators not only help write IEPs; they are also responsible for working with students to implement them. They may do this in special education classes or resource rooms; team-teach with regular education teachers; and collaborate with regular education teachers and other school personnel, contributing expertise to meet the student's individual needs.

Individuals Who Have Special Expertise or Knowledge About a Student

Parents and/or school system employees can invite individuals to participate as members of a student's IEP team based on their especial expertise and/or knowledge about the student. For instance, parents may know a professional with specific expertise in the student's particular disability; an advocate who has a relationship with the student; or a vocational educator who has been working with the student on employment skills. Such individuals are able to discuss the student's individual strengths and needs. The school system may also invite individuals, like paraprofessionals or professionals specializing in related services, who can contribute special expertise and/or knowledge about the student. A significant aspect of IEP development is the related services a student often needs; therefore, professionals specializing in such related services are frequently members or participants in the IEP team. These professionals can include physical therapists; occupational therapists; adaptive physical education instructors; orientation and mobility specialists; ASL interpreters; speech-language pathologists; psychologists; and others.

Material the IEP Team Reviews to Determine What Kinds of Special Education and Related Services a Student Needs

To develop the IEP, the team reviews evaluation results including individual tests given to the student to determine eligibility for services; classroom tests the student has taken; and the observations of parents, teachers, related service providers, paraprofessionals, administrators, and others involved. These help the team characterize the "present levels of educational performance" of the student, i.e., how s/he is currently functioning in school. They develop yearly goals targeting areas of educational need identified through this information. Information specific to the student they discuss includes the student's strongest assets; recent evaluation and/or re-evaluation results; parents' ideas to improve the student's education; and the student's performance on district-wide and statewide standardized examinations. The team's discussion of what the student needs should be guided by how they can help the student progress toward meeting yearly goals; engage in the general education curriculum and make progress in it; be included in participation and education with other students, both with and without disabilities; and participate in nonacademic and extracurricular activities.

Copyright © Mometrix Media. You have been licensed one copy of this document for personal use only. Any other reproduction or redistribution is strictly prohibited. All rights reserved.
This content is provided for test preparation purposes only and does not imply an endorsement by Mometrix of any particular political, scientific, or religious point of view.

Legal Requirements Related to Decisions the IEP Team Must Make Regarding a Student's Placement Within the Continuum of Special Education and Related Services

Once an IEP team has developed and written a student's IEP, where this program will be implemented—i.e., the student's placement—must also be decided. In some US states, the IEP team is also the group that makes placement decisions. In others, a different group may decide student placements. However, in every instance the parents have the legal right to participate as members of the group deciding placement. Placement decisions must abide by the IDEA's requirements for the Least Restrictive Environment (LRE): students with disabilities must be educated together with students without disabilities to the maximum degree possible and fitting. In addition, the IDEA specifies that students with disabilities may only be removed from the regular school setting—to special classes or separate schools—if the severity and/or nature of the student's disability makes education in regular classes, including the use of supplementary services and aids, impossible to attain with satisfactory results.

Integrating Social and Life Skills into Academic Curricula for Students with Disabilities

Many students with disabilities need special education and support to learn daily living skills. With proper instruction, they can obtain and keep meaningful jobs and live in the community; but without specialized instruction, they frequently lose jobs and/or home placements. Life skills include proper attire, grooming, and hygiene; acceptable table manners; financial decision-making; and utilizing transportation to employment. Instruction in financial skills is required by some states, including counting money and making change; managing bank accounts; keeping personal budgets and records; making personal financial decisions; spending and using credit responsibly; estimating and paying taxes; paying bills; and renting/leasing. Household management includes housekeeping; meal preparation; doing/hiring home maintenance/repair; and new appliance warranty registration. Personal care includes obtaining health care, eschewing substance abuse; recognizing common illnesses, knowing prevention and treatment; and nutrition, physical fitness, and weight maintenance. Safety awareness includes recognizing safety/hazard signs, rules, and procedures; unfamiliar sounds and/or smells; and knowing emergency evacuation procedures. Buying, storing, planning, preparing, and eating balanced, appropriate meals are included.

Special Student Factors Whose Consideration by the IEP Team and Inclusion in the IEP Document Are Required by Law If They Exist

The law requires a number of "special factors" for the IEP team to consider as applicable with individual students. If a student's behavior impedes his/her and/or other students' learning, the team must consider effective, positive behavioral supports and intervention techniques to manage, control, or change the behavior. If the student has limited English-language proficiency, the team must consider the student's linguistic need relative to his/her IEP. If a student is blind or visually impaired, the team must provide Braille texts or instruction in Braille, or determine through evaluations the student does not need such instruction. In the latter case, the team must specify any other methods and/or devices the student needs and provide these. The team must consider any communication needs a student may have. For deaf or hard-of-hearing students, the team must consider their communication and linguistic needs, including opportunities for communicating directly with peers and staff in ASL or their other customary communication method(s). The team must also consider any student needs for assistive technology services and/or devices.

Copyright © Mometrix Media. You have been licensed one copy of this document for personal use only. Any other reproduction or redistribution is strictly prohibited. All rights reserved.
This content is provided for test preparation purposes only and does not imply an endorsement by Mometrix of any particular political, scientific, or religious point of view.

Program Placement Settings for Students Receiving Special Education and Related Services

A student's IEP may be implemented in various placement settings according to the individual student's needs. Settings include placement in the regular education class, with supplementary services and aids the student needs; in a special class for all or part of the school day, with other students all also receiving special education and related services; in a special school dedicated to students needing special education and related services; in a hospital; in an institutional facility; and other settings. To fulfill its legal requirements to make sure a student is placed appropriately, a school system can take various actions. For example, it may furnish the student with a suitable program as part of the school system. Or it may contract with an outside agency that can provide the student with an applicable program. Or it may make some other arrangements and/or make use of other mechanisms available to pay for or otherwise provide the student a program appropriate and consistent with the terms of the IDEA.

Daily Living Skills That Students with Disabilities Must Learn Through Special Instruction for Successful Adult Community Living

In addition to skills in dress, hygiene, other personal care, finance, household management, safety awareness, and food preparation, students with disabilities must also receive instruction, integrated into academic curricula in school, in how to purchase and care for clothing. They must be instructed in responsible citizenship, including knowing their own civil rights and responsibilities; obtaining legal aid; reporting crimes; for males, registering with Selective Service at age 18; knowing and obeying laws; knowing about federal, state, and local governments; and voting. Disabled students must also learn about community resources available; how to select and plan leisure activities, appreciate their importance, and participate in them; to plan vacation activities and social events; and practice music, arts, crafts, hobbies, and sports. Students must also be instructed in community navigation, including knowing right from left and front from back; safety and traffic rules; carpooling and other transportation; reading maps; and when applicable, learning to drive and obtaining a driver's license and automobile insurance. Special and regular educators, families, and peers provide instruction.

Prioritizing Areas of the General Education Curriculum for Students with Disabilities

The IDEA and ESEA Acts require all students' access to general education curriculum. Educators can help disabled students by connecting academic content to real-life activities. Achievement standards include the same academic content, but utilize alternate performance indicators still fitting content standards for reading and math. While alternative assessment methods and definitions of achievement standards vary considerably across states, educators in all states must provide instruction effective in helping students with disabilities meet standards. Teachers in some states select which responses are assessed to document progress toward state standards—e.g., portfolio assessments; specific choice-making; sight words; task analyses; generalized responses, like requests; problem-solving; and self-initiation responses. Systematic prompting with feedback, reinforcement, correction, and fading is an instructional support method. In general education settings, systematic instruction to small mixed-ability groups; cooperative learning groups; trials embedded in general education lectures/lessons; observational learning; peer tutors; and self-instruction and problem-solving materials are options. Assistive technology aids symbol use, and can reduce behavior problems and increase social interaction. Special and general educator planning collaboration is vital.

Copyright © Mometrix Media. You have been licensed one copy of this document for personal use only. Any other reproduction or redistribution is strictly prohibited. All rights reserved.
This content is provided for test preparation purposes only and does not imply an endorsement by Mometrix of any particular political, scientific, or religious point of view.

Promoting Student Development and Learning in Students with Autism Spectrum Disorder

Teacher Attitudes and Behaviors Interact with Student Attitudes and Behaviors

Research studies show that when teachers establish supportive relationships with their students; communicate clearly and consistently enforce high expectations of their students academically and behaviorally; and deliver a high quality of pedagogy and instruction to their students, the students are more likely to develop attitudes and behaviors of engagement in their learning, and perceptions of their own academic competence. These student attitudes and behaviors are found in turn to augment student achievement in key academic areas like reading and math. Experts define students' engagement as how much inherent interest they demonstrate in school, and the quantity and quality of their participation in schoolwork. This engagement and participation include both attitudes, like positive values about learning, motivation, interest, enthusiasm, and pride in succeeding, and also behaviors like attention, effort, and persistence. Therefore, students who are engaged pursue activities in and out of classrooms that further learning and/or succeeding. Additionally, they demonstrate curiosity, desire for more knowledge, and emotionally positive responses to school and learning.

Considerations for Educators Regarding Their Expectations and Student Behavior

Researchers have found that teachers are often unprepared for problem behaviors from both nondisabled and disabled students in urban school settings. Some reasons for such problem behaviors include the higher proportions in urban school populations of students from lower socioeconomic levels; of students from families who do not speak English; and of students with special needs. Some researchers have experimented with elementary-level urban schools by introducing a "Good Behavior" game. Teachers were directed to identify acceptable and unacceptable behaviors clearly to their students. Then they were to observe the students during specified periods of time and count the numbers of unacceptable behaviors. The individual student or group of students receiving the smallest number of recorded unacceptable behaviors would win the game. The researchers found that using this technique both increased on-task behaviors and decreased disruptive behaviors in the students. This approach is considered to be generalizable to schools in nonurban settings.

Factors in the Educational Setting That Influence Students' Motivation to Learn

One factor that is found to increase students' motivation to learn is a sense of belonging in their school settings and a sense of having caring relationships. This includes the students' feeling that their families and friends support them and their education, and in school particularly, that their teachers are supportive. Individualizing and personalizing their instruction is one way that teachers accomplish this. Teachers also create caring, supportive social environments in school by demonstrating interest in their students' lives, inside and outside school. Students experiencing such positive interpersonal relationships are found to display more positive attitudes and values regarding school, and more satisfaction with it, and to attend school more, learn more, and report more academic engagement. Another factor is clearly defined, high, consistent, and realistically

Copyright © Mometrix Media. You have been licensed one copy of this document for personal use only. Any other reproduction or redistribution is strictly prohibited. All rights reserved.
This content is provided for test preparation purposes only and does not imply an endorsement by Mometrix of any particular political, scientific, or religious point of view.

attainable teacher expectations of student performance. A third factor promoting students' cognitive engagement is teachers' use of active pedagogical strategies challenging students to tackle new ideas, explain their thinking, defend their decisions, and/or explore alternate methods and solutions, especially through peer collaboration.

Activities Teachers Use That Promote Student Engagement in the Long Term

Educational research has found that students are more likely to experience and demonstrate greater classroom engagement over the long term of their education when teachers assign them to such hands-on, authentic activities as constructing models; planning, implementing, completing, and reporting on projects; participating in role-play exercises; participating in debates on topics relevant to school subjects and activities; and planning and conducting experiments, making conclusions about them, and reporting their results to their classmates and teachers. Studies have also shown that teachers can make the lessons that they teach more relevant and meaningful to students when these lessons draw from and build upon the students' existing background knowledge, cultural backgrounds, and experiences in the real world and life. When the material that they study is personally interesting to students and related to their lives, they both learn more effectively and also enjoy the learning process more.

Instructional Strategy of Modeling to Help Autistic, Cognitively Impaired, and Younger Students Learn to Use Eye Contact, Vocal Tone, and Pronunciation Appropriately in Social Interactions

Many autistic students avoid eye contact, as do some cognitively impaired students and even nondisabled younger students. Often they do not understand its importance and have no practice using it. Some teachers with teaching assistants or aides find it helps to model through conversations with them: the teacher says to the assistant that s/he noticed how the assistant's eyes were looking right at a student's eyes when they were talking; that this showed the student the assistant was listening, and the assistant could see the student was also listening; and praises the assistant for "good eye contact." The assistant replies that good eye contact during conversation is good manners. The same technique can be used to describe appropriate vocal tones for conversations and correct pronunciation. The teacher can follow up by asking students to demonstrate good eye contact when greeting another student. They observe and provide prompts as needed. This is most effective when the teacher immediately rewards the interaction with verbal praise, plus applause from the class.

Establishing Rapport with Students in Early Elementary Grades

Teachers report warm lighting helps create a cozy, "at-home" atmosphere. Many elementary teachers assign a theme for the school year, like bugs, birds, fish, or rocks. They display posters illustrating the theme, including catchphrases expressing their learning strategies; incorporate the theme in first-day handouts, student folders, and parent letters; devise activities around the theme, like reading books to the class about the theme and assigning student pairs/small groups to design an original bug. On first days, teachers assign activities enabling students to move around, become comfortable with the classroom, get acquainted with each other, work collaboratively, and think creatively. They use games—searching for all classmates' names in puzzles or physically finding each classmate and collecting their signatures. Teachers use "brainteasers" to engage students in creative problem-solving. They take inventories of student interests on first days. And they assign students artistic activities—like cutting out and illustrating paper "T-shirts" identifying their preferences, interests, future dreams, past experiences, and adjectives describing themselves.

One way a sixth-grade teacher can get acquainted with new students is to give them surveys about their interests and surveys of Gardner's Multiple Intelligences to get ideas of students' preferences,

Copyright © Mometrix Media. You have been licensed one copy of this document for personal use only. Any other reproduction or redistribution is strictly prohibited. All rights reserved.
This content is provided for test preparation purposes only and does not imply an endorsement by Mometrix of any particular political, scientific, or religious point of view.

strengths, needs, and learning styles. To assess student writing abilities and styles, a pre-assessment can involve writing a letter to the teacher about themselves. The teacher gives no pre-instructions on the steps of writing to discern what they already know how to do independently. The teacher may use her/his district's model for assessing writing. As icebreakers, teachers can assign as homework writing and illustrating a "Me" page, guided by teacher-given questions. They can have each student create a poster using the letters in their first name, filling the page with large "bubble" letters, and filling each letter with information, photos, or drawings about themselves. Then the teacher can display these in the classroom, integrating technology by adding printed digital photos of students to their posters. They can have students create slide shows and revise them at the end of the school year to add what they have learned.

Areas Important to Successfully Relating to and Instructing a High School Class

Experienced high school teachers find that classroom success centers on three crucial areas: establishing rapport with the students; setting the teacher's rules and expectations for the class; and having strategies to promote students' motivation to learn. While teacher education students and new teachers observing experienced teachers may feel they seem to do it by some kind of magic, the experienced teachers say that strategic planning is actually at the heart of establishing a rapport and developing good working relationships with their students. For example, a high school teacher can help to build rapport with a new class of students by presenting oneself as having a "stern yet caring" (as one teacher puts it) presence; set class rules and conduct other activities together *with* the students rather than unilaterally, which helps to establish a classroom community; and communicating one's expectations to the students clearly on the very first day of school.

Engaging Disabled and Younger Students in Paying Attention to Directions

Some experienced teachers use techniques like rhythmic clapping and/or chanting to engage student attention. For example, the teacher demonstrates a loud, rhythmic hand clap and tells the students that when they hear the teacher do this, they should stop what they are doing and imitate the hand clap. The teacher tells the students the clap means s/he has something important to share with them and to copy clapping when the teacher's hands go down, and s/he will know they are done when they make eye contact ("I see you looking at my eyes"). Teachers can chant directions, like "If you hear me, put your hands on your shoulders....If you hear me, put your hands on your hips....If you me, put your hands on your tummy...." Teachers enhance students' attention by modulating their voices. For students who do not pay attention, teachers instruct them aloud to be sure their hands are empty and they are looking at the teacher's eyes. Teachers may need to wait for all students to focus.

Developing Class Rules for Disabled and Nondisabled Students on the First Day

The high school teacher can first establish basic, vital "ground rules" based on what the teacher needs in the classroom. For example, students must arrive on time and be prepared; respect both classmates and classroom materials; and follow directions the first time the teacher gives them. After conveying these rules, the teacher can involve students in collaborating to create class rules. This helps build a class community. The teacher can integrate the opinions and viewpoints of students by asking them simple questions, like why they are there and what they need to achieve their goals. The teacher records student answers, incorporating these in expanding on the ground rules. Involving students gives them a sense of a democratic class community instead of a dictatorship and stimulates processes of critical thinking. Teachers should also give students lists of daily materials needed and examples of acceptable versus unacceptable work, and inform students

Copyright © Mometrix Media. You have been licensed one copy of this document for personal use only. Any other reproduction or redistribution is strictly prohibited. All rights reserved.
This content is provided for test preparation purposes only and does not imply an endorsement by Mometrix of any particular political, scientific, or religious point of view.

how they will assess their work (rubrics, etc.). Teachers should communicate their expectations orally, in print/writing, and visually.

Motivating Teens to Read

Some high school teachers experienced in teaching teens who struggle with reading meet such challenges by getting students excited about reading. They find books their students can relate to and enjoy, and they can begin the school year by reading these books aloud to students. Only after they have stimulated student enjoyment and enthusiasm for reading do they assess students' current reading levels, using instruments like the Scholastic Reading Inventory. Teachers can use a Book Pass activity to help students become familiar with books in their class library and select books with topics interesting to them at suitable levels for independent reading. Small groups (like five each) designate one student timekeeper. Seated in circles, each group member previews the front and back of the book and begins reading that book. The timekeeper announces when 2 to 3 minutes elapse; students write down the book title, pages read, comments, and whether they would like reading it further. Students then pass the books to their right, repeating with another book. They finish with group sharing of individual book comments.

Creating a Safe, Supportive, Positive Classroom and School Climate

Elementary school teachers realize that students will be more engaged in school and learning if it is fun and they are happy. Some teachers help students consolidate what they just learned and/or take a break from schoolwork with a group singing period in the classroom. A few weeks into the school year, once students have gotten to know each other and developed into a cohesive group, some teachers have them vote for an alliterative class name reflecting their interests, ambitions, and/or attitudes. The teacher calls them by this group name when they are lining up to leave the room and at other key moments to reinforce their feelings of belonging and ownership. To encourage and reinforce student responsibility, some elementary teachers assign a job to each student for the week, posting these on a chart on the wall, and all of the students take turns assuming different weekly job rotations.

Communicating Expectations of Students and Regular Routines

Some schools use an acronym like BEST, representing Be respectful, Enjoy learning, Stay safe, and Totally responsible, to help students remember these principles. Some teachers have students negotiate their classroom expectations, keeping them generally consistent with school expectations, and on reaching consensus, they display pictures and words on the walls reflecting these. They also discuss choices and how expectations keep everyone safe. They set routines, posting their daily schedule on the wall and discussing it. Some teachers institute weekly lessons involving behavioral tasks explicitly teaching behavioral expectations aligned with school values, and they post these on the wall. Some teachers use a token economy. For example, each student gets a smiley face on a chart for making good choices; upon accumulating 10, the student can select a prize, which the teacher reports schoolwide to record all recognition of positive behaviors. When students do not meet expectations, some teachers explicitly model and teach expected behavior, like teaching how to apologize sincerely for hitting/kicking, with the victim choosing whether to accept the apology.

Preventing and/or Address Bullying in Schools

In April 2013, the US Department of Justice arrived at a settlement agreement with the Metropolitan School District of Decatur Township, Indiana. This concluded a review of district practices and policies regarding bullying and harassment, prompted by 2011 reports of possible racial targeting at one school. The district arranged to collaborate with the federally funded Great Lakes Equity Center at Indiana University-Purdue University Indianapolis on actions against bullying for disability, race, national origin, color, gender, or religion and promoting safe,

Copyright © Mometrix Media. You have been licensed one copy of this document for personal use only. Any other reproduction or redistribution is strictly prohibited. All rights reserved.
This content is provided for test preparation purposes only and does not imply an endorsement by Mometrix of any particular political, scientific, or religious point of view.

supportive learning environments for all students. Actions include creating a district-wide antiharassment task force to review and revise district harassment/bullying and disciplinary policy and procedures; creating a coherent process to receive, investigate, and monitor bullying/harassment complaints, and track repeating instances involving groups/individuals in special classes; and give students and staff at two district schools school climate assessments, training, and professional development. A Civil Rights Division spokesperson said these affirmative steps provide statewide and nationwide examples. Nationwide work against school bullying also aligns with federal civil rights legislation.

Icebreakers to Get Acquainted with Disabled and Nondisabled Students and Vice Versa

Experienced high school teachers find adolescents are primarily concerned with adjusting to the new setting and getting acquainted with new classmates, and teachers need to start the year by familiarizing themselves well with new students. To help both teacher and students get acquainted, teachers can use icebreaker activities. One involves "matching" index cards based on common interests of the school's student body. For example, teachers make card pairs like Bill Gates and Microsoft; Russell Simmons and Def Jam Records, etc. Each student gets one card and finds the student with a matching card. Then they interview each other. Teachers can suggest questions, like the last school they attended, their favorite book genre, pet peeves, favorite things, embarrassing incidents, hobbies, etc. Following interviews, each student presents information about his/her "match" to the class. Another activity groups and numbers students in fours; each student writes down adjectives describing themselves and alliterative with their names (e.g., "Shy Shannon" or "Bookish Brad"), and take turns introducing themselves and another student using these.

Integrating Technology to Motivate Students to Begin Learning

To prepare and motivate adolescents to learn right away, high school teachers can integrate technology, yet need no more than a video camera and books when they assign projects the first week of school. For example, the teacher can ask the students to choose a book they have recently read and/or is their favorite. The teacher can lead a class discussion about characteristics in TV commercials that make the viewer remember the commercials best, like musical jingles; vivid visual imagery; strong slogans or tag lines; or humorous/incongruous situations. The teacher creates a model for students with a sample commercial. The teacher can then have the students make their own commercials advertising their chosen books. Another example of a project is to assign students to make their autobiographies, using videos about five minutes long. The teacher can guide the students to incorporate details related to their early childhoods; pets, friends, their home lives; their hobbies, what things interest them most, and what their major goals in life are.

Promoting Parental Support

Some teachers implement a practice of using a communication book for each student. These books are sent back and forth between the school and the students' homes for the teacher and parents to write correspondence to one another. Before calling the roll every morning, the teacher checks the communication books for new entries. (This practice likely works best with smaller class sizes.) Some elementary school teachers also invite all students' parents to visit their classrooms in the morning to help by reading or telling stories to the children to get them settled down and ready for the day. Some elementary school teachers regularly send notes to parents with students. For example, one teacher noticed her young students became hungry at midmorning, and the class agreed to schedule a snack period. She sent parents notes asking them to send healthy snack foods, including a list of appropriate, easy-to-prepare snacks. This teacher reported their snack time soon ran smoothly, with children usually eating and doing schoolwork concurrently.

Copyright © Mometrix Media. You have been licensed one copy of this document for personal use only. Any other reproduction or redistribution is strictly prohibited. All rights reserved.
This content is provided for test preparation purposes only and does not imply an endorsement by Mometrix of any particular political, scientific, or religious point of view.

Federal Laws Regarding Students with Disabilities

The IDEA and other federal legislation for students with disabilities mandate that these students be provided physical education. Federal law defines physical education as the development of physical and motor skills; fundamental motor skills and patterns like catching, throwing, walking, running, etc.; and skills in individual and group sports, including intramural and lifetime sports, and in dance and aquatics. The IDEA mandates instruction in the least restrictive environment (LRE) possible. Regarding PE, this involves adaptations and/or modifications to curriculum and/or instruction as it does regarding academic education. In PE, adaptations/modifications assure each student's success in a safe environment. A student's IEP defines placement, which can include one or several options among the general physical education setting alone; this setting but with aid from teaching assistants or peers; a separate PE class setting with peers; a separate PE class setting with assistants; and/or settings with 1:1 student-instructor activities.

Benefits of Including Students with Disabilities in General Education

Educational research has found that both students with disabilities and their nondisabled peers obtain significant benefits from inclusive educational programs. For example, students with disabilities experience more stimulating learning environments via inclusion. They benefit from nondisabled role models of adaptive, communication, and social skills and behaviors. They have more opportunities for making new friends and sharing new experiences with them. They gain greater peer acceptance from being included, and they have a greater sense of membership in a regular class and in the school. Students without disabilities benefit by learning greater acceptance of individual differences among people. They learn to feel more comfort around students with various disabilities. They learn to help their disabled peers, which generalizes to learning to be more helpful to others. They gain leadership skills by providing examples, help, and guidance. And they gain greater self-esteem through modeling helpful leadership behaviors. Thus, inclusive education benefits all students.

Adapting the Physical Environment to Facilitate Learning

For students whose cognitive levels, attention spans, or other differences make large assignments intimidating, teachers can divide these into small, more achievable "chunks" so they are more willing to tackle them and experience some success daily. For students having difficulty taking notes from the blackboard, teachers can offer paper handouts/notes. Distractible students can be seated away from windows, noisy, high-traffic areas, and classmates who encourage chatting. Teachers must implement all adaptations in student IEPs, monitor their effectiveness, and discuss changes with the team if adaptations are not enabling best student performance. With students needing constant reminding of how to follow class practices, teachers can make an enlarged checklist of expectations for their daily assignments/routines and tape it to their binder/desktop, enabling more independent work tracking. Scheduling morning periods daily to check student homework and planners clarifies expectations and allows time to resolve problems and still have productive days. Assignments and assessments can use computers/scribes/time extensions/oral responses as alternatives for students with writing/printing difficulties.

Arranging Physical Space to Accommodate Students with Needs Like Limited Mobility, ADHD, and LDs, and Teaching 1:1 in Small and Large Groups

Teachers must consider all learning community members' needs, including students, teachers, specialists, paraprofessionals, and volunteers. When community members change, last year's arrangement may not work. Teachers must also consider size and layout of their classroom/space, including attached equipment/furnishings, classroom location in the school, and instructional materials. Depending on curriculum and teaching philosophy and approach, teachers may want to

Copyright © Mometrix Media. You have been licensed one copy of this document for personal use only. Any other reproduction or redistribution is strictly prohibited. All rights reserved.
This content is provided for test preparation purposes only and does not imply an endorsement by Mometrix of any particular political, scientific, or religious point of view.

arrange space for large and small groups, teams, cooperative learning groups, and individual instruction. If any student(s) use wheelchairs, teachers must consider accommodating their maneuvering in the room. They must consider preventing distractions for ADHD students. They may lower chalkboards, bulletin boards, and pencil sharpeners, and add bathroom grab bars for wheelchair students, and they may procure more electrical outlets for computers, language masters, and tape recorders for students with LDs or visual impairment. They may place carpet in areas for students needing to sit/lie on the floor periodically. Insurmountable obstacles may dictate extensive remodeling or relocation to different classrooms. Advance planning is hence necessary to allow budgeting and work without interrupting school-year instruction.

Modifications to Games Played That Can Integrate Special-Needs Students

To level the competition, PE teachers can modify activities. They can let special-needs students hit or kick instead of pitching a ball. In volleyball games, they can let students catch and throw the ball and/or let it bounce. Teachers can permit longer time periods equal to student ability for moving to a goal/base. When possible, they can schedule games inside the gym on smooth floors to facilitate movement instead of outdoors in a field. When modifying rules for disabled students, teachers can involve them in the decision-making process. Teachers can reduce distances by moving bases closer together; letting students get closer to the net/goal/target; and letting them serve from midcourt in volleyball/badminton/tennis. Teachers can provide more scoring opportunities by substituting four for three strikes/ten arrows for six/three for two foul shots/etc. They can assign disabled students to be pitchers/goalies/first basemen, or other positions requiring less mobility. Adaptive equipment they can provide includes bigger bats/racquets; bigger/lighter/softer balls; and bigger baskets/goals/bases.

Differential Definition of Instructional Accommodations and Modifications

Accommodations are changes in HOW students learn and are assessed, while modifications are changes in WHAT students are expected to learn. Accommodations can involve teaching methods, materials, assignments, tests, the learning environment, scheduling, time demands, and special communications systems, and they need not change school learning goals. Modifications can involve partial program or course completion; lower than grade-level curriculum expectations; alternative curriculum goals; and alternate assessments. The IDEA mandates that schools give students with disabilities the chance to be included and progress in the general education curriculum, which can require accommodations and/or modifications to accomplish. The IDEA also requires all students receiving special education and related services to have IEPs Section 504 of the Rehabilitation Act that requires that schools provide accommodations to students with disabilities even if they do not have IEPs. The Americans with Disabilities Act (ADA) bans discrimination against the disabled. State laws follow the federal laws in allowing accommodations and modifications for students with disabilities.

Instruction for Differentiated Group Sizes, Separating Areas, Guiding Traffic, and Compensating for Less Than Ideal Classroom Locations

Teachers should allocate areas within their classroom for individualized teaching, and also small and large groups. The teacher and/or learning specialist might need a small-group instruction space. Teaching stations, learning centers, and areas for partner/pair work are good whenever possible. Teachers need to separate/designate noisy and quiet areas, and spaces free of distractions. According to educational research, horizontal and vertical paths must allow teachers to reach any student within eight steps. Wheelchairs require at least 36" to maneuver. Student coats and backpacks must be placed to avoid blocking traffic. Some experts suggest having students turn their desks so the lids open away from them, to keep them from accumulating unwanted/forgotten things inside. If a classroom faces the playground, a busy road, student cafeteria lines, and/or

Copyright © Mometrix Media. You have been licensed one copy of this document for personal use only. Any other reproduction or redistribution is strictly prohibited. All rights reserved.
This content is provided for test preparation purposes only and does not imply an endorsement by Mometrix of any particular political, scientific, or religious point of view.

steady streams of traffic—especially since classroom relocation, even when available, can take extreme effort and a whole year—teachers can adapt existing spaces by putting curtains over windows, closing the door, and hanging visual displays from the ceiling that absorb sound.

Preventing Obstacles for Disabled Students and Helping All Students Make Effective Use of Common Spaces Within the School Building

While teachers have little or no control over their school building's commonly shared spaces, they can instruct their students to work with these. For example, they can teach them the common courtesies of walking quietly on the right side of the hall, and of speaking quietly in the library and cafeteria, auditorium, or cafeteria. This will help students adjust to large spaces inside the building. Teachers can also instruct all students to allow sufficient space for students using wheelchairs to go around corners and not to crowd wheelchairs. This not only helps the students in wheelchairs; it also prevents ambulatory students from being injured by coming too close to wheelchairs. Students in both special and general education programs must be taught to take special care in adhering to rules and guidelines on the playground and in the school gymnasium. Students make successful adaptations to school building spaces when they have learned how to navigate from one place to another, and how to behave in each school area.

Accommodations to Make in School for Students with Disabilities If They Have Difficulty with Self-Control of Their Behavior

Some students with disabilities can require alterations in the learning environment to assist them in managing their behavior. For some, behavior management plans and/or counseling services may be required. There are also classroom accommodations educators can make for students whether or not they have such behavior management plans and/or counseling services. For example, teachers can let students use study carrels or other enclosures to work independently with less distraction. Teachers can assign work that students are able to finish in shorter time durations. Teachers can also allow students to use timers to help them monitor how much more time they have to finish assignments and how much more time they need to complete their work. For students needing structure to promote behavioral self-control, teachers can positively reinforce following classroom rules, list consequences for breaking rules, and ensure students' knowledge of rules and consequences.

Providing More Structure to Students with Disabilities Who Need Support in Exercising Behavioral Self-Control

In addition to posting lists of classroom rules and consequences for breaking them and making sure all students know these, teachers can also make sure to supply students with activities to pursue during free time periods. Students requiring structure are apt to act out during unassigned times without the direction of something specific to do. To prepare students for transitions such as beginning new lessons, going to lunch, moving to other school areas, or changing classes, teachers should follow regular routines and give students prompts about the changes. Teachers may seat some students next to trained peers, teacher's aides, or volunteers to help them attend to lessons. They can also designate "study buddies" who know how to interact effectively with some students to help them when the teacher is otherwise occupied. For pupils who lack behavioral self-control without personal support and attention, the teacher can also conduct 1:1 instruction with certain students and work with others in small groups to address their needs.

Crisis Intervention and Prevention

Three main elements of responding to and preventing crises in schools are: Communication; Direction and Coordination; and Health and Safety. During a crisis, educators communicate: they sound alarms if needed; clarify next steps; give information about the occurrence and first-aid

Copyright © Mometrix Media. You have been licensed one copy of this document for personal use only. Any other reproduction or redistribution is strictly prohibited. All rights reserved.
This content is provided for test preparation purposes only and does not imply an endorsement by Mometrix of any particular political, scientific, or religious point of view.

station locations, etc.; control rumors about the event; interact with the media as needed, and with the school district and community; respond to parent concerns; and keep track of the students and staff. Direction and coordination during a crisis include monitoring and solving problems and directing emergency operations centers. Health and safety during the emergency include directing evacuation, security, search and rescue operations; providing first aid for medical and psychological injuries; and reducing hazards to students and staff. Immediately after a crisis, communication includes dispelling rumors, clarifying crisis sources and impacts, and supplying information on medical and psychological resources available. Direction and coordination include continuing problem monitoring and solving. Health and safety include continuing activities begun during the crisis.

In immediate responses to crises in schools, educators should concentrate on restoring equilibrium for students. Their demeanor should be calm, authoritative, and nurturing; their behaviors direct, informative, and oriented to problem-solving. Educators should address student denial by providing them with accurate information and realistic explanations about what happened and what they can expect. Reassurance should never be untrue or unrealistic. Educators should encourage students to face the factual aspects of a crisis. They should invite students to cope with their emotional responses, and discuss with them their responses and defense mechanisms. They should communicate to students a sense of positive expectations and hope, in that although crises bring changes, they have means of coping with these. Educators can shift students' positions from victims to actors by helping them plan appropriate, realistic, and salutary actions to follow after they separate, building upon demonstrated student coping skills and techniques, and when appropriate, engage them in helping restore equilibrium. They should link students with peers, family, and staff for immediate social support.

Educator response to a crisis in school has three main areas: Communication, Direction, and Coordination, and Health and Safety. In the days and/or weeks following a school crisis, educators continue communication by supplying information and counseling to promote closure to students, school personnel, parents, and other school district and community members. They continue direction and coordination by monitoring and solving problems ensuing from the crisis. They continue health and safety by supplying case management, direct services, and/or referral for longer term treatments as needed to those involved. In efforts to prevent future crises, educators demonstrate communication by conducting debriefing meetings with school staff, parents, other community members, district personnel, and students as appropriate to make clear any deficits in their response to the recent crisis. They demonstrate direction and coordination by applying debriefing analysis to plan possible prevention of additional crises; limit the impacts of inevitable occurrences; and improve crisis response procedures and resources. They provide health and safety education to students, parents, and staff.

Classroom Difficulties Encountered by Many Students with Disabilities in Reading Textbooks and Other Printed Learning Materials and Following Instructional Methods

Many students with various disabilities have difficulties in the classroom due to problems they experience with following the instructional methods and reading and applying the textbooks and other printed or written learning materials used in regular education programs. Educators can help these students to work around such difficulties by providing them with accommodations. One of the most important skills to enable success in school is being able to read. However, many students who have disabilities are not reading at their grade level because of various impediments to their reading skills. Some are still in the process of acquiring fundamental skills in phonics (i.e., the relationship between speech sounds and the alphabetic letters that represent them) and word

Copyright © Mometrix Media. You have been licensed one copy of this document for personal use only. Any other reproduction or redistribution is strictly prohibited. All rights reserved.
This content is provided for test preparation purposes only and does not imply an endorsement by Mometrix of any particular political, scientific, or religious point of view.

recognition. Some students are still in the process of learning how to apply techniques to assist them in comprehension of printed words, phrases, and sentences. In addition, plenty of textbooks, worksheets, and similar learning materials are not well-organized or clearly articulated, constituting further challenges to these students.

Trouble Attending, Following Concepts, and Interpreting Information That Is Delivered Via Oral Presentation, as in Lectures and Discussions

Some students with disabilities have trouble deciphering what they are meant to learn from an oral lecture or discussion on an academic topic. Teachers can make such accommodations as visual aids, like supporting their oral presentations with overhead projectors, large charts, or blackboards. They can give students an overview of a lesson's content before presenting it, and also introduce students to new vocabulary words prior to the lesson. Immediately following an oral lesson or lecture, teachers can give a printed summary of its important points, accompanied by a list of questions for them to answer. To help students with difficulties following ideas in oral lectures and discussions, teachers can break up lectures with discussions or other activities in small groups, and also maintain student engagement by inviting their questions. They can identify the primary parts of steps in the information. They can write important ideas on chalkboards/whiteboards, emphasizing parts using different colors.

Problems Learning Mathematical Concepts and Processes

Some students who have various disabilities have deficient skills in basic arithmetic and may still depend on counting on their fingers beyond the usual age. Some students with disabilities have major problems with remembering fundamental facts related to math. For students who have trouble with understanding mathematical concepts and solving math problems, teachers can provide accommodations such as giving them concrete objects and materials to assist in learning math concepts. Many students who cannot understand abstract ideas solely through mental processes can succeed better when they can process them using concrete, tangible things they can see, touch, and manipulate. Teachers can also highlight or color-code the important words in mathematical word problems for students. They can allow students to utilize charts to plan how they will solve math problems. And they can permit students to use basic fact charts and/or calculators to follow formulas and compute numbers for solving math problems.

Learning Problems Associated with Reading

One common problem for students with disabilities is isolating the main ideas in a book they are reading and/or which parts are important to remember. Teachers can highlight the important concepts and instruct students to read these first. They can give study guides to students for independent reading. They can offer students books on the same subjects at lower grade levels to make the main ideas easier to identify. Some students comprehend information when they hear it, but cannot read it. Teachers can supply books on tape/recorded versions; videos or movies of the information; computer text-to-speech software programs; and/or assign classmates to read printed materials aloud to students. Students with blindness or visual impairments may need specially produced materials and/or equipment to access class information. Teachers can supply books on tape or texts with large print; books and other materials in Braille or embossed formats; and give students equipment like magnifying devices or optical enhancers.

Trouble Taking Notes on and Remembering Ideas in Orally Presented Lessons

When students with various disabilities have trouble with taking notes on the teacher's oral lectures or lessons, the teacher can distribute printed copies of their lecture notes to accompany the oral presentation. They can allow these students to record orally presented class lessons, lectures, and discussions for their review and study. Teachers should repeat important concepts, paraphrase

Copyright © Mometrix Media. You have been licensed one copy of this document for personal use only. Any other reproduction or redistribution is strictly prohibited. All rights reserved.
This content is provided for test preparation purposes only and does not imply an endorsement by Mometrix of any particular political, scientific, or religious point of view.

them to express them in more than one set of words, and provide students with summaries of all the most important points. It is especially helpful if teachers repeat, paraphrase, and summarize at the end of a lesson, lecture, or class discussion. Teachers can help students with taking notes by giving them copies of their overhead projector documents, diagrams, and/or outlines of their lectures. To reinforce the information in oral presentations, teachers should supplement them with charts, diagrams, written/printed text, and/or pictures, and repeat as frequently as needed. Also, for deaf or hard-of-hearing students, teachers should procure a sign-language interpreter or a note-taker.

Difficulties in Writing for Classroom Assignments and Assessments

Students with a number of different disabilities can have difficulty with the fine motor control involved in handwriting. In general, the same kinds of classroom accommodations are required to address disabled student needs for both written assignments and written tests. For example, if a student needs to complete a written assignment using a word processor, s/he will also need the word processor to complete a written test. For students having difficulties with fine motor control, teachers can allow them to write straight into their workbooks instead of on separate paper or on photocopies of the workbook pages. They can permit students to type on typewriters, word processors, or computer keyboards. They can arrange for students to dictate their assignment and/or test responses to scribes, like classmates or teaching assistants, who write down their dictations. Teachers can also allow and provide adaptive equipment for students, such as special pen/pencil holders or grips, pens with erasable ink, and special paper featuring raised/embossed lines or color-coded line ruling.

Difficulties with Expressive Language That Impact Abilities to Complete Written Assignments and Assessment

Many students with disabilities may have good ideas, but have difficulties with expressing these in writing and/or speech. Teachers can provide them with accommodations that can facilitate their use of expressive language. For example, they can allow students to use a thesaurus to look up words that express the ideas they want to convey, and to find additional synonyms and antonyms for words if their actual vocabularies and/or their access to retrieving words they know are limited. Teachers can allow and provide to students specialized word-processing software programs that predict the words that students are trying to express. They can allow students to make use of electronic spelling aids and/or spelling dictionaries to support correct orthography. Teachers should also grade the content of written assignments separately from the writing mechanics in academic subjects (other than English composition, grammar, or spelling). They should additionally allow students with disabilities to correct their grammatical and spelling errors when they are completing written assignments or assessments.

Difficulty in Completing Assigned Work

Some students with disabilities can do the same work as others, but much more slowly. This can cause them to run out of time to finish assignments. Other students have trouble remembering to assemble the materials and resources they will need to complete assignments. For students who have trouble keeping track of their class assignments, teachers can provide accommodations by dividing longer assignments into portions and giving students separate due dates for each portion. Teachers can instruct students to mark their assignments' due dates on a calendar they can see. To accommodate students who work more slowly than others, teachers can assign a smaller total amount of work, while still ensuring that the items or tasks they choose are those necessary for meeting all the learning objectives they have identified. Teachers can allow these students to use instructional materials and resources outside of class. Until students can complete assignments on time, teachers can provide them with reinforcement via partial credit for incomplete or late work.

Copyright © Mometrix Media. You have been licensed one copy of this document for personal use only. Any other reproduction or redistribution is strictly prohibited. All rights reserved.
This content is provided for test preparation purposes only and does not imply an endorsement by Mometrix of any particular political, scientific, or religious point of view.

Difficulty Following Teachers' Instructions

In general, teachers speak, write, or demonstrate to students what they want them to do in school. Some students with disabilities have difficulty attending to spoken, written, or demonstrated information; some with remembering it; and some with both attending and retaining it. Moreover, some students with disabilities have difficulty comprehending and/or applying directions. When students find it hard to remember what they were instructed to do, teachers can provide accommodations by asking them to repeat the instructions in their own words or to demonstrate physically what they were instructed to do. They can also teach these students how to use personal planners or assignment notebooks for keeping track of assignments and tests. When students have difficulty comprehending the teacher's instructions, the teacher can provide accommodations by giving directions broken down into consecutive steps, and furnishing pictures or outlines of them. They can demonstrate for students how to complete sample tasks or problems, and combine oral instructions with pictures, diagrams, and/or printed words.

Difficulties with Organization

Students with attention deficits, cognitive impairments, and other disabilities can be distracted more easily than usual, causing them to confuse or forget the teacher's instructions. Students who find it hard to pay attention to more than one thing at a time frequently encounter difficulty completing complex assignments. Compounding these, some instructional materials are unclear by nature, and materials with excessive details can cause disabled students great confusion. Additionally, many disabled students have trouble storing, finding, and keeping track of classroom materials. Teachers can provide accommodations for confusion with complexity in materials and instructions by color-coding different materials or tasks to help students identify them. They should arrange tasks in clear, uncluttered formats with obvious beginning points and step sequences. To help students keep their materials organized, teachers can provide them with special binders or folders with dividers and different colors for each subject and unit. Teachers can also provide students with checklists of the materials they need for each class, which students keep in/on their binders, desks, or lockers.

Main Categories of Accommodations Permitted on Most Standardized Tests

Five main categories wherein accommodations are permitted on standardized tests are presentation, response, schedule, setting, and assistive technology. Insofar as they are legally allowed on standardized tests, students with disabilities generally need the same kinds of accommodations for classroom and standardized assessments. Accommodations enable students to demonstrate their mastery of skills and knowledge without their disabilities interfering. For students with reading deficits, teachers can read test items aloud to them (excluding reading skills tests). They can supply text-to-speech software to present students with test directions and/or nonreading test items. They can let students read test items to themselves instead of presenting them orally. They can supply Braille or large-print test forms, and/or visual magnifiers, auditory amplifiers, or other assistive technology. To aid in focusing visually on tests, teachers can have students use positioning tools, pointers, blank cards, templates, colored, blank overlays, or transparencies. To decrease auditory distraction, they can give students headphones and "white noise" machines.

Accommodations

Accommodations That Teachers Can Provide in Their Presentation of Classroom or Standardized Tests to Students with Disabilities to Help Them Follow Directions

When students with disabilities are taking classroom and/or standardized tests, they can often have difficulty with accessing, understanding, and/or following the directions in the tests. Teachers

Copyright © Mometrix Media. You have been licensed one copy of this document for personal use only. Any other reproduction or redistribution is strictly prohibited. All rights reserved.
This content is provided for test preparation purposes only and does not imply an endorsement by Mometrix of any particular political, scientific, or religious point of view.

can provide classroom accommodations to these students to facilitate test-taking. For example, they can provide answer forms or test forms with visual symbols, like stop signs, arrows, etc., to guide students in following directions. Some standardized tests already include such symbols for all students. When test directions are presented orally, teachers can provide sign language interpreters for deaf or hard-of-hearing students. When test directions and writing prompts are presented in print, teachers can read these aloud for students with visual impairments, cognitive disabilities, and reading-related learning disabilities. For students who need it, teachers can reread test directions or further explain their meaning. Teachers can also highlight or underline the most important words in test directions and/or test items for students with disabilities.

Accommodations to Students with Disabilities When They Have Difficulty Understanding or Applying Test Directions as They Are Normally Presented

When students with disabilities are not sure what to do on tests, teachers should avoid hinting at right/wrong answers but still accommodate them verbally by encouraging them (e.g., to answer each question and continue working), and they should give them additional examples of test items for practice to ensure they know what to do during actual testing. Most standardized tests prohibit accommodations in presentation that alter the assessed skill; for example, if a test measures reading skills, teachers cannot read items aloud to students. However, certain accommodations are permissible for classroom assessments. For students having difficulty switching among task types, teachers can group similar items and place easiest items first on tests. They can divide matching tasks into smaller groups of 4 to 5 items each. For essay/fill-in-the-blank items, they can provide applicable word lists. Whenever memorization is not required, teachers can let students take open-book tests. On multiple-choice tests, teachers can remove one choice from each question. Teachers can select test questions covering all content required but give fewer total questions.

Accommodations That Students with Disabilities May Receive for Completing State Standardized Tests When They Have Trouble Sustaining Their Attention and Effort, and Some Not Allowed by Standardized Tests but Permitted in Classroom Assessments

When administering state standardized tests, teachers may provide some accommodations to disabled students who struggle to maintain their attention and energy during testing. For example, teachers may monitor student answer sheets to see whether they are putting their responses in the right places. When student responses to extended-response items are partly correct, teachers may give partial credit as designated by the rubrics for these items on state standardized achievement tests. In classroom assessments, teachers may furnish students with prepared outlines, charts, diagrams, and/or webs to help them plan essay or open-ended question responses. Students may demonstrate their skills and knowledge via alternate formats like role-plays, oral interviews, or physical demonstrations. They may be allowed references like thesauruses, dictionaries, or almanacs. They may be allowed concrete manipulatives to do and/or check calculations. Students may retake tests and get credit for improving. Also, some state standardized tests even allow certain grades to retake them.

Accommodations That Students with Special Needs May Require for Taking Tests Related to the Setting of the Assessment, Including an Important Assessment Consideration Related to Assistive Technology

Some students with special needs are so easily distracted that they cannot perform to their ability if they take a test in a large group. Accommodations to address this problem include administering the test to the student in isolation or in a smaller group; allowing the student to take the test in a study carrel or other enclosure; or having the student take the test in another room free of distractions. Other students have physical or sensory disabilities that have an impact on their

Copyright © Mometrix Media. You have been licensed one copy of this document for personal use only. Any other reproduction or redistribution is strictly prohibited. All rights reserved.
This content is provided for test preparation purposes only and does not imply an endorsement by Mometrix of any particular political, scientific, or religious point of view.

ability to take a test. In such cases, schools and teachers need to allow these students to use whatever adaptive equipment or furniture they require to be able to participate in the assessment. One important consideration in allowing the use of assistive technology is that it does not alter the performance of the actual skills being tested. For example, if a test measures skills in reading printed language, a student could not use text-to-speech software for that particular test.

Accommodations That Can Be Allowed for Students with Disabilities Related to the Test Schedule for Typical State Standardized Tests and a Couple for Classroom Assessments

Some students with disabilities need additional time to finish taking a test. Students who work very slowly, those who can work for only briefer periods at a time, and those using certain types of assistive technology may need alterations in testing schedules. Accommodations when administering typical state standardized tests include allowing longer times for students to take the test; dividing a test into smaller portions and allowing students to take each portion on a different day if necessary; permitting students to take short breaks during the testing period; and allowing students to take a test at different times of day if physical conditions and/or medications affect their alertness and attention. Teachers may provide additional accommodations not allowed on standardized tests for classroom assessments. For example, the teacher can give disabled students fewer test questions, as long as they still cover all the same skills and content being assessed. Teachers may also let students review and correct their test answers from the day before.

Student Responses to Test Items Which Teachers Can Provide

Students with various disabilities can have difficulty handwriting test answers, circling or checking multiple-choice answers, filling in bubbles, or solving problems and explaining their solutions. Accommodations often allowed on standardized tests in some states include giving additional space for students to handwrite their answers; allowing students to answer questions orally instead of in writing, to dictate their answers into a sound recorder, or to a scribe or test proctor; or allowing the student to sign his or her test responses to a sign-language interpreter. Students may also be permitted to use word processors or computer or typewriter keyboards to answer test questions, although state standardized tests typically prohibit their using spell-check and grammar-check software when typing. Students may write into their test booklets instead of on separate sheets, create Braille answers on separate paper, or record their answers using speech-to-text software programs. Students are also often allowed to use outlines, charts, and/or diagrams for planning essay or open-ended question responses on tests.

Technology That Can Be Used as Accommodations to Respond to Assessment Tests

Students with various disabilities may need assistive technology to acquire the information they are expected to learn and/or to communicate what they have learned. As long as the purpose of assessment is not defeated, the skills being assessed are not changed, and the student's responses still reflect his or her independent efforts, students can generally use the same assistive technology they use during classroom instruction to complete assessments. For example, a student with a disability might be given an accommodation allowing him or her to use an adaptive calculator for solving mathematics problems on a test. Some state standardized achievement tests allow students in seventh through tenth grades, for example, to use calculators. Another example involves completing answers to essay questions and/or long explanations or answers to questions on tests. Students with disabilities may be permitted to use assistive technology, such as voice recorders to dictate their responses, or word processors to type them.

Copyright © Mometrix Media. You have been licensed one copy of this document for personal use only. Any other reproduction or redistribution is strictly prohibited. All rights reserved.
This content is provided for test preparation purposes only and does not imply an endorsement by Mometrix of any particular political, scientific, or religious point of view.

Unique Accommodations Required by Some Students with Disabilities to Participate in State Testing That Are Not Already Identified by Their State's Education Department

Some students can have disabilities that necessitate more unusual accommodations in order to participate in state standardized achievement testing. Testing accommodations identified as unique usually entail some changes in the existing assessment materials. Typically, states will allow such unique assessment accommodations if their Commissioner of Education has previously approved their use. Parents and teachers can look to the program of educational services to exceptional students in their school district to assist them with making a request for approval of such accommodations. Several examples of unique or unusual accommodations that may be approved for students with disabilities to participate in standardized assessments include: test forms with fewer items on each page; test forms with more space separating each item from the next; test forms with modified or tabbed pages to enable students to turn pages more easily; and having test question and response forms attached to the student's work area to prevent their falling, sliding, or shifting to facilitate reading and writing or marking on them.

Adapting Class Schedules and Time Constraints

Some students who have disabilities can handle the same course content as their peers, but they need more time to do so, or they need their work to be broken up into shorter time periods with breaks in between. Some students with disabilities suffer deterioration in their performance when they feel pressured by time limits. Some also require more time to complete assignments and assessments due to the adaptive equipment they must use in order to participate. Some strategies teachers can use include keeping schedules flexible to allow students with disabilities more time to finish a course. This can include completing the requirements in summer school. Teachers can allow students with disabilities extra time to complete their classwork and take tests. They can assign work further in advance to allow students with disabilities a chance to begin their assignments earlier. Teachers can also supply students with clear schedules of all units, assignments, and tests, and include periodic checkpoints within these schedules to help students monitor their progress.

Scheduling Demands Within Programs, Courses, Assignments, and Assessments

Many students with disabilities learn and/or work at slower speeds than their nondisabled peers. Others perform better without the pressure of rigorous schedules. Teachers can provide them with time- and schedule-related accommodations. For example, some high school students may be given an Incomplete course grade and finish the course in summer school or the next semester. On practice assignments with multiple similar items, students who have the cognitive ability to learn without excessive repetition but need additional time and/or perform poorly under time pressure may be permitted to complete only every other item. Another educator consideration regarding students with disabilities is that in middle school and high school programs, it is particularly critical to assign these students to classes appropriate for them. Teachers of special education are advised that they may facilitate this process by working with their school administrators to ensure that the schedules of assigned classes are able to accommodate the special needs of any students who have disabilities.

NIMAS

The IDEA incorporates the National Instructional Materials Accessibility Standard or NIMAS. The stated purpose of this standard is to "facilitate the provision of accessible, alternate-format versions of print textbooks to pre-K–12 students with disabilities." This standard provides information to assist school IEP teams in deciding how they can electronically provide access to textbooks and

Copyright © Mometrix Media. You have been licensed one copy of this document for personal use only. Any other reproduction or redistribution is strictly prohibited. All rights reserved.
This content is provided for test preparation purposes only and does not imply an endorsement by Mometrix of any particular political, scientific, or religious point of view.

other reading materials to students who have dyslexia and other LDs with reading. Parents who have children with reading disabilities should look at their children's IEPs and/or 504 plans to discover whether they contain anything about eligibility for accessible instructional materials, or AIM. If a student was determined not to be eligible for AIM, parents have the legal right to talk with their school personnel about why not. Parents can advocate for their children with schools by initiating conversations about how their children learn best, and how alternative formats, digital software, and/or readers can sometimes strikingly improve their learning and their motivation and confidence in it.

AIM

AIM stands for Accessible Instructional Materials. Many students with disabilities find reading impossible or difficult because of various disabilities affecting being able to read standard printed materials. AIMs consist of textbooks and other printed educational materials published in special digital formats. These formats provide accommodation to individuals who are blind, visually impaired, have various physical disabilities, and have reading-related learning disabilities (LDs) including dyslexia. Using digital formats enables students with reading and/or print disabilities to hear and see the text simultaneously using a computer, tablet, or other digital device. AIM includes formats like Braille, large print, audio, and digital text. The standard format for digital text files is named DAISY, for Digital Accessible Information System. DAISY allows users to listen to recordings of human voices or electronic speech synthesizers for audio versions of print materials. Accompanying reading software presents text visually at the same time. Today, most young students are comfortable and familiar with electronic voices and adapt easily to using them for reading.

Main Components of Effective Instruction in Reading

According to the National Reading Panel, three main components of effective instruction in reading are (1) phonemic awareness, phonics, and alphabet knowledge; (2) vocabulary, text comprehension, and reading fluency; and (3) reading comprehension strategies. When the National Center for Learning Disabilities surveyed teachers and assistive technology (AT) specialists about digital technologies and digital books, the consensus of their responses identified a number of benefits. These included that digital reading technology affords a whole new world of learning potential for students, and that it affords flexibility among more learning options according to student preferences and learning styles. Teachers and AT specialists also find that digital reading options further the personal achievement, independence, and socialization skills of students. They say digital reading does much to aid students who struggle with decoding printed words. It keeps students' attention for longer time spans. It helps students read at their grade levels. It encourages students to take notes and make annotations to texts. And it corrects students' spelling errors.

Providing Books in Accessible Digital and Audio Formats That Facilitate Reading for Students with LDs and Other Disabilities

Two organizations whose specialty is providing accessible text formats are Bookshare at bookshare.org and Learning Ally at learningally.org. Bookshare is an online library of over 150,000 digital versions of copyrighted textbooks and other books. Learning Ally is an online library of more than 70,000 audio versions of literary works and textbooks, with both recordings of human voices and digitally synthesized voices reading the material. These organizations both have approval from the US Department of Education for providing accessible instructional materials (AIM) to school districts and individual schools. Schools and/or districts can request digital formats or files from these groups for qualifying students with reading or print disabilities. Due to their cooperative missions, qualified members of either organization can more easily gain membership in the other.

Copyright © Mometrix Media. You have been licensed one copy of this document for personal use only. Any other reproduction or redistribution is strictly prohibited. All rights reserved.
This content is provided for test preparation purposes only and does not imply an endorsement by Mometrix of any particular political, scientific, or religious point of view.

Some school districts or schools even pay for memberships in both organizations or either one for students who are found eligible.

Research Evidence Regarding the Use of Text-to-Speech Technology for Reading

Studies suggest that reading technologies that use audio or digital formats can enhance the reading process for students with learning disabilities. When students simultaneously see words and sentences highlighted on the screens of computers, tablets, or other devices and hear them read aloud via text-to-speech (TTS) programs, this is described as "multisensory" or "multimodal" reading. With digital education widespread today, students may learn at home or while on the go as well as in the classroom. In this environment, AT programs are compatible with student learning processes. Some high-quality programs include Read Write Gold by TextHelp; Read: OutLoud by Don Johnston; and Kurzweil 3000 by Cambium. For iPads and other Apple devices, the large online digital library Bookshare offers an application ("app") called Read2Go, which enables its members to download and read its digital books on their devices. Students can digitally navigate through books' tables of contents, chapters, pages, and paragraphs.

Print Books That Present Challenges to Representation in Digital Formats

According to the National Center for Learning Disabilities, certain visual images in printed books—for example, mathematical concepts, charts, and graphs—cannot be accurately represented using text-to-speech software programs. This presents a limitation to what students with reading or other disabilities can access compared to the original printed book versions. However, progress in technology is addressing this need. The organization Benetech is the parent group of the extensive online library known as Bookshare (bookshare.org). Benetech has a division called the DIAGRAM Center. At the DIAGRAM Center, designers of digital technology have created a new web application tool named POET. POET is an open-source application that enables crowd sourcing of verbal descriptions of visual images. In addition, it facilitates the process of creating descriptions of visual images for Digital Accessible Information System or DAISY file format, the standard format for digital text files. The progress of this and similar technology developments afford increased access to text for students with disabilities.

Research Findings About the Prevalence of Studies on Teaching the Respective General Education Curriculum Content Areas of Literacy, Math, and Science to Special Education Students with Severe Developmental Disabilities

Comprehensive literature reviews find nearly twice as much research exists about teaching literacy as math, and four times more about math than science. One commonality among these areas is that using behavior analysis principles is effective for teaching them all to severely developmentally disabled students. For example, using task analysis to break down the instruction of multistep (chained) tasks and using time delay for teaching separate tasks are both highly effective for teaching academic content. These techniques are used in systematic instruction, which studies show is an effective overall teaching strategy for these students. Systematic instruction has been used to teach feeding, toileting, dressing, safety, and many other functional skills, and academic skills as well. Systematic instruction procedures define observable, measurable target skills; collect intervention data to prove new skill acquisition; apply behavioral principles and techniques like systematic prompts and fading, error correction, and differential reinforcement to aid transfer of learned skills; and effect behavioral changes that can be generalized across skills, materials, people, and contexts.

Copyright © Mometrix Media. You have been licensed one copy of this document for personal use only. Any other reproduction or redistribution is strictly prohibited. All rights reserved.
This content is provided for test preparation purposes only and does not imply an endorsement by Mometrix of any particular political, scientific, or religious point of view.

Assistive Technology Programs That Allow Students with Reading/Learning and Other Disabilities to Read Books Digitally

Today, students can download and read books digitally on tablets, other devices, and computers from online digital libraries, which even offer apps (applications) for downloading to digital devices. Students can interact with, manipulate, and change settings in digital reading matter, including the sizes and colors of the fonts, both in the text and in hypertext links; choosing between male or female voices in audio versions of text; adjusting the speed of the readers' speech in audio text; turning on and off the read-aloud function in books with both visual and audio text; setting bookmarks in books; and changing the appearances of background displays in digital books. Some software programs and portable devices incorporate graphic organizers to aid comprehension and studying; note-taking tools to aid in essay writing; built-in scanners to copy and upload/download documents and pictures; support tools for outline writing; dictionaries, spell-checkers; keyword searches; bibliographers; voice recorders, voice recognition; and Acapela Voices, which reads text aloud translated into Spanish and other languages for ESL/ELL students.

Teaching Core Concepts and Content in Science According to State Standards

Recent educational research studies have shown that teachers, when trained in a specific task analysis, could teach developmentally disabled students to conduct science experiments. Some researchers have used graphic organizers to teach science core content to students with autism in middle school. Others taught science vocabulary and concepts to similar students using explicit instruction of descriptors. And some have taught the steps of scientific inquiry lessons, and science concepts that the learners generalized to new materials, to students with moderate intellectual disabilities. Research has shown that time delay and similar strategies for special educators to teach math and science vocabulary across multiple academic content areas is effective with high school students having moderate and severe developmental disabilities. Other researchers have recently investigated teaching early science concepts and vocabulary to elementary school students with severe DDs. They find even at lower ages/grades and more severe disabilities, students learned comprehension of both scientific vocabulary and concepts, meeting the criteria of state standards for progress through science lessons in the general education curriculum.

Ways Wherein English as a Second Language Classes Differ from Other Classrooms

American classrooms where students are learning English as a new language demand much more interaction between students and teachers than other classrooms generally do. Many activities assigned in ESL classes involve group work, which necessitates moving desks, getting up, and moving around, which must be kept in mind for disabled students. Teachers should also be sensitive to the diversity of most ESL classes, which often include students from different countries and of various ages. ESL teachers can help by educating themselves in advance about any specific disabilities incoming students to their classes have. They should ensure their classes are inclusive, by providing accommodations and/or services needed by disabled students, and communicating this to students clearly in their course syllabi and in other ways. They should discuss with disabled students how their needs and accommodations might change, and any help or adjustments such changes could necessitate.

Tips for ESL Teachers to Approach Having Students with Disabilities in Their Classes

Depending on the type and extent of a disability and the classroom situation, students with various disabilities can find everyday classroom activities difficult, e.g., active learning that involves getting up and engaging in different physical actions; making physical and oral presentations; or

Copyright © Mometrix Media. You have been licensed one copy of this document for personal use only. Any other reproduction or redistribution is strictly prohibited. All rights reserved.
This content is provided for test preparation purposes only and does not imply an endorsement by Mometrix of any particular political, scientific, or religious point of view.

participating in group or class discussions. ESL teachers can exercise their creativity by adapting the activities they design and assign to allow more universal student access, while still attaining the same learning goals. When an ESL teacher has a student with a disability in the class, the teacher should communicate the same expectations and standards for academic achievement and personal behavior that s/he has for all students. The majority of students with disabilities appreciate being treated with the same educational standards and teacher expectations as a sign of respect from the teacher. ESL teachers should also ask their disabled students regularly for feedback about what things in class work and do not work for them, and how things that do not work may be adjusted or modified.

Communication Skills and Instruction for Students Who Are Blind or Visually Impaired

While teachers routinely use visual aids like pictures, flash cards, graphs, charts, and pointing at objects in the room while saying "this" or "that," they must realize these are not accessible to blind or visually impaired students. They must provide them with additional tactile versions and/or verbal descriptions. Students with low vision may not be able to see writing on blackboards/whiteboards, in workbooks, etc. They should be seated at the front of the room and allowed to bring their own magnifying devices. Before class, teachers can provide handouts to these students in Braille, large print, audio formats, or electronic formats depending on their preferred format, and/or give students additional prompts during class. When presenting visual information, teachers should spell new vocabulary words aloud; print using large, clear letters; use larger sized fonts in overheads and handouts; and read aloud as they write, which benefits all students. When drawing or displaying pictures, teachers should verbally describe their contents.

Proactive Measures That Teachers of ESL (English as a Second Language) Can Take to Accommodate Students with Disabilities in Their Classrooms

ESL teachers with disabled students should discuss their needs and accommodations with the students. They should also discuss these with their teaching assistants, aides, school office staff, and other support staff, and also request that they help with accommodations for these students. Teachers must observe privacy regulations and not disclose disability information with faculty, staff, or other students, except in regard to accommodations that are needed. In the United States, the law requires schools, agencies, and other organizations to provide the same accommodations to international students with disabilities as they do to US citizens; ESL teachers in America should comply with this legal requirement. All world nations have organizations that provide access to local resources for people with disabilities. ESL teachers with disabled students can contact these groups for resources and advice. Regardless of the type of disability, teachers should concentrate on the individual student's abilities and strengths.

Enhancing Communication Skills for Students Who Have Mobility Disabilities

When assigning group activities, teachers may need more flexibility and time for assembling groups and moving furniture. Teachers should consider this in assigning groups/pairs, without restricting variety among student partners/classmates. Students with limited/no use of their arms cannot perform common classroom behaviors like jotting down new vocabulary words, looking words up in dictionaries or encyclopedias, or even raising their hands. Teachers need to provide them with alternative methods, like a scribe to take notes, orally saying "yes"/"no" instead of raising hands, etc. Teachers can collaborate with students on alternative means to get teacher attention. Students in wheelchairs may arrive late and/or need to leave early because of weather, transportation service, architectural barriers, or other factors outside their control. Teachers should discuss with students whether their disability requiring accommodation or behavioral factors cause late arrivals/early departures, defining expectations and resolving issues accordingly. Teachers should

Copyright © Mometrix Media. You have been licensed one copy of this document for personal use only. Any other reproduction or redistribution is strictly prohibited. All rights reserved.
This content is provided for test preparation purposes only and does not imply an endorsement by Mometrix of any particular political, scientific, or religious point of view.

ensure other students realize wheelchairs/other adaptive equipment constitute personal space and respect it. Teachers and students should sit when interacting with students of shorter stature or students in wheelchairs.

Ensuring That Students with Low Vision or Blindness Have Equal Access to Content

When school assignments involve large amounts of reading, students with low vision often experience eye fatigue and need to rest their eyes frequently. Teachers can permit them breaks during class and/or give them extensions on due dates for reading assignments. Teachers should ensure student access to alternative media formats like Braille, audio recordings, or large print. Some students bring laptops or other computerized devices with text-to-speech, large print, or Braille conversion software; teachers should provide their teaching content in electronic formats for these students. They should also discuss with them whether any websites the teacher uses as lesson supplements are incompatible with students' special software, and consider adjusting their curriculum to use compatible sites. Teachers should also keep classroom layout consistent to facilitate student orientation and navigation. Teachers sharing classrooms can try to enlist the other teachers' cooperation and assistance. Tactile and/or audio rather than visual cues more effectively get these students' attention. Teachers can also instruct other students to say their names before speaking during group discussions.

Improving Communication Skills for Deaf/Hard-of-Hearing (HOH) Students

Even deaf/HOH students who use spoken English are apt to have problems during class activities involving faster reaction times, like listen-and-repeat exercises. Teachers can give them more time to repeat, and also try to eliminate background noises—including cross-talk from other students—as possible. Fire alarms, other audio emergency signals, and PA speaker announcements are not usually accessible to deaf students. Teachers can accommodate them by flicking the overhead lights on and off, waving a hand, or touching them on the shoulder to get their attention before announcements or during alarms. Viewing videos of movies and TV programs is an activity often used and enjoyed in classrooms in general and even more so in ESL classes. However, teachers should be sure the videos include English closed captions or subtitles. This benefits comprehension for both deaf/HOH and ESL students. If captions/subtitles are unavailable for a video, teachers can procure sign language interpreters or speech-to-text note-takers. HOH students often comprehend video images better than audio practice.

Some deaf/hard-of-hearing students learn written English and speech reading to understand hearing people, but communicate using sign language and do not learn speech. Others want to learn speech and have pronunciation difficulties due to their hearing loss. For students who want to use spoken English, teachers can find technological help. For example, microphones equipped with FM systems not only amplify speech sounds, but also send them directly to the student's hearing aids. Teachers can also repeat what other students say if they are out of microphone range, which benefits all students. For deaf students who communicate using sign language, teachers can engage the services of sign language interpreters; they can additionally learn several simpler signs themselves to facilitate basic communication with these students. Interpreting can be challenging for international students, because sign language is not universal but varies among countries. In this case, speech-to-text services may be better. Teachers should always directly address the student rather than the sign language interpreter/STT assistant.

Teachers should seek means of utilizing visual aids as supplements to all their lessons. They should wait to allow time for students to view both the signs of a sign language interpreter or the text of speech-to-text software programs, and also the visual aid the teacher presents. Teachers should be

Copyright © Mometrix Media. You have been licensed one copy of this document for personal use only. Any other reproduction or redistribution is strictly prohibited. All rights reserved.
This content is provided for test preparation purposes only and does not imply an endorsement by Mometrix of any particular political, scientific, or religious point of view.

mindful whether they are standing between the student and interpreter. Teachers can also use color-coding, e.g., different pen colors to represent different parts of a sentence—like red for subjects or blue for verbs. They can use geometric shapes to adapt concepts visually and use their fingers to represent different subjects or different tenses when conjugating verbs. Since some deaf/hard-of-hearing students speech read, teachers should not stand in front of windows or other places that interfere with this. Seating in front of the room or circular seating wherein students can see both the teacher and classmates can help hearing-impaired students always see who is speaking. Decreasing background noise from open windows, large groups, fans, or cross-talk helps students follow class discussions.

Improving Communication for Students with Chronic and Mental Health Disabilities

Some students have different conditions like diabetes, asthma, seizure disorder, multiple sclerosis, arthritis, or anxiety, depression, obsessive-compulsive disorder, or bipolar disorder. Individual differences in symptoms complicate such chronic disabilities. Due to the condition, medication side effects, and/or the environment, students may feel/perform better/worse at certain times of the day/on certain days. This can influence attendance, attention, and memory. Teachers should permit students flexibility in taking breaks, extend time for finishing assignments, allow note-takers, adjust schedules, and let students make up missed tests as necessary. Some students with chronic conditions need rest at home for days/weeks, but may be able to study and do homework there. Teachers can design and adhere to a good syllabus to inform students what to do if they miss classes. Some students have sensitivities to sensory stimuli like temperature changes, lights, or sounds, or they have other conditions affecting classroom participation and/or social interactions. Teachers should make time to acquaint themselves with each student's unique circumstances and which accommodations help them most.

Teaching Communication Skills

Some students have difficulty controlling their speech muscles secondary to cerebral palsy; some progressive illnesses cause speech problems; and traumatic brain injuries can cause aphasia, a language processing problem. Some students stutter, and some have voice disorders secondary to cleft palate/lip, vocal nodules/polyps, etc. Students who cannot speak functionally use electronic voice synthesizers or visual-manual communication boards/books. Others can speak, but less quickly, clearly and/or fluently than normal. Many students have milder articulation disorders that still affect their communication. Teachers not understanding a student should not say/pretend they do, but allow them to repeat; they are accustomed to it. Teachers should not finish their sentences for them, but give them time for self-expression, promoting self-confidence. Teachers must adjust their expectations for oral assignments/tests. They can also seek alternative means for students to attain class goals, e.g., hand-raising, writing, or group-texting question answers and slower discussion speeds. For students with communications assistants, teachers should address the student, not the assistant.

Things to Keep in Mind When Instruction in Communication Skills Includes Students Who Have Cognitive and Learning Disabilities

An ESL teacher may find that students with traumatic brain injuries or ADHD encounter difficulty in class, especially if the teacher presents information using only one format, modality, or approach. Teachers should use multimodal teaching approaches and alternative assessment formats. Utilizing a variety of instructional methods, e.g., lectures, games, small group assignments, or paired work, will make it easier for these students to find which technique(s) are most effective for them. Students with LDs often perform better in one modality and worse in another, e.g., excelling at spoken skills but struggling with written skills. Teachers can accommodate these students by

Copyright © Mometrix Media. You have been licensed one copy of this document for personal use only. Any other reproduction or redistribution is strictly prohibited. All rights reserved.
This content is provided for test preparation purposes only and does not imply an endorsement by Mometrix of any particular political, scientific, or religious point of view.

offering them a variety of ways to demonstrate their learning, like doing assignments in artistic or oral formats. Teachers should also realize that individual differences give every student's neurological deficit a unique presentation, so they must discover solutions case by case. ESL teachers need to understand students' abilities/skills in their native languages to differentiate errors due to disabilities from those naturally due to learning a second language.

Students with learning and cognitive disabilities are increasingly common in today's classrooms and quite common in ESL classrooms where they can substantially affect how students learn English. Standard instructional methods for language are usually less effective for students with learning disabilities, autism spectrum disorders (ASDs), and various other neurological deficits. Teachers are responsible for modifying their teaching styles to facilitate learning, and ESL teachers to facilitate learning a new language. In ESL, students with LDs must not only process words and symbols; they also contend with various difficulties remembering/retrieving words, articulating speech sounds, fluency, organizing thoughts, constructing sentences, and thinking abstractly. Teachers should focus not on student deficits, but strategies many students have developed independently to compensate. Teachers can provide accommodations like more time for activities and tests; note-takers; and tutors. Neurological deficits that affect social skills, as with ASDs, can make group/pair activities challenging. Teachers should provide structure and lead classes deliberately, clarifying the goals and purposes of each segment of the class.

Behaviors Related to Communicating with Others

An important part of communicating with other people is being able to recognize emergency situations and respond timely and appropriately. This can be difficult for students with intellectual disabilities, behavior disorders, and other conditions. Among those who do not recognize an emergency situation, some will always require supervision, while others can be taught certain basics, such as the smell of smoke; the sight of fire, flooding, or a person needing emergency medical attention; and what to do, like calling 911. Some students with disabilities can recognize emergency situations but may panic. Educators can use explicit, systematic instruction, including task analysis steps and behavioral shaping and chaining, to help them develop strongly entrenched procedures to follow. With enough practice, repetition, and reinforcement, many students with disabilities can implement these series of behaviors instead of panicking. Students with autism spectrum disorders often need explicit instruction in the meanings/purposes of social cues (like facial expressions, vocal intonations, gestures, body language, and verbal expressions) and how to respond appropriately.

Components of Self-Confidence

Many students with disabilities are aware of their disability, which can undermine their self-confidence. They often feel they are different and do not fit in socially and have experienced rejection, ridicule, and bullying by other students. Additionally, experiencing failure at tasks their nondisabled peers complete easily can lower their self-esteem. Teachers can offer explicit instruction, asking students to identify good qualities they possess; help them develop positive affirmations they can understand, repeat, and believe; and provide plentiful positive reinforcement for every small success and for admirable efforts regardless of outcome. They can have students describe how they think others see them, and collaborate to develop strategies to improve their own and others' images of them. They can teach students to accept and offer praise and criticism appropriately with others. Students may also need training in wearing clothing appropriate to different social situations and answering and using telephones properly. The more students master such social skills, the more self-confidence they will develop.

Copyright © Mometrix Media. You have been licensed one copy of this document for personal use only. Any other reproduction or redistribution is strictly prohibited. All rights reserved.
This content is provided for test preparation purposes only and does not imply an endorsement by Mometrix of any particular political, scientific, or religious point of view.

Interpersonal Skills

For students with disabilities to interact well with their classmates and others, one key area is in social conversations as well as in class discussions. Students must learn both to listen to others, which includes not only refraining from interrupting them, but also listening attentively to what they say, and to respond appropriately to what others say. Students with intellectual disabilities may, for example, change the subject completely instead of saying something that continues the topic. Teachers can give explicit instruction. For example, they can ask the student to repeat or paraphrase what another student just said; then ask her/him what possible things s/he could say in return on the same topic; have her/him demonstrate; and give positive reinforcement. Another area is forming and maintaining close relationships and friendships with others. Teachers can counsel students by asking them who shares particular interests, activities, and/or personal characteristics with them; helping them identify and implement behaviors for establishing and keeping relationships and friendships; and monitoring their progress by inquiring periodically.

Socially Responsible Behavior

Some students with cognitive disabilities may not have a good sense of personal possessions and boundaries. Consequently, they may take others' belongings; not take turns with others; or go ahead of others in lines. One facet of socially responsible behavior is respecting others' property and rights. Teachers can point out other students' showing such respect; explicitly show intellectually disabled students how to do the same; and give ample positive reinforcement whenever they do. Students with behavior disorders like oppositional defiant disorder will defy/ignore authority and directions. Teachers can establish behavioral contracts with them whereby they gain rewards meaningful to them for complying with clearly defined terms of what to do and not do. Students with ADHD easily act on impulse and become distracted, interfering with following directions. Behavior modification techniques or cognitive-behavioral therapy, sometimes in conjunction with medication, can help. Students also must learn to recognize valuable personal characteristics (e.g., honesty, kindness, or bravery); their personal roles in society; and social etiquette and proper behavior in public.

Social and Personal Skills

For all people with and without disabilities, it can be challenging to get along with others. One of the commonest reasons that adults are fired from jobs and students have problems in school is inadequate social and personal skills. Students with various disabilities that affect learning often do not learn through observation and imitation as others do. Teachers need to instruct them explicitly in areas like self-awareness. They must teach them to identify their own physical and psychological needs, abilities, interests, and emotions by asking them questions; showing them how to point to pictures representing various feelings, actions, events; or teaching them descriptive vocabulary. Teachers need to guide students to learn to identify and demonstrate knowledge of their physical beings and their relationship to and interaction with space, objects, and other people. They need to help students properly utilize, care for, and maintain hearing aids, glasses, braces, crutches, wheelchairs, or walkers. Teachers can also help disabled students learn appropriate strategies for coping with life stressors.

Attaining Independence

Many students with disabilities have had things done for them that they could not accomplish alone and may have become habituated to passively waiting for others to initiate activities. Educators can help them achieve more independence by first explicitly teaching a student needed skills, giving prompts for each step, and then systematically fading the prompts so the student gradually performs tasks/activities with less and less help, direction, and guidance. Depending on the

Copyright © Mometrix Media. You have been licensed one copy of this document for personal use only. Any other reproduction or redistribution is strictly prohibited. All rights reserved.
This content is provided for test preparation purposes only and does not imply an endorsement by Mometrix of any particular political, scientific, or religious point of view.

disability and activity, some students ultimately achieve full independence, while others can do more than before with less assistance. Students also must learn to take responsibility for their behaviors. Teachers/specialists can help students navigate the community by teaching orientation, mobility, street directionality, how to use public transportation, or strategies for coping with getting lost or with timetable changes when traveling. They can also teach them to follow safety procedures. They can counsel them in choosing friends and provide behavioral procedures for choosing clothing and getting to school on time.

Problem-Solving Skills

As much as some students with disabilities may want to be completely independent, some disabilities dictate that they will need help with some things at times. A crucial behavior included among problem-solving skills is having the judgment, willingness, and ability to ask for help when they really need it. Educators can help in one on one, small group, or whole class settings by initiating discussions wherein students identify situations they have experienced when they needed help; what they did; what they could have done instead; and discriminate situations where they could have succeeded independently from those where this was impossible. Some students can benefit by learning from the experiences their classmates share. Teachers/specialists can assess and teach student skills for identifying problems, give them practice in predicting the consequences of events/actions, develop various alternatives for responding to problems, and evaluate their relative effectiveness. They can also work with students individually and in groups on developing their own goals, plans, and solutions to problems.

School-Wide Positive Behavioral Support Program

School-wide positive behavioral support programs are typically divided into tiers along a continuum, based on how students respond behaviorally to intervention. In the first tier, all students in the school/system/district are given positive behavioral supports, such as giving positive rewards to reinforce exemplary and acceptable academic and social behaviors, which are implemented by all staff members in all school settings. This universal tier is known as primary prevention. The second tier of secondary prevention is for students whose behaviors do not respond to the behavioral supports given in the first tier, putting them at risk for disciplinary issues. These students are placed in a specialized group, where they receive more intensive behavioral measures. The third tier of tertiary prevention is for students identified as being at high risk of antisocial behaviors resulting in disciplinary problems and possible harm to themselves and/or others. These students receive individualized behavior management plans that are the most specialized and utilize the most intensive interventions.

School-Wide Positive Behavioral Support (SWPBS)

Four integrated parts of SWPBS programs are data, practices, systems, and outcomes. The data educators collect about students' academic and social behaviors support the decisions they make about the academic and behavioral interventions and practices to use. The practices educators choose have science-based evidence of being effective for achieving the educational outcomes they desire. These practices support the desired student behaviors. The systems that educators establish support the most effective and efficient implementation of their chosen practices. These systems support implementation by supporting the behavior of the school personnel. The desired outcomes educators identify are observable and measurable, and the data they collect support these measurements. The students' outcomes in turn support the students' academic achievement and social competence. Well-implemented SWPBS makes learning environments less dangerous, exclusionary, aversive, and reactive, and more preventive, inclusive, engaging, and responsive. Disciplinary and classroom management issues like lateness, attendance, and antisocial behavior

Copyright © Mometrix Media. You have been licensed one copy of this document for personal use only. Any other reproduction or redistribution is strictly prohibited. All rights reserved.
This content is provided for test preparation purposes only and does not imply an endorsement by Mometrix of any particular political, scientific, or religious point of view.

are addressed. Student behaviors needing more specialized interventions receive better support. And all students' academic motivation and performance are optimized.

SWPBS is not a practice, intervention, or curriculum per se. It is rather an operating framework for decision-making, toward the goal of assuring access for all students to the most effective possible teaching and behavioral interventions and practices. It guides a school's choice, integration, and application of evidence-based best practices to realize all students' best academic and behavioral outcomes. Six principles guiding SWPBS are: establishing a continuum of behavioral and academic supports and interventions based on science; utilizing real data for problem-solving and decision-making; organizing environments to prevent problem behaviors from occurring or developing; encouraging and teaching pro-social behaviors and skills; accountability and fidelity in implementing evidence-based behavioral practices; and universal screening and continuous monitoring of student performance and progress. Four interrelated elements of SWPBS are: data for making decisions; measurable outcomes, which data evaluate and support; practices backed by evidence they attain from the outcomes; and systems that support implementing the practices with effectiveness and efficiency.

Problem-Solving Procedures and How to Apply Them to Conflict Resolution

The teacher introduces the topic to students by explaining that where a conflict exists, a problem exists, and that having a way to think about and try to solve a problem helps. The teacher writes three steps on the board and goes over each step with the students: (1) Define the problem; (2) Brainstorm solutions; and (3) Choose a solution and act upon it. The teacher explains that before solving a problem, people must agree to work out the problem; that for problem-solving to work, they must agree not to call names, yell, or otherwise escalate the conflict. For step (1), the teacher encourages the students to define the problem in a way that does not place blame upon others. For step (2), the teacher encourages the students to think of as many possible solutions as they can. For step (3), the teacher advises the students that they should pick a "win-win" solution wherein all parties benefit and nobody loses.

To help younger and disabled students learn how to resolve conflicts, the teacher can first teach them a three-step problem-solving approach consisting of defining the problem, brainstorming solutions, and choosing and implementing a solution. The teacher then gives students a script for a "fight"/conflict and puppets if appropriate for the students, and then has some students volunteer to act out the conflict script. Then they review the problem-solving approach. Once students agree on one or more solutions, have the volunteer players act out their choice(s). Students who are able may then work in small groups to create and perform their own conflict resolution sketches for the class. The teacher then leads a class discussion, asking the students: (1) Which things in the sketches caused the conflict to escalate; (2) Which things people can say to each other to show they want to stop fighting and solve the problem; and (3) Whether any of the students have experienced similar conflicts in their own lives and how they resolved those conflicts.

Difficulties That Students with Special Needs Encounter in Trying to Complete Activities of Daily Living (ADLs)

Many of us take activities of daily living for granted. Because we have long ago learned to do them automatically, we do not realize how complex they actually are by involving many different steps. This complexity, however, can baffle special-needs students who have not achieved automaticity. Task analysis provides a solution by separating tasks into smaller, more manageable steps. Educators must also provide support, like going over each step with the student to ensure their understanding; helping with steps the student cannot do independently; answering student questions; and monitoring that they complete all steps correctly and in the right sequence. Daily life

Copyright © Mometrix Media. You have been licensed one copy of this document for personal use only. Any other reproduction or redistribution is strictly prohibited. All rights reserved.
This content is provided for test preparation purposes only and does not imply an endorsement by Mometrix of any particular political, scientific, or religious point of view.

skills tasks can easily be connected with general education curriculum. For example, reading care instruction tags on clothing and directions on soap packages when doing laundry and discussing it with others connect with English. Measuring laundry soap, reading washing machine and dryer dials and numbers, sorting and counting clothes, and estimating washing and drying times connect with mathematics. This also applies to cooking, meal preparation, etc.

Many special-needs students encounter difficulty processing information communicated verbally; initiating activities independently; maintaining attentional focus; and completing each step in a multiple-step task. When instructing special-needs students in ADLs, educators find a valuable resource in picture cards because these convey information visually instead of only verbally; they are naturally amenable to task analysis by using one picture card for each step in a task and arranging cards in the correct sequence; and they can be integrated into visual/graphic schedules, functional communication systems, and/or story strips. "Reminder strips" are short strips of picture cards that help students follow sequential steps when they cannot remember these without visual cues. For example, for hand-washing, a reminder strip placed above a sink can include individual pictures (with word captions) of turning on water, soap, lathering hands, turning off water, and drying hands on a towel, respectively. Many online resources offer printable cards, some designed for students to color themselves, which increases their engagement, enjoyment, and ownership in the learning process.

To function independently in the home or community, special-needs students must learn such ADLs as selecting clothes suitable for the day's weather and activities; doing grocery shopping for the week; performing personal hygiene like toileting, bathing, brushing teeth, etc.; organizing and doing household chores; managing money and paying bills; taking out garbage and retrieving trash/recycling bins; cooking a simple meal; doing laundry; and others. Task analysis breaking a task down into individual steps is effective for special-needs students who otherwise have difficulty remembering all a task's parts and sequence. For example, doing laundry can be broken down into 10–12 steps. Before giving all steps to the student and supervising following them, the educator must follow these steps: Write down the steps, in chronological sequence. Assess what parts of steps the student can already do independently. Assess what steps/partial steps the student can do partly or with some adult assistance. Teach the student the steps that s/he cannot already do. Evaluate whether the instruction was effective for the student's learning.

Teaching the Daily Life Skill of Washing a Load of Laundry

(1.) Take the laundry hamper to the laundry room. (2.) Empty the hamper onto the table/floor. (3.) Sort laundry into colors and whites. (4.) Open the washing machine. (5.) Put one sorted pile (or as much of it as will fit easily) into the washer. (6.) Add laundry soap. (7.) Turn on the washer. (8.) Wait until the machine is done. (9.) Open the washer. (10.) Take the laundry out and look to make sure everything is clean. (11.) If not, remove soiled pieces and put them back into the washer for another cycle. (12.) Put laundry in the dryer.* (13.) Choose the right setting for the fabric type. (14.) If needed, set the length of drying time. (15.) Turn the dryer on. *[Alternative: Hang laundry on the clothesline to dry.] (16.) When laundry is dry, remove each piece from the dryer/clothesline. (17.) Fold each piece and put it into the hamper. (18.) Put away the clean laundry in the right closets, drawers, etc.

Teaching Students with Autism Spectrum Disorders (ASDs)

To increase progress toward independent living, two of many important areas are time management and hygiene. While parents commonly wake their children, when they get older teaching them to use an alarm clock/clock-radio frees them from depending on parents. For students with ASDs, parents may need some trial-and-error experimentation with different

Copyright © Mometrix Media. You have been licensed one copy of this document for personal use only. Any other reproduction or redistribution is strictly prohibited. All rights reserved.
This content is provided for test preparation purposes only and does not imply an endorsement by Mometrix of any particular political, scientific, or religious point of view.

loudness, sounds (e.g., beeps or buzzes or music, and music types) as many are hypersensitive to sensory stimuli. For those capable, advanced skills include setting the alarm independently and deciding when to set an alarm for by estimating the time they need. Parents/educators can also teach students to use a watch/clock to manage home/school task completion. Students having difficulty with numbers can benefit from graphic visual timers. Students also need to develop hygiene routines for bathing, using deodorant, grooming, and dressing. Many ASD students naturally have rigid behavior, find routines comforting, and are amenable to daily bathing/showering (which is easier long-term than every 2–3 days) and specific instructions, like washing each area four times.

To prepare children with disabilities for more independent living as they grow up, parents and educators can start teaching young children responsibility for their belongings. For example, when young children bring their toys with them in the car or to others' homes, they can be taught a routine to find the toy before leaving, take it to the car, and bring it inside when arriving at home. As they get older, this routine can be transferred to backpacks, school supplies, digital devices, and phones. Adults can also teach young children to employ visual cues for remembering duties. For example, they can keep medications in specific locations as reminders to take them at the specified times. They can use Post-it notes on their backpacks reminding them to pack lunch and/or bring permission slips and completed assignments to school. Adults can begin teaching food preparation and how to make noncooked snacks and sandwiches to young children. As they grow, adults can teach them to follow recipes, safely utilize kitchen tools, and cook.

Official Legal Precedent for Including School-to-Work Training in Education

President Clinton signed the School to Work Opportunities Act of 1994 (Public Law 103-239) into law. This law is a joint initiative by the US Department of Education and Department of Labor. In transitions from school to work (STW), students with disabilities may need help with environmental accommodations; job accommodations; assistive technology devices; and additional supports for full participation in STW programs based in schools and/or communities. Key issues affecting success or failure in the workplace are related to social skills, for both nondisabled and disabled workers. In fact, 75 percent of job loss within the nondisabled population is attributed to poor social interactions. Disabled students also need good awareness of their own strengths and weaknesses to succeed at work, and skills for compensating for their deficits and making the most of their talents. Survey research with employers hiring disabled workers indicates that they want employees who are dependable, on time, can follow basic directions, and get along with their coworkers.

Helping Students with Disabilities Prepare for Living Independently When They Grow Up by Teaching Them Daily Life Skills Beginning in Early Childhood

Adults can help many students with cognitive, behavioral, emotional/social, and mental health disabilities prepare for daily life. For example, for telephone skills, they can first teach young children to answer the telephone, and then take and deliver messages. As they grow, adults can help them progress with skills like calling 411 for phone numbers; calling stores in advance to ask if they have certain products in stock; calling restaurants to order takeout or delivered food; or calling technical support for help with computer issues. Adults can teach young children about walking to nearby neighborhood places; teach middle children about riding bicycles to destinations and taking public transportation when ready; and help adolescents and young adults learn to drive when appropriate. They can teach children as they grow to carry house keys, cell phones with important numbers, and money when leaving home; and personal safety, like judgment about hand-shaking versus hugging/kissing; protecting their personal information online and money in public; and what to do if followed/approached by strangers.

Copyright © Mometrix Media. You have been licensed one copy of this document for personal use only. Any other reproduction or redistribution is strictly prohibited. All rights reserved.
This content is provided for test preparation purposes only and does not imply an endorsement by Mometrix of any particular political, scientific, or religious point of view.

Jobs That Educators Can Create in and Around School Grounds to Help Teach Students with Disabilities About Career Awareness

To help prepare students with disabilities for futures in the workplace, educators can provide work experience in/around school. They can instruct them in doing laundry for the art room, gymnasium/pool, or lower grades' classrooms. Students can learn to sweep, vacuum, mop, wipe chairs and tables, and refill condiment containers in the cafeteria. Teachers can instruct students, sometimes with assistance from the custodial staff, in janitorial tasks like taking out garbage, dusting, cleaning, floor-waxing/buffing, painting, or refilling soap and paper towel dispensers. They can also enlist groundskeeper staff to help teach students seasonal outdoor tasks like weeding, mulching, mowing grass, and raking leaves. With the cooperation of office staff, teachers can instruct students in clerical tasks like preparing mail, making copies, filing, and data entry. Students can learn to help maintain school buses by vacuuming and washing. They can learn to restock vending machines; collect and count the money and deliver it; recycle materials; or construct and paint scenery and run lights for school plays/assemblies.

Introducing Elementary Age Students with Disabilities to Career Awareness and How Teachers Can Use Workplace Field Trips

When working with students with disabilities at the elementary school level, career development includes making students aware of workers in the community, and also helping them comprehend individual uniqueness, work's role in life, and fundamental knowledge about various jobs. Teachers can develop programs engaging students in activities involving adult workplaces and familiarize students with the kinds of social interactions they will experience after leaving school. Educators can also teach young students skills related to employment in the classroom, and then reinforce those skills in situations that expose them to workplace experience. Teachers can plan 1 to 3 hour field trips to visit different workplaces in their community. To prepare students, teachers can make them familiar with basic career information. After field trips, teachers can ask students questions like: What are the working environment and conditions? What abilities and skills do the jobs require? Do jobs observed primarily involve things, people, ideas, or information? Where/how can you learn skills for this occupation? Are you interested in this occupation? Why/why not?

Overall Transition Planning Process

Transition planning helps students with disabilities and their families consider students' lives after high school; identify long-term goals; tailor high school learning for acquiring skills and contacts they will need to meet those goals; and with allocation to local school districts of funding and services supporting transition processes. Students and adults invest in students' future well-being by planning for postsecondary life. The IDEA's Indicator 13 is a provision that students with disabilities age 16 and above must have IEPs including postsecondary transition plans. The US Department of Education's Office of Special Education Programs (OSEP) requires states to develop six-year State Performance Plans, based on about 20 indicators, and submit indicator data in Annual Performance Reports for Indicator 13 by February 2011. The National Secondary Transition Technical Assistance Center (NSTTAC) has developed the I-13 Checklist to aid state data collection. States may use their existing monitoring systems; however, this checklist can be used instead, or to evaluate those systems, or as a supplement, and is approved by the OSEP.

Guiding Postsecondary Transition Planning and Goals

When planning postsecondary transitions for significantly disabled students, adults should consider whether the student is able to express his/her interests. If not, educators should obtain information from parents/caregivers for planning transitions. They should consider the student's special health care needs. They must account for any challenges or needs that keep the student

Copyright © Mometrix Media. You have been licensed one copy of this document for personal use only. Any other reproduction or redistribution is strictly prohibited. All rights reserved.
This content is provided for test preparation purposes only and does not imply an endorsement by Mometrix of any particular political, scientific, or religious point of view.

from working outside of home. Transition planners must determine who can provide training and/or education to help the student's transitions. They must determine what the student can already do without others' assistance. And they must also consider what else the student could do if s/he had help from a habilitation training specialist, a job coach, a caregiver, or other service provider(s). Additional ideas for transition planning include connecting students and their families with other students who have similar disabilities and their families; identifying peer mentors for students; supplying the resources the student needs; and inviting others who can make valuable contributions to join the transition planning team.

The IDEA requires all students with disabilities to have postsecondary transition plans included in their IEPs when they are age 16 and older. When setting goals for students with disabilities to make transitions from school to work, job training and/or higher education, and community living, a few general criteria include that the goals should reflect expectations that are both high and realistic for the student. These goals should also reflect an approach for some kind of forward progress rather than a dead-end situation. When establishing postsecondary goals, the goals and objectives may be of mixed character, reflecting the ability, endurance, and stamina levels of the individual student. The transition plan can and should include external supports as needed. Transition plans can begin with more general goals and incorporate more specific details as the student comes closer to graduation. These goals may change from one school year to the next. Changes can range from minor alterations to major differences, depending on the individual student and situation.

Vocational Assessment and Planning for Postschool Transitions

Employment preparation for disabled students contains the same essential components as for nondisabled students: assessing and establishing skills; exposure to career possibilities; and awareness of aptitudes and interests. However, greater and more individualized supports for these components are involved with disabled students. Successful school-to-work transition programs require transdisciplinary, comprehensive vocational assessment to identify student skills and needs by teachers, psychologists, counselors, and representatives from vocational rehabilitation and social services agencies and community mental health/intellectual disabilities departments as well as the students, parents, employers, and business organizations. Assessment should cover academic, daily living, personal, social, occupational, and vocational skills (including performance tests and situational assessments); career maturity; vocational interests; and vocational aptitudes. A number of standardized instruments are available for assessing the latter two. Three major goals for students to learn in school activities for vocational preparation are: understanding themselves, their abilities, interests, and values; understanding the world of work; and learning good decision-making skills. These enable informed, realistic work-related decisions, and are also the main elements of career maturity.

Common Subjects Taught in School-to-Work (STW) Curricula

Some common STW curriculum subjects include employment-related functional academics; independent living skills; and interpersonal skills, since social skills are critical for nondisabled and disabled workers alike to get and keep jobs. Many opportunities connect school with work so students gain employment experience. Students can get unpaid/paid work experience through internships, structured for practically applying academic knowledge in jobs; job shadowing in one-day workplace visits and observing an employee in a specific job; or adult mentors, who serve as role models by communicating information about workplace norms, giving consistent, caring guidance and support, reviewing progress regularly, and establishing high expectations. Co-op programs combine technical and career classwork with part-time work during school years, with expectations for employers to provide and students to learn defined in training agreements. Community members visit schools on Career Days to share their experiences with interested

Copyright © Mometrix Media. You have been licensed one copy of this document for personal use only. Any other reproduction or redistribution is strictly prohibited. All rights reserved.
This content is provided for test preparation purposes only and does not imply an endorsement by Mometrix of any particular political, scientific, or religious point of view.

students. Teachers can learn of academic job preparation through unpaid/paid workplace programs. Additional opportunities include apprenticeships, on-the-job training, field trips, class speakers, school-sponsored enterprises, and health care "clinicals."

Copyright © Mometrix Media. You have been licensed one copy of this document for personal use only. Any other reproduction or redistribution is strictly prohibited. All rights reserved.
This content is provided for test preparation purposes only and does not imply an endorsement by Mometrix of any particular political, scientific, or religious point of view.

Working in the Professional Environment

History of the Philosophy of Special Education

Special education is a relatively new development in human history. Historically, people with disabilities received little or no education and were frequently placed into asylums or hospitals. The ancient Greek and Roman civilizations viewed disability as an evil omen, punishment from the gods. They viewed people as unable to change. Plato and Aristotle recommended euthanizing disabled infants. Cicero cited need for military superiority as reason to rid society of "defectives." The city/state took charge of soldiers disabled by combat. Due to ancient Greek and Roman philosophies, children born with disabilities were often drowned, "dashed against the rocks" as Homer described, thrown off cliffs, left to die on hilltops, chained up, or locked away. And fathers had the right to end a disabled child's life. In historical Christianity, while various physical ailments were treated as ritual impurities in the Old Testament, the New Testament shows Jesus healing the disabled, emphasizing their need for help and the goodness of helping them.

In Medieval times (c. 500–1500 AD), society had a rigid caste system with royalty at the top, and no education for the masses. Some people with disabilities were exterminated; others were exploited as clowns, "fools," or servants. Generally, the disabled experienced ridicule for their differences. During the Renaissance (c. 1300–1700), when interest in knowledge was reborn, the Catholic Church made the disabled wards of the state, caring for them in isolation. They received more humane treatment, but initially no education. By the Enlightenment (c. 1650–1800), philosophers like John Locke believed all knowledge was acquired through the senses and all human beings were equal. Enlightenment philosophers believed humanity did not exist without education, increasing potential opportunities. During the Renaissance, in 1578, Spanish explorer Pedro Ponce de León first documented the education of royal deaf children. In 1760 during the Enlightenment, the French Abbé de L'Épée established the first institute for the deaf. In 1829 (the Regency era), Louis Braille invented his tactile reading/writing system for the blind.

In the 1900s, the emphasis regarding disabilities was more biological than psychological or social. Hence many early pioneers of special education were both physicians and educators. Practitioners followed the medical model, and children with disabilities received institutional care. Between the 1900s and 1950s, laws made education compulsory, and educators created schools and classes for children who were blind, deaf, and mentally disabled. Following World War II, the special education system was established, with an organization parallel to the general education system. In the first of four main periods of special-needs education, children with blindness and deafness were most likely to receive instruction, while many children with other disabilities were still excluded from schools. In the second period, children with disabilities were segregated into homogeneous groups and received medical care and rehabilitation. The third period focused on normalizing and integrating the disabled into the community. In the fourth period, laws have mandated educational equality and inclusion rather than segregation in educational services for all children.

Classic "Special" Characteristics of Special Education

Characteristics of "classic" special education include special settings; for example, segregated schools, classes, or resource rooms. Children are considered special, as evidenced by the way they are categorized, which determines their eligibility for special education and related services. "Classic" special education includes special teachers as well; whether they are trained and/or have experience or not, they are designated as special education teachers. Special education also includes therapists and other specialists trained to assess and remediate various conditions that qualify children for special education and related services. Special education traditionally involves a

Copyright © Mometrix Media. You have been licensed one copy of this document for personal use only. Any other reproduction or redistribution is strictly prohibited. All rights reserved.
This content is provided for test preparation purposes only and does not imply an endorsement by Mometrix of any particular political, scientific, or religious point of view.

special teacher-student ratio: classes typically contain fewer students than general education classes, and more teachers per student. Another characteristic of special education is special teaching methods and tools; for example, Braille for the blind, sign language for the deaf, or communication boards/books/systems/software for the nonverbal. Special education also includes special goals, such as integration into the social life of the community, and special programs for teaching needed skills not normally needed by other students.

Jean-Marc Gaspard Itard

Itard was a French doctor and educator, among the first to propose and prove special teaching methods could help educate children with disabilities. From 1801–1805, Itard used systematic instructional techniques to teach communication and daily living skills to a boy named Victor, discovered in the woods, seemingly without human rearing. Itard's work was made more famous by director/actor François Truffaut in his 1970 film *L'Enfant Sauvage* (*The Wild Child*). Itard's goals were to socialize Victor, improve his awareness of environmental stimuli, expose him to ideas, teach him to communicate, and advance his thinking from concrete/simple to abstract/complex. Some successes included increased regularity and control in Victor's eating, sleeping, and personal hygiene; improved senses of taste and touch; and increased range of interests. Victor learned to sequence objects and utter a few single-syllable words. However, he never developed connected speech or emotional attachments, and longed for his previous life. Some speculate Victor had intellectual disability or autism, which would also explain why he was likely abandoned at an early age.

Maria Montessori

Maria Montessori (1870–1952), an Italian doctor and educator, developed an entire philosophy of education with procedures based on its principles. Today there are many Montessori schools worldwide. While the Montessori method is intended for the general education of all children, it has many benefits for children with disabilities and inclusive education. It is based on the way children naturally learn through exploring and experience. Montessori aimed to enable children's optimal exploration and independent learning. To this end, she proposed the concept of the "prepared environment," a learning environment designed to facilitate this learning process. This environment features an uninterrupted continuum of learning experiences. Montessori schools divide classrooms into multiple-age groups: parent and infant for ages 0–3; preschool, ages 3–6; lower elementary, ages 6–9 and upper elementary, ages 9–12; and middle school, ages 12–14. However, this series of classrooms comprise a "flow" experience, wherein the child continuously constructs and builds upon his/her learning throughout the program. Classroom materials each isolate various single qualities/concepts like color, shape, or size.

Édouard Séguin

French doctor Séguin had studied with Jean-Marc Itard, who insisted that children with disabilities could learn via special instruction. In 1848 Séguin came to America, where he developed influential principles for educating intellectually disabled and other special-needs children. In his programs, he emphasized presenting combined physical and intellectual tasks to help disabled children develop self-reliance and independence. He developed the physiological method, consisting of sensory training (particularly tactile) utilizing concrete materials, and also motor training, featuring movement from the simple to the complex, age-appropriate and functional activities, and activities involving both work and play. The major elements that made up the foundation of Séguin's educational philosophy and programs for instructing children with disabilities were: frequently changing activities; task analysis; discrimination between the senses and the intellect; sensory stimulation; physical education; and education with employment as an outcome. One can see from

Copyright © Mometrix Media. You have been licensed one copy of this document for personal use only. Any other reproduction or redistribution is strictly prohibited. All rights reserved.
This content is provided for test preparation purposes only and does not imply an endorsement by Mometrix of any particular political, scientific, or religious point of view.

these elements the importance of Séguin's contributions, as these are all still prominent aspects of special education today over 150 years later.

Advantages and Disadvantages of Segregated Settings

In some cases, special schools and classes are still used today; however, in America and many other countries, laws mandate inclusive education for students with disabilities. Before this legislation, segregation was more the norm than the exception, yielding both advantages and disadvantages. Some advantages include: giving students with disabilities more chances of success; fostering cooperation instead of competition; being able to learn physical and social skills in accepting, understanding settings; staff with specialized training, specialized equipment, and specialized services; more opportunities to improve skills needed for greater participation in more inclusive settings; easier student access to individual attention; and more opportunities to meet other students with the same disability. Disadvantages include: developing "disabled" values, attitudes, and behaviors; lowered expectations in students, parents, and educators; resistance to transferring learned skills to regular settings; depriving disabled and nondisabled children of the benefits of interacting; less preparation for future living; greater lifelong expenses; more interactions with adults than with children; and performance standards separate from "normal" standards.

Medical Model Versus the Social Model of Disability

Historically, early models of special education were based on the medical model of illness. As special education developed, the medical model came to be gradually replaced by the social model. Some key differences in these models are: The medical model viewed the child as defective, whereas the social model values the child as a unique individual. The medical model focused on diagnosing and labeling children by their disabilities; the social model strives to identify children's strengths and needs. The medical model focused on impairment; the social model focuses on identifying obstacles and developing solutions. The medical model dictated segregation and alternative services for the disabled; the social model dictates making necessary resources available to the disabled within inclusive settings. The medical model resulted in being excluded permanently from normal schools and society, or inclusion only if the individual eventually seemed sufficiently "normal" in appearance and behavior; the social model welcomes diversity. The medical model effected no social change; the social model causes society to evolve.

Culturally and Linguistically Diverse Students in Special Education Programs

For the past 30 plus years, court cases and other legal actions have been filed against the special education system over excessive placement of culturally and linguistically diverse students in disability programs. ESL, low-income, African-American, Latino, and Native American students are commonly overrepresented, particularly in programs for LDs, mild intellectual disabilities, and emotional/behavioral disorders. The National Center for Culturally Responsive Educational Systems (NCCREST) advises parents to consult school administrators and/or parent advocates to investigate whether their school has this problem, because researchers disagree about formulae for assessing overrepresentation. However, they also offer one formula for calculating overrepresentation probability: using low-income students as an example, divide their number placed in (for example) LD classes by their total number in the school = percent placed in LD; calculate the same percentage of average income students in LD classes the same way; and divide the low-income percentage by the average income percentage. A result of + 1.0 indicates equal probabilities of special education placement; > 1.0 indicates greater placement probability for lower income students.

Copyright © Mometrix Media. You have been licensed one copy of this document for personal use only. Any other reproduction or redistribution is strictly prohibited. All rights reserved.
This content is provided for test preparation purposes only and does not imply an endorsement by Mometrix of any particular political, scientific, or religious point of view.

Principle Related to Behavior Management

The Council for Exceptional Children's Code of Ethics states this principle: "Special education professionals participate with other professionals and...parents in an interdisciplinary effort in the management of behavior." No one approach works with all students in all situations. While classroom management interventions may be ideally designed and implemented, not addressing individual children's needs and wants limits their effects. Hence one/several students in a class/setting may need behavior management strategies targeting specific behaviors. Cognitive interventions can affect emotional behaviors and psychomotor interventions can influence cognitive and affective development. Educators, parents, and others frequently ask about changing individual and group student behaviors; whether to punish or ignore behaviors; whether to discuss behaviors with students; and whether interventions are ethical, harmful, or effective. CEC suggests an educator activity like the following. Small groups list target behaviors and individual/group interventions, discussing whether these treat students with dignity, teach new skills, and support/need environmental analysis; whether student responses are clear to everybody, including students; whether educators respond sequentially to target behaviors (e.g., the second time a behavior occurs).

International Declarations That Address Children's Rights to Inclusive Educations

Internationally, in 1948, the Universal Declaration of Human Rights addressed rights to inclusive education, as did the UN Convention on the Rights of the Child in 1989. In 1990, the World Declaration for Education for All addressed inclusion. In 1993, the Standard Rules on the Equalization of Opportunities for Persons with Disability established rights of disabled people to equal opportunities in education and employment. In 1994, UNESCO (the United Nations Educational, Scientific, and Cultural Organization) issued the Salamanca Statement and Framework for Action on every child's basic rights to education, stating that educational systems and programs should address children's diversities; special-needs students require adaptations enabling regular school access; and inclusive regular schools most effectively fight and prevent discrimination and make society inclusive. Significant US laws include Section 504 of the 1973 Rehabilitation Act; the Education for all Handicapped Children Act (EHA) (1975/1986); the Americans with Disabilities Act (ADA, 1990); the Individuals with Disabilities Education Act (IDEA, 1997/2004); and the No Child Left Behind (NCLB, 2001) Act.

Trends Related to Technology, Inclusion, and Early Intervention

Technological progress has afforded increased opportunities for both students and teachers in special education. Computer software programs enable students with speech and language and visual disabilities to convert text to speech; hearing-impaired students to convert speech to text; and ESL students to read translations in their native languages. Websites offer students more independent schoolwork at their own pace; multimodal presentations for LD students; and the ability for ADHD students to alternate among shorter units and topics. Students with auditory processing difficulties, and teachers needing more instructional materials, can access more graphic/visual stimuli online. The Internet also facilitates student/parent/teacher access to advocates, support groups, and organizations. Trends are increasingly toward inclusion, with more students mainstreamed than ever. Special classes and schools exist when needs require/parents prefer, but the IDEA's LRE requirement moves more students into regular education classes/curricula/schools. Whereas learning disabilities were previously identified and services recommended in upper-elementary grades or later, today screening, assessment, identification, and intervention are advised by early childhood or even earlier.

Copyright © Mometrix Media. You have been licensed one copy of this document for personal use only. Any other reproduction or redistribution is strictly prohibited. All rights reserved.
This content is provided for test preparation purposes only and does not imply an endorsement by Mometrix of any particular political, scientific, or religious point of view.

Classroom and Behavior Management Techniques

According to researchers (e.g., Smith & Rivera, 1995), to establish/maintain classroom order, teachers should develop positive atmospheres and foundations of positive learning environments; use preventive techniques; develop collaboration with parents and other professionals around disciplinary issues; make sure interventions are appropriate to the problems they address; and regularly evaluate student progress. The goal of behavior management strategies is self-discipline, defined as gaining control over one's behavior in varied situations with various groups and individuals. Some ethical concerns include questions like these: Who decides who will manage behavior and whose behavior will be managed? How can others control behavior managers? Which interventions will be used, and who decides on accepted interventions? For what goals/purposes will interventions be implemented? Are/should children be free to make choices? Are student actions observable, measurable, repeated, and congruent with behavioral principles? In schools: Can externals—educators, peers, parents—change student behavior? Who decides which/whose behaviors to change? What interventions are used in classrooms? And who monitors them?

Professional and Ethical Guidelines Related to Behavior Management

Educators should always explore alternate behavioral interventions before considering any aversive methods. When considering/planning behavioral interventions, educators should first explore any possible injury or side effects these could cause. Before arranging contingencies to apply to student behaviors, educators should discern whether the student understands the contingency. Anyone implementing any behavioral intervention with a student must both have sufficient training in the procedures and feel comfortable applying the intervention. Interventions should be backed by empirical evidence of their effectiveness; be consistent with student programs and parental input; and have written informed parental consent. Behavioral intervention programs must be closely monitored and thoroughly documented. Procedures of legal due process and committee reviews should be followed. Behavioral interventions/programs should comply with the IDEA's Least Restrictive Environment requirement. Interventions should be commensurate with relative seriousness of the behavior; afford student opportunity to succeed; respect individual student worth and dignity; be fair; and address the principle of normalization (disabled students have rights to lives as close to normal as possible).

Under its ethical principle regarding behavior management, the Council for Exceptional Children (CEC) includes the following: (1) Professionals must use only behavioral procedures and disciplinary techniques they have been told to use, and that do not compromise individual student dignity or exceptional students' fundamental human rights (e.g., corporal punishment). (2) Professionals must specify clearly in the student's IEP any goals and objectives related to behavior management. (3) Professionals must comply with rules, statutes, and policies of state and local agencies regarding appropriately applying behavioral and disciplinary practices. (4) When they perceive a coworker's behavior as detrimental to special education students, professionals must take sufficient measures for preventing, discouraging, and intervening with those actions. (4) Professionals must avoid using aversive methods, unless repeated uses of other techniques were ineffective, and then only after consulting with parents and applicable agency officials.

Areas Wherein Children Have Rights Educators Must Observe

According to the Council for Exceptional Children, children have rights in the areas of normalization, fairness, and respect. The principle of normalization means that a person with a disability has the right to develop a life that is as close as possible to that of normal persons. The principle of fairness includes not only basic fairness, but also the due process of law. Educators must determine whether a specific intervention they choose for modifying a student's behavior is fair to the student as an individual. The principle of respect means the student has the right to be

Copyright © Mometrix Media. You have been licensed one copy of this document for personal use only. Any other reproduction or redistribution is strictly prohibited. All rights reserved.
This content is provided for test preparation purposes only and does not imply an endorsement by Mometrix of any particular political, scientific, or religious point of view.

treated as a human being rather than a statistic or an animal. Educators must measure any intervention in light of this principle. For example, physical or psychological punishment, segregation or isolation, medication, shock, restraints, or other punishments usually violate this principle. Ethics encompassing these principles dictate that in behavior management procedures, the means do NOT justify the end unless the principles of normalization, fairness, and respect have been met.

Legal Requirements of School Districts and Some of the Legal Rights of the Parents

Under current federal laws, all public school districts are required to invite parental participation in meetings regarding the evaluation, identification, and placement of their children in special education; notify parents in writing of any intentions to identify/assess/place their child in special education or change their identification/assessment/placement; notify parents in native languages/formats they understand; inform parents of resources available to help them understand written school notifications; and give parents copies of their legal rights and responsibilities and all procedural safeguards. Parents have the right to give written consent for referral, evaluation, re-evaluation, and placement in special education of their children; review all educational records regarding these; have interpreters supplied when they are not native English speakers; contribute input to all assessments, conversations, and decisions, initially and/or subsequently; request independent evaluations not paid by them if they disagree with district evaluation/diagnosis; participate in eligibility determination and placement; receive copies of evaluations, reports, and eligibility determination documents; and receive regular progress reports during their children's special education program placement.

Special Education Ethical Code Addressing Confidentiality

The National Association of Special Education Teachers (NASET)'s Code of Ethics contains six principles. Principle 5 states: "NASET Members collaborate with parents of children with special needs and community, building trust and respecting confidentiality." Under this principle, subsection 5-E states, "NASET Members respect the private nature of the special knowledge they have about children and their families and use that knowledge only in the students' best interests." (2006/2007, NASET) The Family Educational Rights and Privacy Act (FERPA, 1974, aka Buckley Amendment) is the primary legislation delimiting accessibility and disclosure of student records. Privacy regarding student participation in evaluation, analysis, and surveys is defined by the Grassley Amendment (1994) to the Goals 2000: Educate America Act of 1994. Records of student drug and alcohol treatment kept by any entity receiving federal funding have protection under the Drug Abuse Office and Treatment Act (1976). In addition to these laws, the Individuals with Disabilities Education Act (IDEA, 1997/2004) protects the confidentiality of records for students receiving special education and related services.

Communicating and Collaborating with Students and Their Families

A school's principal should advocate strongly for the well-being and interests of culturally and linguistically diverse students receiving special education and related services. Parents and teachers should consider how the principal shows her/his commitment in this respect. A school's curriculum should reflect the viewpoints, contributions, and experiences of diverse linguistic and ethnic groups. Parents should consider whether a school's principal and staff blame diverse students or their families for different educational performance levels, and whether schools pressure diverse families to embrace school values, or work to incorporate cultural and language differences into their instructional programs. It is important to look for ways in which school administrators and staff demonstrate respect for language and cultural differences. Parents will want to consider whether the environment of a given school is orderly and safe for their children.

Copyright © Mometrix Media. You have been licensed one copy of this document for personal use only. Any other reproduction or redistribution is strictly prohibited. All rights reserved.
This content is provided for test preparation purposes only and does not imply an endorsement by Mometrix of any particular political, scientific, or religious point of view.

Additionally, a school should demonstrate high expectations and provide sufficient achievable curricular challenges, both supported by evidence, for all of its students.

Approaches to Prevent Student Problems in Learning and Behavior

A school should recognize and incorporate cultural and linguistic differences in their practices related to assessment, curriculum planning and design, and instruction. Considering the demographics of American society today, all/most schools should have ESL programs. Classroom instruction and other school functions should include languages other than English. Schools should have support systems in addition to special education, such as tutoring programs, teacher assistance teams, and bilingual education programs. Schools should collaborate with their communities in established programs. They should also support their teachers via professional development offerings that respond to needs expressed by faculty members and continuing collaboration and consultation of teachers with other professionals. Educators should build upon students' existing knowledge and use interactive discourse to promote both fundamental and higher order student skills for reading, math, and writing. Schools should systematically and continually evaluate student progress and the quality of their programs. Decision-making should include all relevant stakeholders. School educators should include cooperative learning methods and thematic instructional techniques in their teaching.

Assessment Regarding Eligibility for Special Education Services

The assessment stage is when professionals collect data used to determine or rule out disability; therefore, parents and cultural diversity experts should be included in the assessment team. Assessment plans should always include multiple instruments and settings to be comprehensive and reflect multiple perspectives and approaches. How student difficulties are addressed and what consequences result across various settings should also be considered. Suspected disabilities in ELLs should be assessed in a student's dominant language. Educators should gather data on student proficiency and educational achievement in both his/her first language and English. Assessment teams must obtain parental perceptions, beliefs, values, and expectations about children's learning/behavioral challenges. Schools should avoid interpreters and test translations. However, if these are unavoidable, they should document interpreter skills; ensure multiple formal and informal assessments and information sources; use peers from normative groups; and, if tests are invalidated, seek performance patterns rather than absolute scores. With behavioral referrals, educators should consider obtaining more information to corroborate interpretations of projective instruments, which can be subjective.

Eligibility Determination and Placement in Special Education Programs/Services

Parents of culturally and linguistically diverse backgrounds should become involved in all stages of the special education process if their children are referred. In addition to being included on referral and assessment teams, parents as well as cultural diversity experts should be included in decision-making for eligibility determination and placement. This team should consider whether a student's difficulties are caused by a possible disability, cultural/social differences, or both. Immigration, switching schools, and school absences should be considered. Evidence of different sources of student difficulty should be provided. If a student is identified with a disability, parents should determine whether the school has specific plans for reviewing the student's circumstances in the future, determining whether the student might be reclassified. If a student is determined eligible for special education, parents should know whether team members work for placement in the least restrictive environment and seek proof/evidence of such efforts. They should find out if students with the same disability type and age are placed in similar programs and why..

Copyright © Mometrix Media. You have been licensed one copy of this document for personal use only. Any other reproduction or redistribution is strictly prohibited. All rights reserved.
This content is provided for test preparation purposes only and does not imply an endorsement by Mometrix of any particular political, scientific, or religious point of view.

Considerations Related to the Special Education Referral Process

Because diverse students are frequently overrepresented in special education referrals, their parents should be included on referral teams, as well as persons with expertise regarding cultural diversity. Educators should review these factors before recommending comprehensive evaluations: the school and classroom climate; all attempts at pre-referral intervention and their results; any temporary problems in the classroom, home, and/or community; educator effort in building on students' cultural experiences and knowledge and their strengths; and observations by parents when possible, and by qualified others with knowledge of cultural differences, of the student's current classroom—particularly if the referral is for behavior management, as these problems can be influenced by teacher behavior management approaches. In addition, it is only appropriate to refer ESL/ELL students if: students have good communication skills in their native languages but are behind peers in English, and instructional adaptations have been implemented; students are academically proficient in English, receive effective reading instruction, and still demonstrate significant reading problems; and/or effective ESL or bilingual instruction do not improve academic English-language skills.

Collaboration with General Educators

As all teachers have various strengths and needs, special educators should share these. General educators are likely less familiar with specialized resources for matching practices to student skill levels when these are far beneath grade level; special educators are likely less acquainted with the richness of grade-level projects and activities. Both types of teachers can pool their knowledge of proactive/preventive and disciplinary techniques, and two pairs of eyes can better prevent misbehavior and identify desirable behavior to reinforce. General educators have training in using and instructing students with many kinds of software; special educators contribute working familiarity with assistive technology. For routine planning, special and general educators can help each other develop simple student routines. While structure and content often easily combine in general education, special-needs students must learn how assignment directions are structured before addressing assignment contents. Teachers can use tracing/matching routines to plan independent student activities. Praise motivates teachers as well as students: collaborating special and general educators should regularly praise each other's successes verbally.

When collaborating, teachers must schedule *at least* one weekly planning session, even if it must be after school. Co-teachers will fail through unmet expectations and lack of communication without such planning. As in any relationship, co-teachers do not know everything about one another. They must share their ideas and experiences, not only to succeed in teaching their students, but to understand their own teaching and learning processes and to experience job satisfaction. Teacher collaboration processes will undergo changes, just as students discover new concepts over time through their teachers and their instructional methods. While these changes mean that co-teachers and students alike will encounter surprises and adjustments, they also mean that teachers will develop better ways of meeting student needs. Collaboration also affords teachers new perspectives. They can take advantage of these by making focused observations and asking reflective questions whenever not directly occupied in instructional delivery. Taking brief but specific notes helps co-teachers discuss observations later, troubleshoot/problem-solve, fine-tune instruction, and communicate student successes.

Collaborating with Community Agencies

When special education students have already had interactions with some government departments like the juvenile justice system, the mental health system, or the department of social services, those agencies may initiate contact with schools/teachers. In other cases, educators may need to contact them. Community agencies dedicated to children with disabilities and all those

Copyright © Mometrix Media. You have been licensed one copy of this document for personal use only. Any other reproduction or redistribution is strictly prohibited. All rights reserved.
This content is provided for test preparation purposes only and does not imply an endorsement by Mometrix of any particular political, scientific, or religious point of view.

working with/for them serve as liaisons/links to public and private schools and government departments, local officials, and legislators. Some community agencies offer services like direct representation; educators can invite them to IEP meetings and due process mediations and hearings on behalf of disabled students and their families to ensure effective advocacy, information, and support. Teachers can help get parents training on their rights and special education services from community agencies. Community agencies can provide professional educators and families with consultations on technical assistance for students with disabilities. If parents and school districts disagree, educators can enlist mediation services from some community agencies to prevent escalation into court cases.

Working with General Education Teachers Regarding Curriculum and Volunteers Regarding Data Collection

Many special educators, such as special education resource teachers, often teach students in multiple grades. To support their students' various educational needs, the special education teacher must know the general education curriculum. When this teacher works with multiple grade levels, s/he has to know multiple different curricula. This teacher must also collaborate with all students' general classroom teachers to ensure s/he supports what they teach. This entails both making time and being organized to speak with each teacher individually. Special education teachers must also provide data for each student, to document instruction that implements the student's IEP and document their reports of student success or difficulty in each area. They must monitor data collection, analyze data, and adjust instruction accordingly. They need the cooperation of general education teachers in collecting data when they are not in the general classrooms with students. While parents/others may volunteer to help collect data, special education confidentiality laws can prohibit volunteers without permission from the parents of every student in class.

Tips for Special and General Educators Who Collaborate in Classrooms to Make the Most of Their Co-Teaching in Meeting Student Needs

Regardless of which co-teacher is leading a lesson/activity at the time, both should be actively interacting with students, which includes physical movement: one's viewpoint is narrowed when sitting at one's desk/in a classroom corner, whereas moving about enables a global view. Co-teachers should determine shared organizational goals and periodically review these. During the school year, considering organization is often sacrificed under time pressures; however, small enhancements in organization can have major influences. Co-teachers can examine their total classroom environment for smooth flow of activities and how well students stay organized. Special educators can contribute techniques to establish regular external structures for students with deficits in executive functioning who do not generate such structure internally. They can help general education teachers with monitoring students and supporting their organizational needs through simple structures incorporating task analysis for following step-by-step routines, visual cues, and instruction in self-monitoring routines. Co-teachers should reflect on their entire process, analyze it, and respond. They can experiment with co-teaching methods they could not use individually.

Challenges and Considerations for Special Education Teachers in Working with Other Professionals, Teaching Aides, Assistants, and Paraprofessionals

When educational research investigates high turnover rates among special educators, some researchers have thought the voluminous paperwork in special education was responsible, only to hear from some special education teachers that they attribute turnover more to being appreciated less than general education teachers. Special education teachers often must coordinate their schedules with art teachers, music teachers, physical education teachers, and 10–20 other teachers, and also show consideration to physical therapists, occupational therapists, and speech-language

Copyright © Mometrix Media. You have been licensed one copy of this document for personal use only. Any other reproduction or redistribution is strictly prohibited. All rights reserved.
This content is provided for test preparation purposes only and does not imply an endorsement by Mometrix of any particular political, scientific, or religious point of view.

pathologists, as well as accounting for lunch and recess when making resource schedules. Even minor changes in general education teachers' schedules can alter the special education teacher's whole day or week. Most special education teachers are enormously grateful to their aides, assistants, and paraprofessionals; however, the reality is they must also devote significantly more time and effort to train them and create daily schedules for them. A teacher's aide differing in opinion from the teacher's, especially if the aide is older/more experienced than the teacher, presents an additional challenge to teamwork, for which the teacher is responsible.

Standards for the Credentials and Employment of Special Education Professionals

Some of the Council for Exceptional Children practice standards for special education professionals in credentials and employment include: represent oneself accurately, legally, and ethically regarding their expertise and knowledge to prospective employers; assure that those representing themselves and/or practicing as special education administrators, teachers, and related service providers have the qualifications of professional credentials; operate within their limits of professional skills and knowledge, and appropriately seek consultation and/or support from sources outside themselves as necessary; comply with contractual terms of employment; comply with policies and contracts of local education agencies for notifying them when terminating their positions; advocate for supportive and suitable educational conditions, and for staffing resources sufficient to keep absences of support staff or substitute teachers from causing special education services to be denied; and get professional help for personal problems affecting work performance.

CEC's Standards Applying to Special Education Professionals in the Areas of Credentials and Employment

In addition to nine others, the CEC (Council for Exceptional Children) identifies standards for special education professionals that include: documenting and reporting objectively any deficits in resources, and offering solutions for these to their supervisors/administrators; evaluating employment applicants and grievances objectively, without discrimination; utilizing established procedures to resolve professional workplace problems; expecting their responsibilities to be conveyed to coworkers, and assuring their understanding and respect of those responsibilities; requesting clear written statements of their employment conditions, duties, and responsibilities; participating actively in planning, management, and evaluation of special education programs and general education programs, and in associated policy development; expecting sufficient support and supervision for special education professionals, and for programs delivered by qualified professionals in special education; and expecting there to be clearly defined chains of accountability and responsibility regarding the supervision and administration of professionals in special education.

Tools Whereby Special Educators Can Engage in Self-Assessments of Their Own Work

Many school districts and systems have created self-assessment rubrics or instruments for special educators. These instruments generally list specific standards for an array of required skills and knowledge, including operational definitions that describe what knowledge, skills, and behaviors the special educator should demonstrate. These descriptions are accompanied by incremental rating scales. The educator reads each competency and checks a box corresponding to whether s/he thinks s/he, for example, models it, adjusts upon reflecting, and is a resource for others (the highest score); or works independently to apply the competency across settings and self-initiates planning (the second highest); applies the competency with support and shows emerging self-initiation of planning (the middle score); understands and tries to apply the competency, and uses resources for improving his/her teaching (the second lowest); or is aware of the competency but

Copyright © Mometrix Media. You have been licensed one copy of this document for personal use only. Any other reproduction or redistribution is strictly prohibited. All rights reserved.
This content is provided for test preparation purposes only and does not imply an endorsement by Mometrix of any particular political, scientific, or religious point of view.

has no experience in and/or does not demonstrate it (the lowest score). Another example states competence areas for self-rating as highly effective, effective, minimally effective, or ineffective.

Standards for the Professional Development of Special Education Professionals

In the area of professional development, the Council for Exceptional Children (CEC) has standards that include: systematically keeping individualized plans for their own professional development, designing these to increase their own skills, knowledge, and cultural competence to sustain high competency levels; keeping current in their knowledge of laws, policies, and procedures related to their practices; systematically and objectively evaluating themselves, their coworkers, and their programs and services to enhance their professional performance continually; advocating for effective, schoolwide professional development and individual professional development plans being provided by their employing agencies; participating in supervised, systematic field experiences for special education professional candidates as a part of their educator preparation degree and certification programs; and functioning as mentors for other special educators in whichever times, places, and circumstances that their doing so is appropriate.

Special education professionals cannot allow their training, knowledge, and expertise to remain at the same level throughout their working lives as when they received their degrees and certification and began working. They must continually update, improve, and expand their skills, both to remain current in this dynamic, changing profession and to grow as educators. Special education professionals acquire and apply knowledge about developmental levels and readiness for various instructional interventions. They learn about research evidence-based instructional strategies, and then apply these for teaching fundamental skills in literacy and numeracy to students with special needs. They know how to individualize their instruction for each student, and they continue to learn new strategies and techniques to improve this individualization process. They assess student progress on an ongoing basis and refine their assessment techniques to increase their accuracy and applications to adjustments and modifications in their instructional approaches. They make use of data and continually inform themselves of newer data from emergent research to apply to their problem-solving endeavors. They prepare students to become independent.

Improving Professional Skills and Engaging in Lifelong Professional Growth

A number of organizations offer professional development courses. For example, the National Association of Special Education Teachers (NASET) has many classes. Professionals can learn more about modifications for alternative assessments; the annual and triennial review processes; assistive technologies for students with disabilities; ADHD, anxiety disorders, autism, pervasive developmental disorders, bipolar disorder, depression, Down syndrome, eating disorders, emotional disturbances, epilepsy, LDs, intellectual disabilities, orthopedic impairments, multiple disabilities, PTSD, Rett syndrome, schizophrenia, speech-language disorders, spina bifida, Tourette syndrome, traumatic brain injuries, blindness and visual impairments, deafness and hearing impairments, and deaf-blindness; auditory processing disorders; developmental and psychological disorders in special education; criteria for eligibility determination for special education services related to each disability; educational implications of some disorders; factors influencing curriculum for special-needs students; identification of high-risk students in classrooms; developing, writing, implementing, reviewing, and modifying IEPs; medications; services related to special education; team transitional planning; and helping students cope with disasters and violence.

Copyright © Mometrix Media. You have been licensed one copy of this document for personal use only. Any other reproduction or redistribution is strictly prohibited. All rights reserved.
This content is provided for test preparation purposes only and does not imply an endorsement by Mometrix of any particular political, scientific, or religious point of view.

Strategies for Special Educators to Reflect on Their Own Effectiveness in Their Work

Research finds viewing video recordings of their teaching practices in combination with collaborative professional development courses and activities helps teachers enhance and change their practices. In one pilot study (Osipova, et al, 2011) teachers viewed many video recordings of themselves teaching throughout the school year. They self-reflected, noting what they did effectively, generating suggestions for future teaching, and rating their instruction. The researchers found this process altered teachers' initial self-reflections overestimating their practices to more critical self-examinations. It changed teachers' self-reflection comments, vague at first, to more specific descriptions. Teachers particularly realized they attended to certain students and not others. Because not all teachers apply what they learn in professional development to their classroom practices, researchers find guided/coached critical self-reflection instrumental for changing teacher beliefs about learning and teaching, which are frequently unspoken and even unconscious. Teachers are more likely to change their practices once they change their beliefs, and also when they view themselves as learners. Video self-reflection affords self-analyses with multiple foci, and also repeated self-analyses of teaching practices.

Professional Advice for Parents Whose Child Is Diagnosed with an ASD

The National Institute of Mental Health recommends that, because remembering everything they need to know about the most helpful available resources is difficult, parents should keep notebooks and write everything down. Keeping records of physicians' reports and evaluations helps document needs for special services. The more parents learn, the better they can advocate for their child. For children under age 3, each US state has an early intervention program and determines its lead agency. Services are detailed in an Individualized Family Service Plan (IFSP). The IDEA 2004 law requires public school districts to provide children with disabilities a free and appropriate public education, including special services from speech and occupational therapists, school psychologists, social workers, and nurses or aides as needed. The law also requires public schools to develop Individualized Education Programs (IEPs) for children in special education programs. Parents should participate as members of the team developing the IEP.

Considerations for Families Having One Child with an ASD Who Are Wondering Whether or Not to Have Another Child

Some psychologists describe risks of autism in a second child as a "genetic lottery." Research finds that the chance of having a child who will be diagnosed with ASD is one in 150 to one in 100. The probability of having a second child with ASD is more than 5%. While this is a serious consideration, still, the probability of having a normal child is 90%. Psychologists note the impact of individual differences on families: Some cope well with autism; others are overwhelmed. Some with more than one ASD child appreciate each child's uniqueness; others regret having another child; others feel renewed after having a second, non-ASD child. Although having an ASD sibling can be difficult for a typical child, many children with special-needs siblings develop tolerance and maturity superior to that of the general population, becoming their best model, teacher, and advocate, which is something for parents to consider.

Advice from a Family Therapist for Parents of Children with ASD

Through the advocacy organization Autism Speaks, Dr. Kathryn Smerling offers these five tips for parents of ASD children: (1) Take advantage of all available community services. Practitioners/providers can teach and help parents. Parents gain strength from the people they meet. They should be informed and learn to be their child's best advocates. (2) Parents should discuss their feelings, not avoid them. Conflicting emotions are normal. Parents should try not to

Copyright © Mometrix Media. You have been licensed one copy of this document for personal use only. Any other reproduction or redistribution is strictly prohibited. All rights reserved.
This content is provided for test preparation purposes only and does not imply an endorsement by Mometrix of any particular political, scientific, or religious point of view.

displace their anger at the disorder onto their family members. (3) Parents should support and spend quality time with all family members, and not let preoccupation with ASD consume their entire lives. (4) Parents should love their ASD child for who he is, not compare them to other children, and proudly celebrate each small success, focusing on their abilities, not disabilities. (5) Parents should become engaged with the autism community. Other parents provide support; advocacy empowers parents and is productive.

Dr. Kathryn Smerling offers this advice to siblings: They should accept and be proud of their ASD sibling. They should also know it is okay to feel positive and negative feelings about them. Talking openly and comfortably about autism with peers will make them comfortable too, while being embarrassed will make them feel awkward about it. Being angry/upset for long times does not change circumstances, only increasing siblings' unhappiness. Additionally, they should realize their parents may also have such feelings. Smerling advises siblings to spend time alone with their parents; they also need to feel important. She points out they would need this even if their sibling did not have ASD. She also recommends finding an activity they can do together with their ASD sibling, which creates connection and closeness between them. This will enhance their relationship, and will be rewarding for both the ASD sibling and the typical sibling.

Collaborative Programs of Excellence in Autism

The Collaborative Programs of Excellence in Autism research program (CPEA) is funded by the National Institute of Child Health and Human Development (NICHD) and the National Institute on Deafness and Other Communication Disorders (NIDCD) Network on the Neurobiology and Genetics of Autism, which are both agencies of the National Institute of Mental Health (NIMH). The CPEA program has recently been conducting research studies of the largest group in the world of individuals with autism spectrum disorders who have been definitively diagnosed as such, based on their comprehensive developmental and genetic profiles. Data the CPEA produces will be analyzed at a data coordination center. The CPEA program has centers that are located at Boston University, Massachusetts; University of California (UC) Davis; UC Irvine; UCLA; Yale University, Connecticut; University of Washington, Seattle; University of Rochester, New York; University of Texas, Houston; University of Pittsburgh, Pennsylvania; and University of Utah, Salt Lake City.

National Institute of Mental Health (NIMH)

NIMH advises that when professionals recommend any treatment program for their ASD child, parents should ask them the following things: How effective the program has been for other ASD children; how many children in this program have progressed to regular schools, and how they have performed there; whether the program's staff have training and experience working with autistic children and teenagers; how the program's activities are planned and organized; whether the program's daily routines and schedules are predictable; how much individual attention their child will be given; how progress is measured in this program; whether the child's behavior will be carefully observed and documented; whether the program affords tasks and rewards that are personally motivational to their child; whether the program's environment is designed for minimal distractions; whether the program prepares parents to continue treatment at home; what the program costs, where it is located, and the time commitment required.

Children's Health Act of 2000

The Children's Health Act of 2000 established the Interagency Autism Coordinating Committee (IACC). Charged by Congress with developing a 10-year agenda for autism research, IACC presented its "matrix/roadmap" at the first Autism Summit Conference in 2003, defining research priorities for years 1-3, 4-6, and 7-10. IACC includes directors of five NIH agencies: National Institute of Mental Health (NIMH), National Institute of Neurological Disorders and Stroke, National Institute

Copyright © Mometrix Media. You have been licensed one copy of this document for personal use only. Any other reproduction or redistribution is strictly prohibited. All rights reserved.
This content is provided for test preparation purposes only and does not imply an endorsement by Mometrix of any particular political, scientific, or religious point of view.

on Deafness and Other Communication Disorders (NIDCD), National Institute of Child Health and Human Development (NICHD), and National Institute of Environmental Health Sciences (NIEHS). It also includes representatives from the Health Resource Services Administration, National Center on Birth Defects and Developmental Disabilities (part of the Centers for Disease Control), Agency for Toxic Substances and Disease Registry, Substance Abuse and Mental Health Services Administration, Administration on Developmental Disabilities, Centers for Medicare and Medicaid Services, US Food and Drug Administration, and US Department of Education.

Studies to Advance Autism Research and Treatment (STAART) Network

The STAART Network was established by the Interagency Autism Coordinating Committee (IACC), a group composed of directors of five NIH agencies concerned with developmental disabilities, neurological disorders, communication disorders, mental health, child health and human development, and environmental health; and representatives from eight other government agencies related to health resource services, developmental disabilities, disease registry, mental health, Medicare and Medicaid, education, and food and drugs. Eight network centers make up the STAART Network, each conducting its own combination of studies and also participating in multi-center clinical trials. Fields of research include genetics, developmental neurobiology, and psychopharmacology. Center locations are at Yale University in Connecticut; University of South Carolina, Chapel Hill; University of Washington, Seattle; University of California, Los Angeles (UCLA); Mount Sinai Medical School, New York; Kennedy Krieger Institute, Maryland; Boston University, Massachusetts; and University of Rochester, New York. STAART data gathered will be analyzed by a data coordination center.

Copyright © Mometrix Media. You have been licensed one copy of this document for personal use only. Any other reproduction or redistribution is strictly prohibited. All rights reserved.
This content is provided for test preparation purposes only and does not imply an endorsement by Mometrix of any particular political, scientific, or religious point of view.

MTTC Practice Test

1. Which of the following is a sign of atypical gross motor development in a child?

a. The child cannot sit up without support by the age of 5 months.
b. The child cannot pull up on furniture to stand around 9 months.
c. The child cannot raise his or her head while lying on the stomach by 2 months.
d. The child cannot walk independently past the age of 24 months.

2. In typical cognitive development, when are children most likely to understand abstract concepts?

a. By around 11 to 12 years of age
b. By around 9 to 10 years of age
c. By around 7 to 8 years of age
d. By around 5 to 6 years of age

3. In psychosocial development, during which of Erikson's stages is a child typically most occupied with the tasks of making new friends and succeeding in school?

a. Trust versus mistrust
b. Autonomy versus shame or doubt
c. Initiative versus guilt
d. Industry versus inferiority

4. Which of the following milestones in normal language development occurs latest?

a. Babies develop different crying sounds to express different needs.
b. Babies use their eyes to follow the directions of sounds they hear.
c. Babies make gurgling sounds when playing with parents and alone.
d. Babies turn to look in the directions of the sounds that they hear.

5. In normal sensory development, which of these represents the correct sequence from earliest to latest?

a. Full taste sensitivity; identifying some foods by smell; distinguishing sizes and shapes by touch; hearing the full range of sound frequencies; full visual acuity
b. Full visual acuity; hearing the full range of sound frequencies; identifying some foods by smell; full taste sensitivity; distinguishing sizes and shapes by touch
c. Hearing the full range of sound frequencies; full taste sensitivity; full visual acuity; distinguishing sizes and shapes by touch; identifying some foods by smell
d. Identifying some foods by smell; full taste sensitivity; full visual acuity; distinguishing sizes and shapes by touch; hearing the full range of sound frequencies

6. Which of these is accurate about a student with a diagnosis of Asperger's syndrome?

a. This student will have more intellectual impairments than others on the autism spectrum.
b. This student has a diagnosis of a separate disorder that is not part of the autism spectrum.
c. This student is more impulsive with shorter attention than others on the autism spectrum.
d. This student is more likely to function highly than many others do on the autism spectrum.

Copyright © Mometrix Media. You have been licensed one copy of this document for personal use only. Any other reproduction or redistribution is strictly prohibited. All rights reserved.
This content is provided for test preparation purposes only and does not imply an endorsement by Mometrix of any particular political, scientific, or religious point of view.

7. Of the following, which is most characteristic of speech–language development in autism spectrum disorder (ASD) students?

a. Being completely nonverbal or only speaking in echolalia (i.e., repeating what others say)
b. Having advanced vocabulary and fluent speech but difficulty with two-way conversations
c. Being able to conduct normal conversations but having singsong or quirky speech patterns
d. Having all of these characteristic

8. Among effects of autism spectrum disorder (ASD) on receptive language development, which of these is MOST common?

a. Students with ASD understand emotional content like humor and sarcasm better than technical jargon.
b. Students with ASD understand word meanings better than nonverbal facial and body language cues.
c. Students with ASD who have difficulty noticing or understanding nonverbal content cannot learn this.
d. Students with ASD typically can interpret social customs better than emotions from nonverbal signals.

9. What is MOST accurate regarding the implications of autism spectrum disorder (ASD) for various aspects of an individual's life?

a. Career is most severely affected as ASD individuals cannot focus attention for long.
b. Family life shows profound impacts as many ASD individuals do not experience love.
c. Social relationships are significantly affected by ASD difficulties with social behaviors.
d. Recreation is an especially problematic area because individuals with ASD lack leisure interests.

10. Which of the following is MOSTLY an educational implication of autism spectrum disorder (ASD) student characteristics?

a. Educators will need to use strategies to help ASD students with transitions between activities.
b. Educators will need to amplify all of the sensory modalities to secure ASD students' attention.
c. Educators will need to need to initiate and sustain direct eye contact to engage ASD students.
d. Educators will need to provide great numbers and varieties of activities to keep ASD students' interest.

11. Regarding formative and summative assessments, which is true?

a. Standardized measures are only summative assessments.
b. Portfolio assessments are only for formative assessments.
c. Formative assessment has a cyclical and interactive nature.
d. Summative assessment informs ongoing student progress.

12. Which of the following is a common drawback of standardized achievement tests?

a. The information they offer about student performance is premature.
b. They have good consequential validity but often lack internal validity.
c. The measurements they provide are irrelevant to classroom practice.
d. They tend to construct overrepresentation but lack construct validity.

Copyright © Mometrix Media. You have been licensed one copy of this document for personal use only. Any other reproduction or redistribution is strictly prohibited. All rights reserved.
This content is provided for test preparation purposes only and does not imply an endorsement by Mometrix of any particular political, scientific, or religious point of view.

13. Of the following, which is more characteristic of an informal assessment than a formal one?

a. Standard scores
b. Percent correct
c. A percentile
d. A stanine

14. Classroom modifications, accommodations, and intervention-based assessments with an autism spectrum disorder (ASD) student are most typical of which stage of the individualized education plan (IEP) process?

a. Pre-referral
b. Referral
c. Identification
d. Implementation

15. Which of the following is an example of a classroom accommodation for an autism spectrum disorder (ASD) student?

a. Giving the student fewer questions on a test
b. Giving the student more time to take the test
c. Giving the student fewer items for homework
d. Giving the student a calculator for a math test

16. In the behavioral portion of evaluation to determine autism spectrum disorder (ASD), which of these would NOT normally be included?

a. Short attention span
b. Stereotypical behaviors
c. Object attachment or preoccupation
d. Atypical responses to sensory stimuli

17. Which of these is true regarding diagnosis of autism spectrum disorder (ASD) and eligibility for special education services?

a. Eligibility refers to a specific disorder like autism.
b. Diagnoses are based upon the federal Individuals with Disabilities Education Act (IDEA) law.
c. Eligibility is determined in public school systems.
d. Diagnosis must be made through a team effort.

18. When communicating an autism spectrum disorder (ASD) student's assessment results to parents, which of these applies?

a. Parents typically understand the implications of an ASD diagnosis immediately.
b. Only share results; it is inappropriate to offer resources to parents at this time.
c. There are no reasons to plan further steps beyond communicating test results.
d. Visuals, examples, and descriptions are helpful for communicating with adults.

Copyright © Mometrix Media. You have been licensed one copy of this document for personal use only. Any other reproduction or redistribution is strictly prohibited. All rights reserved.
This content is provided for test preparation purposes only and does not imply an endorsement by Mometrix of any particular political, scientific, or religious point of view.

19. Which of the following is an accurate definition of *continuum of services* regarding special education services for autism spectrum disorder (ASD) students?

a. Services must be programmed to ensure continuity of their services from one grade to the next.
b. A range of services must be available to serve each student in their least restrictive environment.
c. Special education services must progress along a continuum as student skills continually advance.
d. Students must be provided a continuum of services enabling smooth transitions among activities.

20. When creating a transition plan for an adolescent with autism spectrum disorder (ASD), which of the following is MOST appropriate?

a. Describing present levels of student functional and academic performance is best left to educators.
b. Developing the student's individualized education plan (IEP) goals and developing the student's postsecondary goals are separate.
c. Identify the resources, services, activities, instruction, and personnel for meeting post-school goals.
d. Information concerning logistics for plan implementation and monitoring should be addressed later.

21. When conducting a functional behavioral analysis, what is the most important goal?

a. To determine the purpose of the behavior
b. To define the behavior without a purpose
c. To identify a way to eliminate the behavior
d. To isolate ways of modifying the behavior

22. In a positive behavioral support plan, which of the following occur prior to the behavior?

a. Antecedents
b. Setting events
c. Reinforcements
d. Both (A) and (B)

23. When collecting data to monitor autism spectrum disorder (ASD) student progress in a positive behavior support plan, which of the following refers to how long it takes the student to initiate a new learned behavior?

a. Frequency
b. Duration
c. Latency
d. Prompt

24. To collect data for monitoring student progress, which must the data collector do first?

a. Set a goal to indicate intervention success
b. Decide how to summarize student progress
c. Decide how long the intervention is going to last
d. Collect pre-intervention data to calculate a baseline

Copyright © Mometrix Media. You have been licensed one copy of this document for personal use only. Any other reproduction or redistribution is strictly prohibited. All rights reserved.
This content is provided for test preparation purposes only and does not imply an endorsement by Mometrix of any particular political, scientific, or religious point of view.

25. Which is true about visual representations used to help autism spectrum disorder (ASD) students manage their classroom activities?

a. ASD students will need their same preferred systems for every situation.
b. Some students will need different visual systems for different situations.
c. ASD students will focus on prominent images in pictures, not small details.
d. Picture communication symbols work better in colors than black and white.

26. Regarding the international no symbol of a red circle containing a diagonal red line, what has research found relative to autism spectrum disorder (ASD) students?

a. ASD students do not understand this visual symbol of an abstract concept.
b. ASD students comprehend it as meaning *do not do that* but nothing else.
c. ASD students have understood it as a warning not to run out of doorways.
d. ASD students have not comprehended schedule changes with the symbol.

27. For an ASD student with limited verbal development and below age- or grade-level cognitive development who can copy, match, and sequence letters, which modification would be most appropriate to a weekly 20-word spelling test, with words dictated by the teacher in a fifth-grade general education classroom?

a. Have this student type the words into a computer software program using its spell-checker.
b. Give this student 10 of the spelling words instead of all 20, and make it oral instead of written.
c. Excuse this student from the test, and have him or her write every word in a sentence instead.
d. Make a test sheet for this student wherein he or she completes two to three omitted letters in each word.

28. To differentiate instruction for a nine-year-old autism spectrum disorder (ASD) student, the teacher gives the student a story map to complete when reading. The map has lines labeled *Title, Characters, Setting – When, Setting – Where, Problem, Events,* and *Solution to the Problem*. How does this help the student?

a. It will help the student by enhancing reading comprehension.
b. It will help the student by enabling improved reading fluency.
c. It will help the student to make inferences regarding the text.
d. It will help the student by stimulating background knowledge.

29. With respect to principles of effective, research-based early intervention with autism spectrum disorder (ASD) students, which of the following is accurate?

a. Strategies for maintenance and generalization of learned skills are necessary.
b. If ASD is seriously suspected, intervention must wait until definitive diagnosis.
c. Early intervention should be only 7 to 10 hours a week to avoid overstimulation.
d. Because ASD children have rigid behaviors, intervention should be unstructured.

30. In early intervention with autism spectrum disorder (ASD), Applied Behavior Analysis (ABA) focuses in which of the following?

a. Problem behaviors
b. Remediating problem behaviors
c. Both prevention and remediation
d. Neither prevention nor remediation

Copyright © Mometrix Media. You have been licensed one copy of this document for personal use only. Any other reproduction or redistribution is strictly prohibited. All rights reserved.
This content is provided for test preparation purposes only and does not imply an endorsement by Mometrix of any particular political, scientific, or religious point of view.

31. Various antecedent-based interventions are included among many specific versions of Applied Behavior Analysis (ABA). Which of the following is NOT also a type of ABA intervention?

a. Discrete Trial Training (DTT)
b. Pivotal Response Training (PRT)
c. Auditory Integration Training (AIT)
d. Functional Communication Training (FCT)

32. Regarding incorporating assistive technology into their educational programs, what results has research discovered about autism spectrum disorder (ASD) students' daily computer use integrally to curriculum?

a. Computer use improves fine motor skills and reduces self-stimulatory acts.
b. Computer use increases focused attention but not overall attention span.
c. Computer use extends in-seat behavior and decreases generalization skills.
d. Computer use decreases agitation and increases perseverative responses.

33. Of the three main functions of language, which is most social and most difficult for autism spectrum disorder (ASD) children to develop?

a. Behavioral regulation
b. Social interaction
c. All of these
d. Joint attention

34. Which of the following is true about Functional Communication Training?

a. It is a method of training that is not behavioral in its orientation.
b. It replaces inappropriate behavior with effective communication.
c. It can be used without first making a functional behavior analysis.
d. It has been found to have the greatest effect with older children.

35. Regarding the Social Thinking treatment for autism spectrum disorder (ASD) students, what is accurate?

a. Good social skills depend on being engaged in a social interaction.
b. Good social skills involve producing the socially expected behavior.
c. Good social skills can be taught to the nonverbal with this method.
d. Good social skills do not require any particular vocabulary to learn.

36. A child with a social communication disorder or pragmatic communication disorder rather than an autism spectrum disorder is more likely to have which of the following?

a. Reading, writing, grammar, and vocabulary problems
b. Repetitive or stereotypical patterns of behavior
c. Restricted numbers or types of interests and activities
d. Any or all these

37. When teaching self-management to autism spectrum disorder (ASD) students, which of these is most accurate?

a. The student self-observes and self-records behaviors.
b. The student self-observes, while the teacher records.
c. The student always receives a prompt from a teacher.
d. The student never receives a prompt from a teacher.

Copyright © Mometrix Media. You have been licensed one copy of this document for personal use only. Any other reproduction or redistribution is strictly prohibited. All rights reserved.
This content is provided for test preparation purposes only and does not imply an endorsement by Mometrix of any particular political, scientific, or religious point of view.

38. In Positive Behavioral Intervention and Support (PBIS) programs, among the prevention, educational, and response components, which of the following are used in the response component?

a. Antecedent-based interventions, visual schedules, and functional communication systems
b. Differential Reinforcement of Incompatible (DRI) behavior and prompting by teacher
c. Differential Reinforcement of Other (DRO) behavior and Discrete Trial Training (DTT)
d. Instruction in self-management techniques, extinction, and use of adult scripts

39. Which of these is accurate regarding a crisis intervention plan in a Positive Behavioral Intervention and Support (PBIS) program?

a. A student behavior constituting a crisis does not necessarily pose a danger to the self or others.
b. A crisis intervention plan should prevent the behavior from escalating rather than correcting it.
c. A crisis intervention plan prevents escalation and corrects behavior in the least intrusive ways.
d. A crisis intervention plan is meant to preserve a safe environment, not to correct the behavior.

40. To teach safety skills to autism spectrum disorder (ASD) children for travel and community outings, which of the following is most applicable?

a. Children will acquire the needed skills once you tell them.
b. Modeling the skills is better than just talking about them.
c. It is safer to do some things for them than to teach them.
d. Role-playing, reviewing, and feedback will not help them.

41. Of the following state and local vocational and employment resources among adult services that autism spectrum disorder (ASD) individuals can access after high school, which typically represent primary, direct funding sources?

a. Departments of Vocational Rehabilitative Services
b. Employment Service Organizations (ESOs)
c. Community Service Boards
d. (A) and (C) but not (B)

42. To obtain community services, transition-aged youth with autism spectrum disorder (ASD) may be eligible for which of the following Medicaid waivers?

a. The Individual and Family Developmental Disabilities (DD) Support Waiver only
b. The DD and Day Support Waivers but not the Intellectual Disabilities (ID) Waiver
c. The Technology Assisted but not Elderly or Disabled with Consumer Direction Waiver
d. All five Medicaid Waivers

43. Researchers have found which of the following parental concerns not as prominent as the others upon initially receiving diagnosis of an autism spectrum disorder (ASD) in their child?

a. Deficits in socialization and communication
b. Developmental delays and cognitive disabilities
c. Discussing treatment options with clinicians
d. Stereotypical or repetitive interests and behaviors

Copyright © Mometrix Media. You have been licensed one copy of this document for personal use only. Any other reproduction or redistribution is strictly prohibited. All rights reserved.
This content is provided for test preparation purposes only and does not imply an endorsement by Mometrix of any particular political, scientific, or religious point of view.

44. According to research studies, what are some things parents want educators to do to improve individualized education plan (IEP) meetings for their children?

a. Parents find it burdensome to receive IEP objectives weeks before the meeting.
b. Parents would rather educators fill out IEP forms before meetings to save time.
c. Parents feel educators should encourage them to bring along an IEP advocate.
d. Parents want their children's IEP planning meetings to be shorter in duration.

45. What has research found about the roles of families in the education of children with autism spectrum disorder (ASD)?

a. Parents need closer educational involvement for children with ASD than many other disorders.
b. Children with ASD transfer and generalize learning about equally in institutions as in the home.
c. Parents cannot learn Applied Behavior Analysis (ABA) techniques for teaching their children at home.
d. Parents can learn home teaching methods and not need periodic consultation or ongoing support.

46. When students with autism spectrum disorder (ASD) are placed in special education and related services, which related services are they less likely to receive compared to those they most often receive?

a. Speech–language therapy services
b. Behavior management services
c. Occupational therapy services
d. School social work services

47. A general education teacher identifies an issue with a student having autism spectrum disorder (ASD). A team consisting of three elected teachers, a referring teacher, other specialists, and parents as indicated develops alternatives for intervention and then selects the most appropriate intervention. This is a description of which type of collaborative team in a school?

a. Student-Centered Problem-Solving Team
b. The Teacher Assistance Team
c. The Multidisciplinary Team
d. The Interdisciplinary Team

48. In the history of special education, at what time was the Autism Society of America founded?

a. 1940s—as a reaction against the exclusion and institutionalization of children with disabilities
b. 1965—parent advocacy groups and the Civil Rights Movement reflected shifting societal attitudes
c. 1973—in the Rehabilitation Act passed that year, when Section 504 banned educational discrimination
d. 1975—as a result of the enactment of Public Law 94-142 (EHA) that year, now called the IDEA

Copyright © Mometrix Media. You have been licensed one copy of this document for personal use only. Any other reproduction or redistribution is strictly prohibited. All rights reserved.
This content is provided for test preparation purposes only and does not imply an endorsement by Mometrix of any particular political, scientific, or religious point of view.

49. Numbers of children with autism spectrum disorder (ASD) served in schools has increased dramatically in recent decades. To inform the professional development of educators working with ASD students, the National Professional Development Center (NPDC) on Autism Spectrum Disorders promotes classroom use of evidence-based practices. What are its criteria for evidence-based practices?

a. Established efficacy through peer-reviewed scientific research in two high-quality experimental or quasi-experimental studies with group designs
b. Established efficacy through peer-reviewed scientific research in five high-quality studies with single-subject designs by three different researchers or groups
c. Established efficacy through peer-reviewed research in scientific journals fitting any one of these, lacking critical design flaws and demonstrating experimental control
d. stablished efficacy through peer-reviewed scientific research combining one high-quality experimental or quasi-experimental study with a group design and three high-quality studies with single-subject design done by at least three different researchers or groups overall

50. What is correct regarding regulations for protecting the confidentiality of information about students with autism spectrum disorder (ASD)?

a. Information is only shared with personnel who can benefit ASD students and their families.
b. Personnel providing the information, not its recipients, must protect it from being disclosed.
c. Individual ASD student information may be given to other students or parents in some cases.
d. When educators discuss confidential ASD student information, there is no location regulation.

Copyright © Mometrix Media. You have been licensed one copy of this document for personal use only. Any other reproduction or redistribution is strictly prohibited. All rights reserved.
This content is provided for test preparation purposes only and does not imply an endorsement by Mometrix of any particular political, scientific, or religious point of view.

Answer Key and Explanations

1. D: Normally developing children should be able to walk independently by the time they are two years old and often walk earlier. It is normal for a child not to be able to sit up unsupported at five months (A): Babies do not develop this ability until around seven months old. Children generally start to use furniture to pull up to a standing position (B) by around one year old. While lying on their stomachs, babies normally can raise their heads up when around three months old (C).

2. A: According to Piaget's theory of cognitive development, children typically develop the ability to understand abstract concepts during the stage of Formal Operations in preadolescence or adolescence. Children around 9 or 10 (B) and 7 or 8 years old (C) are typically in the stage of Concrete Operations (c. 7–11 years), when they can perform logical and mathematical mental operations as long as they have concrete objects to refer to or manipulate. Children around 5 to 6 years of age (D) are typically in the Preoperational stage (c. 2–7 years), when they have achieved symbolic representation, as evidenced by pretend or make-believe play, but think intuitively, not logically, and are egocentric, with difficulty understanding others' viewpoints.

3. D: Erikson's stage focusing on the nuclear conflict of trust versus mistrust (A) is during infancy, when children whose needs are met fully and consistently develop a sense of trust in the world; not having their needs met adequately causes mistrust. The stage of autonomy versus shame and doubt (B) is during toddlerhood, when children learn to control their bodies, resulting in feelings of independence when succeeding; if they fail, they feel ashamed and doubt themselves. The stage of initiative versus guilt (C) is during preschool years, when children explore and learn to assert power over their environments. When successful, they develop a sense of purpose; when exerting too much power, causing destruction and parental disapproval, they develop guilt feelings. In the stage of industry versus inferiority (D), children begin attending formal school; their worlds widen from parents and family to new relationships. Addressing new academic and social demands, they either succeed, developing a sense of competence, or fail and feel inferior.

4. D: Babies typically begin turning to look in the direction of sounds they hear at ages of seven months to one year. They develop different types of cries to express different needs (A) at birth to three months. They follow sounds using their eyes (B) and make gurgling sounds when playing with parents and alone (C) at four to six months old.

5. C: Babies normally detect the full range of sound frequencies at ages of four to eight months. Newborns differentiate sweet, sour, salty, and bitter tastes, developing full taste sensitivity at 12 to 19 months. Newborns focus on things 8 to 15" away and have limited color vision. Babies see 3' away by one month; discriminate among basic colors by two months; develop depth perception at three to seven months, full color vision at four to seven months, and full adult visual acuity by two years. Newborns can differentiate hot and cold and feel pain. Babies tell different textures apart by mouth and hands at one to nine months. Children distinguish sizes and shapes by touch at preschool ages. Newborns can differentiate the smell of their mothers' breast milk from that of other mothers; children can identify some foods by smell around five years old.

6. D: Asperger's syndrome is a high-functioning form of autism spectrum disorder (ASD). Students with this diagnosis will not have more intellectual impairments (A). This is not a separate disorder from ASD (B); it is included. Impulsivity and short attention spans are not characteristic (C) of Asperger's syndrome or of ASDs in general; they are more characteristic of attention deficit hyperactivity disorder (ADHD).

Copyright © Mometrix Media. You have been licensed one copy of this document for personal use only. Any other reproduction or redistribution is strictly prohibited. All rights reserved.
This content is provided for test preparation purposes only and does not imply an endorsement by Mometrix of any particular political, scientific, or religious point of view.

7. D: Autism spectrum disorder (ASD) student speech development includes a wide range of variation. Roughly half of ASD students are completely nonverbal (A). The other half range from being limited to echolalia (A) to demonstrating advanced vocabularies and fluent speech in monologues on preferred subjects but having difficulty with the give-and-take of two-way conversations (B) to initiating and maintaining normal conversations albeit with slightly quirky or singsong speech patterns (C) and everything else in between.

8. B: Students with autism spectrum disorder (ASD) most commonly have difficulty understanding the emotional content in others' communication, like humor or sarcasm. They are more likely to master technical jargon (A) in subjects that interest them than be able to interpret affective nuances. They are more likely to understand literal and concrete word meanings than nonverbal communication (B). However, they often can learn (C) to observe and understand it through explicit instruction. They are likely to have equal difficulty interpreting both social customs and emotions when communicated through nonverbal signals (D).

9. C: Autism spectrum disorder (ASD) individuals frequently have difficulty noticing, interpreting, and using socially acceptable behaviors. This affects social relationships. Many ASD individuals can have careers in suitable occupations: Typically, they can focus attention for long periods (A) and hence can excel at some kinds of work; however, they can have difficulty being interrupted, making transitions, or otherwise shifting or dividing their attention. ASD individuals do feel love (B) but may express it differently than others. ASD individuals do not lack all leisure interests (D): They may display more limited repertoires of interests but can enjoy recreational activity within those few preferences.

10. A: Autism spectrum disorder (ASD) students typically have difficulty making transitions between activities. They often focus intense attention on a single activity for long periods and react very aversively to interruptions or changes. Amplifying sensory modalities (B) is one of the worst things to do: Many ASD students find sensory input painful. If anything, educators may need to dampen or minimize sensory stimuli. Many ASD students avoid eye contact themselves and find this visual input from others difficult to modulate; teachers can use gentle reminders with physical proximity when appropriate but should not force it. Students may be listening even when not looking. A common ASD characteristic is narrowly restricted activities and interests; teachers do better identifying their favorites and offering these consistently, not overwhelming them with many different ones (D); students can shut down or act out in response. Educators may explore variations on favored activities for very gradually expanding repertoires with some students.

11. C: Formative assessment is cyclical, interactive, conducted during instruction, and used to inform and improve further instruction. While it is generally more informal in character than summative assessment, it does include standardized measures (A), for example, curriculum-based measurements like oral reading fluency tests. Summative assessment measures student achievement of learning objectives after instruction rather than ongoing progress (D) during instruction as formative assessment does. Portfolio assessments, which collect student work over time, can be used both as formative assessments to monitor student progress and growth and also as summative assessments (B) for evidence of learning as well as large-scale standardized tests, end-of-unit tests, and course grades.

12. C: One disadvantage of large-scale standardized achievement tests is that, because they are written at the state or national level to compare student performance with norms, they are unrelated to practices in actual classrooms. Another common drawback is obtaining information about student performance too late to address it, not too early (A). Another criticism is they lack consequential validity; that is, their scores are misapplied as accountability measures to determine

Copyright © Mometrix Media. You have been licensed one copy of this document for personal use only. Any other reproduction or redistribution is strictly prohibited. All rights reserved.
This content is provided for test preparation purposes only and does not imply an endorsement by Mometrix of any particular political, scientific, or religious point of view.

teacher performance-related compensation or student retention, despite not being designed for such uses. However, approved standardized tests do not often lack internal validity, that is, items within one test not correlating with each other (B). These tests are more likely to demonstrate construct under-representation; this is, they cannot cover the entire content area, rather than overrepresentation, and typically do have construct validity, that is, measuring what they were intended to measure (D).

13. B: Scores like the percent of items answered correctly, percentage of words read correctly, 15 out of 20 questions answered correctly, rubric scores, and running records are typical of informal assessments, which are performance driven, content driven, performance based, and criterion referenced. They are used to monitor progress and inform instruction. Standard scores (A), percentiles (C), and stanines (D) are typical of formal assessments, that is, standardized tests, which are data driven and norm referenced. They are used to compare student performance to grade or age norms, identify strengths and weaknesses compared to peers, and assess overall student achievement.

14. A: During the pre-referral stage, teachers would collaborate with family; use modifications and accommodations in the regular classroom to test their effectiveness and assist student learning; and evaluate instructional intervention effectiveness and monitor student progress using intervention-based assessment to avert unneeded testing and placement. During the referral (B) stage, if pre-referral procedures are ineffective, the student is referred for comprehensive, multidisciplinary evaluation. In the identification (C) stage, evaluation results are used to determine the disability and its type. In the eligibility stage, evaluation results are used to determine student eligibility for special education services. The individualized education plan (IEP) development stage follows. Once the student's IEP is developed, it is applied during the implementation (D) stage.

15. B: Giving the student more time to take a test is an example of a classroom accommodation. Giving the student fewer questions on the test (A), giving the student fewer homework items (C), and giving the student a calculator for a math test (D) are all examples of classroom modifications. Additional modification examples include changing curriculum based on student needs or using weighted grading. Accommodations involve teaching and measuring the same skills but through changing classroom procedures (e.g., American sign language [ASL] interpreters for Deaf students, text-to-speech software for blind students, large-print text for visually impaired students); modifications change the actual work done or how it is done.

16. A: Assessment to determine autism spectrum disorder (ASD) includes formal testing of intellectual and adaptive functioning; educational functioning and performance evaluation; communication evaluation; developmental history; and behavioral evaluation. The behavioral portion would include (B), (C), and (D); social participation and interaction with peers and adults; ability to relate to others; resistance to change, and so on, but would not typically include short attention span (A), which is not usually associated with ASD.

17. C: Eligibility for special education services is only determined in public school systems, whereas diagnoses are typically made in the private sector. Diagnosis refers to a specific disorder like autistic disorder, Asperger's syndrome, and so on, but eligibility does not (A); it refers to a broad category of disability. Eligibility is based on the federal the Individuals with Disabilities Education Act (IDEA), but diagnoses are not (B); they are based on a set of criteria, such as in the Diagnostic and Statistical Manual of Mental Disorders (DSM), when the individual's symptoms match enough of them. Eligibility must be determined through team effort, but diagnosis can be made by a team or an individual (D).

Copyright © Mometrix Media. You have been licensed one copy of this document for personal use only. Any other reproduction or redistribution is strictly prohibited. All rights reserved.
This content is provided for test preparation purposes only and does not imply an endorsement by Mometrix of any particular political, scientific, or religious point of view.

18. D: Experts advise educators and other evaluators to use adult learning strategies, including visuals, examples, descriptions, and demonstrations when communicating assessment results to parents. Additional advice includes remembering that parents require repetition and time for fully comprehending the implications of an autism spectrum disorder (ASD) diagnosis (A); offering parents resources for getting more information, support, and services (B); and planning (in writing) concrete next steps (C) and sharing these with parents, for example, making follow-up appointments or calls to discuss the diagnosis further.

19. B: The meaning of *continuum of services* in special education is that services must range from least to most restrictive to provide environments that are least restrictive for each student according to their needs and abilities. What is least restrictive for one student will be too restrictive for another and vice versa. This term does not refer to service continuity between grades (A) or to transitions among activities (D). Of course, services must progress according to student progress (C); however, this is not the meaning of the term. Moreover, autism spectrum disorder (ASD) students do not all advance continuously, regularly, or steadily. Some reach and stay at a certain level; some regress and then recoup; some advance rapidly enough to skip stages or levels; and some progress with different rates at different times.

20. C: A transition plan for an adolescent with autism spectrum disorder (ASD) should include the student and parents, as well as educators and therapists, in describing present levels of functional and academic performance (A). The student's expressed postsecondary goals should be taken into consideration in developing the individualized education plan (IEP) to enable the student to achieve those goals; the two are not separate (B). The transition plan should include a description of all transition services, instruction, activities, personnel, and resources needed for meeting these goals (C). Logistical information for implementing and monitoring the transition plan should not be left for later (D) but be included in the plan—for example, a time line for meeting goals; identification of agencies or people to assist with goals; description of role coordination; and a plan to identify post-school supports, services, and funding for them.

21. A: It is called a *functional* behavior analysis because its goal is to determine the behavior's function, that is, purpose. Every behavior has a purpose—to get something or get away from something. Defining the behavior operationally is important during functional behavior analysis (FBA) but not without also identifying its purpose (B). FBA is not conducted to find a way to eliminate a behavior (C); it is done to determine why the student is engaging in the behavior. Pinpointing ways to modify the behavior (D) is important but not done during FBA; it is done after the FBA is completed, based on the behavior's identified purpose. Modification aims to fulfill the same purposes but through more-adaptive behaviors.

22. D: Antecedents (A) occur immediately before a behavior and trigger it quickly. Setting events (B) occur earlier before a behavior and activate it slowly. These must be identified in functional behavior analysis before developing a positive behavioral support plan. Reinforcements (C) occur after a behavior, making the individual more likely to repeat it. In positive behavioral support plans, more-desirable replacement behaviors are immediately presented with reinforcements rewarding the replacement behavior, increasing its probable repetition. Also, the problem behavior is proactively prevented if possible; if not, events that previously reinforced the problem behavior are eliminated if possible, and only the replacement behavior is reinforced.

23. C: Latency refers to how long it takes the student to initiate a behavior (e.g., how long to execute a new replacement behavior after a teacher prompt to help determine when to fade the prompt). Frequency (A) refers to how often the student engages in a behavior. Duration (B) refers to how

Copyright © Mometrix Media. You have been licensed one copy of this document for personal use only. Any other reproduction or redistribution is strictly prohibited. All rights reserved.
This content is provided for test preparation purposes only and does not imply an endorsement by Mometrix of any particular political, scientific, or religious point of view.

long a behavior lasts. Prompt (D) refers to the level of support it takes for the student to perform the behavior.

24. D: The first step is to collect data before implementing the intervention to establish a baseline. Student performance during and after intervention must be compared to baseline levels to evaluate progress. The next step is to decide how long the intervention is going to last (C). This should be a duration enabling sufficient data collection to show intervention success. The next step is to set a goal that will indicate success if the student reaches it by the end of the intervention (A). The next step is to decide how to summarize student progress (B). This may be the average (mean) or middle (median) of the last several data points or a pre-identified goal, for example, X consecutive days, weeks, or months with zero maladaptive behavior incidents, or 10 percent maladaptive behavior incidents or fewer, or 90 percent adaptive behavior responses; or X number out of X total tests with a score of 90 percent, and so on. Evaluating intervention results is the last step.

25. B: Some autism spectrum disorder (ASD) students need different visual systems for different situation; for example, one student might need line drawings to communicate needs or feelings but actual concrete objects for a visual schedule to provide more information about what will happen next, and where he or she is going, and to maintain focus during transitions. Another student might need photos to identify people but objects to express needs. Thus (A) is incorrect. (C) is incorrect: ASD students may focus on some minuscule, barely visible detail in a picture, while teachers see only the dominant image. Hence, they should use unambiguous, uncluttered pictures, avoiding personally taken photos. Picture communication symbols work better for ASD students in black and white, not colors (D): Many ASD students with aversions or preferences for certain colors will focus on a color to the exclusion of processing the picture's meaning.

26. C: Research has found the international no symbol very beneficial to communicate this abstract concept to autistic students in multiple ways. For one, it has been used to prevent them from darting out through doorways. Its visual, nonverbal nature is understood by many autistic students (A). They not only understand it to mean *no, do not do that* but other things as well (B), like communicating that something they request is not currently an option (e.g., the student shows a picture symbol of something he or she wants; the teacher draws this symbol on the picture with a dry-erase marker, saying, "No, not now.") Another effective use has been to help autism spectrum disorder (ASD) students understand schedule changes (D): Teachers put the symbol on the picture or label for a scheduled activity to show that, though it usually happens at that time, today it will not.

27. D: Having this student complete blanks of a few letters within each word is most appropriate because he or she can copy, match, and sequence letters. (A) is less appropriate for a fifth grader with below grade-level cognitive development. Reducing the number of words might help this student, but an oral instead of written test (B) would not, considering the student's limited verbal development. (C) would also be harder, not easier, for a student with limited verbal skills.

28. A: By having to identify the main elements of the story in the story map, the student will gain better reading comprehension. Completing a written story map will not improve fluency (B); for this, the student would need to be read to and practice reading aloud. The map will not help with making inferences (C); guided questioning requiring the student to predict what will happen next, speculate about characters' motivations, and so on, would help with that. The map will not activate existing knowledge (D); open-ended questions asking the student to relate or compare events, characters, or experiences in the story to similar ones in his or her own life would help with that.

Copyright © Mometrix Media. You have been licensed one copy of this document for personal use only. Any other reproduction or redistribution is strictly prohibited. All rights reserved.
This content is provided for test preparation purposes only and does not imply an endorsement by Mometrix of any particular political, scientific, or religious point of view.

29. A: Research shows it is not only important to teach new adaptive and academic skills but also to implement strategies enabling autism spectrum disorder (ASD) children to maintain their functional application and generalize them to new situations and settings. Because these skills did not come naturally to these children, maintenance strategies are necessary, and those whose attention and interests are narrowly focused and limited will not necessarily generalize new skills on their own. If ASD is seriously suspected, intervention should not wait for definitive diagnosis (B) but begin immediately. Early intervention should actively engage a child at least 25 hours a week (C) year-round, be planned systematically, and target individualized goals to be effective. ASD children need highly structured interventions (D), including clear physical boundaries to avoid distraction, visual schedules for activities, and predictable routines.

30. C: Applied Behavior Analysis (ABA) focuses on both preventing (A) and remediating (B) problem behaviors in individuals having autism spectrum disorder (ASD). Research studies find it most effective for early, intensive intervention, that is, before children are five years old, though it can be used with all ages and developmental levels. Therefore (D) is incorrect.

31. C: Auditory Integration Training (AIT) is not a type of Applied Behavior Analysis (ABA). It is an intervention claiming to address autism spectrum disorder (ASD) auditory processing and sound sensitivity difficulties and offer accompanying benefits to communication, behavior, and quality of life. Several research studies have been made of this intervention method; however, presently no scientific evidence exists that it retrains ASD individuals' auditory systems or improves their functioning. A few of many kinds of ABA with strong scientific evidence of effectiveness are Discrete Trial Training (DTT) (A), Pivotal Response Training (PRT) (B), and Functional Communication Training (FCT) (D).

32. A: Research has found that using computers every day as an essential part of the curriculum improves the fine motor skills of autism spectrum disorder (ASD) students and also reduces their self-stimulation behaviors. Computer use increases both their focused attention and their overall attention spans (B). Using computers increases both the in-seat behavior of ASD students and also their generalization skills (C) for transferring from computer activities to related noncomputer ones. ASD students also benefit from using computers with both lower rates of agitation and less perseveration (D).

33. D: The communication function of behavioral regulation (A) is the easiest and earliest to develop: Children communicate to request or protest or reject objects, help, or action. Social interaction (B) is of middle difficulty among the three: Children communicate to request comfort or social routines like playing games; greet others (saying hello or good-bye); call attention to themselves; or "show off" in games, for example, dress up, peekaboo, and so on. The most difficult communicative function for autism spectrum disorder (ASD) children to develop is joint attention (D), for example, commenting on something, requesting information from others, or giving information to others. Therefore, these are not all the same (C).

34. B: Functional Communication Training (FCT) is a behavioral training method (A); it is one of a number of categories of Applied Behavior Analysis (ABA). It requires a functional behavior analysis to be conducted first (C) to determine the function of a disruptive or inappropriate behavior. If an autism spectrum disorder (ASD) individual is using the behavior to communicate something, then FCT can help by teaching more socially appropriate, effective replacement behaviors for communicating. While FCT can be used with all ages, it has been found very effective with young children (D) having limited linguistic and cognitive skills.

Copyright © Mometrix Media. You have been licensed one copy of this document for personal use only. Any other reproduction or redistribution is strictly prohibited. All rights reserved.
This content is provided for test preparation purposes only and does not imply an endorsement by Mometrix of any particular political, scientific, or religious point of view.

35. B: According to Michelle Garcia Winner, her Social Thinking treatment teaches autism spectrum disorder (ASD) students to produce behaviors that are socially expected in given situations, which are perceived as good social skills. She says having these skills does not depend on being involved in a social interaction (A); for example, when a teacher is speaking, and students do not talk, their behavior is expected and perceived as a good social skill. Social Thinking is a language-based learning approach; as such, it is not suitable for nonverbal individuals (C). Winner developed a social-thinking vocabulary accompanying her method to address the absence of vocabulary (D) for explicitly and behaviorally defining social expectations. For example, ASD students do not know what to do if told to "be respectful." Social-thinking vocabulary uses language like "Think with your eyes" rather than "Make eye contact," or "Keep your body and eyes in the group" rather than "Pay attention."

36. A: Children with social communication disorder, also called pragmatic communication disorder, can be differentially diagnosed from children with autism spectrum disorders (ASDs) because they do not exhibit the repetitive or stereotypical behavior patterns (B) or restricted numbers or types of interests or activities (C) typical of ASD students along with ASD's social communication problems. However, while some children only have social communication disorder, others with social or pragmatic communication disorder also may have other language difficulties, for example, problems with reading, writing, grammar, or vocabulary (A). Therefore, (D) is incorrect as (B) and (C) are characteristic of ASD but not social communication disorder.

37. A: When teaching self-management to autism spectrum disorder (ASD) students, the teacher explains and models self-observation and self-recording and gives the student a simple, explicit yes or no observational checklists for self-recording (e.g., Was I sitting in my seat? Was I doing my assignment? Was I following class rules?). The student then keeps records—not the teacher (B)—which would not be self-management. The teacher does initially prompt the student to record behavior, but once this is established, prompts are gradually faded via longer or fewer time intervals. Hence, prompting is neither always (C) nor never (D) used.

38. D: In the prevention component of Positive Behavioral Intervention and Support (PBIS), antecedent-based interventions, visual schedules, and functional communication systems (A) are used to keep challenging behaviors from happening. In the educational component, Differential Reinforcement of Incompatible (DRI), prompting (B), Differential Reinforcement of Other (DRO), and Discrete Trial Training (DTT) (C) are used to teach the student new, more-effective behaviors to replace challenging behaviors. In the response component, when challenging behaviors do occur, educators respond so as not to reinforce or escalate these, including teaching students self-management, using extinction (planned ignoring of attention-seeking behaviors) and following adult scripts promoting nonemotional, nonpunitive, and nonverbal or minimally-verbal staff responses to challenging behaviors.

39. C: A crisis is defined as a student behavior that does pose danger to self or others (A). In a Positive Behavioral Intervention and Support (PBIS) program, the crisis intervention plan should seek the least-intrusive ways for preventing a problem behavior from escalating and correcting the existing behavior (B) while keeping the environment safe (D).

40. B: Adults should never assume autism spectrum disorder (ASD) children will acquire needed skills simply through being told about them. Research shows that, not only children with ASD, but people in general, demonstrate very poor correlation between what they hear or say and do. Children with ASD especially must repeatedly practice safety skills in actual environments. They also learn more easily if adults model or demonstrate skills rather than just tell them (B). Adults should not do things for ASD children (C), particularly things they find themselves always doing for

Copyright © Mometrix Media. You have been licensed one copy of this document for personal use only. Any other reproduction or redistribution is strictly prohibited. All rights reserved.
This content is provided for test preparation purposes only and does not imply an endorsement by Mometrix of any particular political, scientific, or religious point of view.

them; these are the most important things to teach children to do independently for times adults will not be available. Helpful methods for teaching safety skills include role-playing; reviewing skill steps; and giving simple, positive, explicit feedback (D). Repeat practice until children perform all skills correctly without prompting.

41. D: State Departments of Vocational Rehabilitative Services (A) receive federal grants under the 1973 Rehabilitation Act. Employment Service Organizations (ESOs) (B) are typically not primary funding sources; some receive funding from Departments of Vocational Rehabilitative Services. Community Services Boards (C), State Departments of Behavioral Health and Developmental Services, and Behavioral Health Authorities are local and state agencies serving individuals with disabilities through Medicaid Waiver program funding.

42. D: There are five Home and Community-Based Services Medicaid Waivers for which transition-aged youth with autism spectrum disorder (ASD) may be eligible: the Individual and Family Developmental Disabilities (DD) Support Waiver (A); the Day Support Waiver; the Intellectual Disabilities (ID) Waiver (B); the Technology Assisted (Tech) Waiver; and the Elderly or Disabled with Consumer Direction (EDCD) Waiver (C). These provide community living, employment, and funding supports for individuals whose disabilities would require them to live in institutional settings without such services.

43. B: Some researchers surveyed numerous parents about the areas of most concern to them when initially receiving diagnosis of autism spectrum disorder (ASD) in their child and how well they felt diagnosing clinicians addressed those concerns. They found parents were most concerned about deficits in socialization and communication (A); stereotypical, repetitive interests and behaviors (D); and being able to discuss treatment options with diagnosing clinicians (C). The researchers identified additional potential problems associated with ASD, including medical issues, coexisting psychiatric disorders, developmental delays, and intellectual disabilities (B). Parents were not as concerned about these as about the ASD core deficits (A, D), which they felt diagnosing clinicians only addressed well about half the time, and about discussing treatment options.

44. C: Multiple researchers conducting studies from 2005 to 2008 received similar feedback from parents they surveyed about how educators could improve individualized education plan (IEP) meetings. Parents wanted to receive copies of their children's IEP objectives a few weeks ahead of time (A), so they could review them and prepare questions for the meeting. Parents did not want educators to fill out IEP forms in advance of meetings (B); they wanted to give their input first and be involved in writing their children's IEP goals and objectives. They wanted educators to encourage them to bring along an advocate familiar with the IEP process (C). They also wanted them to allow enough time for IEP meetings, not less (D).

45. A: Research studies show that, because children with autism spectrum disorder (ASD) frequently have difficulty transferring and generalizing skills to other occasions or settings, parents must be more closely involved in their education than the parents of children with many other disorders. Studies have found children returning to homes prepared to support their learning demonstrated better maintenance of intervention gains than children returning to institutions that did not continue the treatment techniques (B). Behavior analysts have taught parents Applied Behavior Analysis (ABA) basics, making them integral educational team members; many parents developed into teachers of great skill (C). However, research also finds that parents do need periodic expert consultations as well as ongoing support (D).

46. D: Students with autism spectrum disorder (ASD) are most likely to receive speech–language therapy services (A), behavior management services (B), and occupational therapy services (C) in

Copyright © Mometrix Media. You have been licensed one copy of this document for personal use only. Any other reproduction or redistribution is strictly prohibited. All rights reserved.
This content is provided for test preparation purposes only and does not imply an endorsement by Mometrix of any particular political, scientific, or religious point of view.

schools more often than social work services (D) and other related services when they are placed in special education and related services.

47. B: A Student-Centered Problem-Solving Team (A) is a building-level collaborative team that helps teachers to accommodate students who have behavioral or learning issues in the classroom. A Teacher Assistance Team (B) of three elected teachers, a referring teacher, and when indicated, other specialists and parents, addresses a student issue defined by a general education teacher; develops alternatives for interventions; and then selects the most suitable one. A Multidisciplinary Team (C) includes members representing various disciplines and perspectives relevant to the student's needs; it meets less often than the Interdisciplinary Team (D), which has similar composition to the Multidisciplinary Team but meets more often.

48. B: In the 1940s (A), parents began reconsidering the traditional institutionalization of children with autism spectrum disorder (ASD) and other developmental disabilities, many keeping children at home and finding local settings for their education. In the 1950s and 1960s, an overall attitudinal shift in society, reflected in the Civil Rights Movement including *Brown v. Board of Education* prohibiting racial segregation in education, included changing attitudes toward disabilities. The rejection of educational segregation influenced attitudes about disability as well as race; the concept of normalization emerged. A number of parent advocacy groups emerged around this time, including the Autism Society of America, founded in 1965 (B). The Rehabilitation Act, with Section 504 prohibiting discrimination in education, was passed in 1973 (C), and the Individuals with Disabilities Education Act (IDEA, formerly Education for all Handicapped Children Act [EHA]/Public Law 94-142) passed in 1975 (D), guaranteeing inclusive education and special education services to students with disabilities, both after the Autism Society of America's foundation.

49. C: The National Professional Development Center (NPDC) on autism spectrum disorder's (ASD's) criteria require any one of the descriptions in (A), (B), or (D) to be considered an evidence-based practice for individuals with ASD. The center defines *high-quality studies* as ruling out alternate hypotheses, lacking critical design flaws that confound the results, and demonstrating experimental control at least three times per study.

50. A: Regarding regulations to protect the confidentiality of the identities of and information about students with autism spectrum disorder (ASD), educators can only share oral or written information about ASD students with personnel who can benefit the students or their families by having that information. Personnel who provide the information and also those who receive it must protect it from being disclosed (B). Under no circumstances may information about an individual ASD student be given to other students and parents (C). The regulations stipulate that, when educators discuss confidential ASD student information, they must do so in secured locations (D).

Copyright © Mometrix Media. You have been licensed one copy of this document for personal use only. Any other reproduction or redistribution is strictly prohibited. All rights reserved.
This content is provided for test preparation purposes only and does not imply an endorsement by Mometrix of any particular political, scientific, or religious point of view.

How to Overcome Test Anxiety

Just the thought of taking a test is enough to make most people a little nervous. A test is an important event that can have a long-term impact on your future, so it's important to take it seriously and it's natural to feel anxious about performing well. But just because anxiety is normal, that doesn't mean that it's helpful in test taking, or that you should simply accept it as part of your life. Anxiety can have a variety of effects. These effects can be mild, like making you feel slightly nervous, or severe, like blocking your ability to focus or remember even a simple detail.

If you experience test anxiety—whether severe or mild—it's important to know how to beat it. To discover this, first you need to understand what causes test anxiety.

Causes of Test Anxiety

While we often think of anxiety as an uncontrollable emotional state, it can actually be caused by simple, practical things. One of the most common causes of test anxiety is that a person does not feel adequately prepared for their test. This feeling can be the result of many different issues such as poor study habits or lack of organization, but the most common culprit is time management. Starting to study too late, failing to organize your study time to cover all of the material, or being distracted while you study will mean that you're not well prepared for the test. This may lead to cramming the night before, which will cause you to be physically and mentally exhausted for the test. Poor time management also contributes to feelings of stress, fear, and hopelessness as you realize you are not well prepared but don't know what to do about it.

Other times, test anxiety is not related to your preparation for the test but comes from unresolved fear. This may be a past failure on a test, or poor performance on tests in general. It may come from comparing yourself to others who seem to be performing better or from the stress of living up to expectations. Anxiety may be driven by fears of the future—how failure on this test would affect your educational and career goals. These fears are often completely irrational, but they can still negatively impact your test performance.

Elements of Test Anxiety

As mentioned earlier, test anxiety is considered to be an emotional state, but it has physical and mental components as well. Sometimes you may not even realize that you are suffering from test anxiety until you notice the physical symptoms. These can include trembling hands, rapid heartbeat, sweating, nausea, and tense muscles. Extreme anxiety may lead to fainting or vomiting. Obviously, any of these symptoms can have a negative impact on testing. It is important to recognize them as soon as they begin to occur so that you can address the problem before it damages your performance.

The mental components of test anxiety include trouble focusing and inability to remember learned information. During a test, your mind is on high alert, which can help you recall information and stay focused for an extended period of time. However, anxiety interferes with your mind's natural processes, causing you to blank out, even on the questions you know well. The strain of testing during anxiety makes it difficult to stay focused, especially on a test that may take several hours. Extreme anxiety can take a huge mental toll, making it difficult not only to recall test information but even to understand the test questions or pull your thoughts together.

Copyright © Mometrix Media. You have been licensed one copy of this document for personal use only. Any other reproduction or redistribution is strictly prohibited. All rights reserved.
This content is provided for test preparation purposes only and does not imply an endorsement by Mometrix of any particular political, scientific, or religious point of view.

Effects of Test Anxiety

Test anxiety is like a disease—if left untreated, it will get progressively worse. Anxiety leads to poor performance, and this reinforces the feelings of fear and failure, which in turn lead to poor performances on subsequent tests. It can grow from a mild nervousness to a crippling condition. If allowed to progress, test anxiety can have a big impact on your schooling, and consequently on your future.

Test anxiety can spread to other parts of your life. Anxiety on tests can become anxiety in any stressful situation, and blanking on a test can turn into panicking in a job situation. But fortunately, you don't have to let anxiety rule your testing and determine your grades. There are a number of relatively simple steps you can take to move past anxiety and function normally on a test and in the rest of life.

Physical Steps for Beating Test Anxiety

While test anxiety is a serious problem, the good news is that it can be overcome. It doesn't have to control your ability to think and remember information. While it may take time, you can begin taking steps today to beat anxiety.

Just as your first hint that you may be struggling with anxiety comes from the physical symptoms, the first step to treating it is also physical. Rest is crucial for having a clear, strong mind. If you are tired, it is much easier to give in to anxiety. But if you establish good sleep habits, your body and mind will be ready to perform optimally, without the strain of exhaustion. Additionally, sleeping well helps you to retain information better, so you're more likely to recall the answers when you see the test questions.

Getting good sleep means more than going to bed on time. It's important to allow your brain time to relax. Take study breaks from time to time so it doesn't get overworked, and don't study right before bed. Take time to rest your mind before trying to rest your body, or you may find it difficult to fall asleep.

Along with sleep, other aspects of physical health are important in preparing for a test. Good nutrition is vital for good brain function. Sugary foods and drinks may give a burst of energy but this burst is followed by a crash, both physically and emotionally. Instead, fuel your body with protein and vitamin-rich foods.

Also, drink plenty of water. Dehydration can lead to headaches and exhaustion, especially if your brain is already under stress from the rigors of the test. Particularly if your test is a long one, drink water during the breaks. And if possible, take an energy-boosting snack to eat between sections.

Along with sleep and diet, a third important part of physical health is exercise. Maintaining a steady workout schedule is helpful, but even taking 5-minute study breaks to walk can help get your blood pumping faster and clear your head. Exercise also releases endorphins, which contribute to a positive feeling and can help combat test anxiety.

When you nurture your physical health, you are also contributing to your mental health. If your body is healthy, your mind is much more likely to be healthy as well. So take time to rest, nourish your body with healthy food and water, and get moving as much as possible. Taking these physical steps will make you stronger and more able to take the mental steps necessary to overcome test anxiety.

Copyright © Mometrix Media. You have been licensed one copy of this document for personal use only. Any other reproduction or redistribution is strictly prohibited. All rights reserved.
This content is provided for test preparation purposes only and does not imply an endorsement by Mometrix of any particular political, scientific, or religious point of view.

Mental Steps for Beating Test Anxiety

Working on the mental side of test anxiety can be more challenging, but as with the physical side, there are clear steps you can take to overcome it. As mentioned earlier, test anxiety often stems from lack of preparation, so the obvious solution is to prepare for the test. Effective studying may be the most important weapon you have for beating test anxiety, but you can and should employ several other mental tools to combat fear.

First, boost your confidence by reminding yourself of past success—tests or projects that you aced. If you're putting as much effort into preparing for this test as you did for those, there's no reason you should expect to fail here. Work hard to prepare; then trust your preparation.

Second, surround yourself with encouraging people. It can be helpful to find a study group, but be sure that the people you're around will encourage a positive attitude. If you spend time with others who are anxious or cynical, this will only contribute to your own anxiety. Look for others who are motivated to study hard from a desire to succeed, not from a fear of failure.

Third, reward yourself. A test is physically and mentally tiring, even without anxiety, and it can be helpful to have something to look forward to. Plan an activity following the test, regardless of the outcome, such as going to a movie or getting ice cream.

When you are taking the test, if you find yourself beginning to feel anxious, remind yourself that you know the material. Visualize successfully completing the test. Then take a few deep, relaxing breaths and return to it. Work through the questions carefully but with confidence, knowing that you are capable of succeeding.

Developing a healthy mental approach to test taking will also aid in other areas of life. Test anxiety affects more than just the actual test—it can be damaging to your mental health and even contribute to depression. It's important to beat test anxiety before it becomes a problem for more than testing.

Study Strategy

Being prepared for the test is necessary to combat anxiety, but what does being prepared look like? You may study for hours on end and still not feel prepared. What you need is a strategy for test prep. The next few pages outline our recommended steps to help you plan out and conquer the challenge of preparation.

Step 1: Scope Out the Test

Learn everything you can about the format (multiple choice, essay, etc.) and what will be on the test. Gather any study materials, course outlines, or sample exams that may be available. Not only will this help you to prepare, but knowing what to expect can help to alleviate test anxiety.

Step 2: Map Out the Material

Look through the textbook or study guide and make note of how many chapters or sections it has. Then divide these over the time you have. For example, if a book has 15 chapters and you have five days to study, you need to cover three chapters each day. Even better, if you have the time, leave an extra day at the end for overall review after you have gone through the material in depth.

If time is limited, you may need to prioritize the material. Look through it and make note of which sections you think you already have a good grasp on, and which need review. While you are studying, skim quickly through the familiar sections and take more time on the challenging parts.

Copyright © Mometrix Media. You have been licensed one copy of this document for personal use only. Any other reproduction or redistribution is strictly prohibited. All rights reserved.
This content is provided for test preparation purposes only and does not imply an endorsement by Mometrix of any particular political, scientific, or religious point of view.

Write out your plan so you don't get lost as you go. Having a written plan also helps you feel more in control of the study, so anxiety is less likely to arise from feeling overwhelmed at the amount to cover.

Step 3: Gather Your Tools

Decide what study method works best for you. Do you prefer to highlight in the book as you study and then go back over the highlighted portions? Or do you type out notes of the important information? Or is it helpful to make flashcards that you can carry with you? Assemble the pens, index cards, highlighters, post-it notes, and any other materials you may need so you won't be distracted by getting up to find things while you study.

If you're having a hard time retaining the information or organizing your notes, experiment with different methods. For example, try color-coding by subject with colored pens, highlighters, or post-it notes. If you learn better by hearing, try recording yourself reading your notes so you can listen while in the car, working out, or simply sitting at your desk. Ask a friend to quiz you from your flashcards, or try teaching someone the material to solidify it in your mind.

Step 4: Create Your Environment

It's important to avoid distractions while you study. This includes both the obvious distractions like visitors and the subtle distractions like an uncomfortable chair (or a too-comfortable couch that makes you want to fall asleep). Set up the best study environment possible: good lighting and a comfortable work area. If background music helps you focus, you may want to turn it on, but otherwise keep the room quiet. If you are using a computer to take notes, be sure you don't have any other windows open, especially applications like social media, games, or anything else that could distract you. Silence your phone and turn off notifications. Be sure to keep water close by so you stay hydrated while you study (but avoid unhealthy drinks and snacks).

Also, take into account the best time of day to study. Are you freshest first thing in the morning? Try to set aside some time then to work through the material. Is your mind clearer in the afternoon or evening? Schedule your study session then. Another method is to study at the same time of day that you will take the test, so that your brain gets used to working on the material at that time and will be ready to focus at test time.

Step 5: Study!

Once you have done all the study preparation, it's time to settle into the actual studying. Sit down, take a few moments to settle your mind so you can focus, and begin to follow your study plan. Don't give in to distractions or let yourself procrastinate. This is your time to prepare so you'll be ready to fearlessly approach the test. Make the most of the time and stay focused.

Of course, you don't want to burn out. If you study too long you may find that you're not retaining the information very well. Take regular study breaks. For example, taking five minutes out of every hour to walk briskly, breathing deeply and swinging your arms, can help your mind stay fresh.

As you get to the end of each chapter or section, it's a good idea to do a quick review. Remind yourself of what you learned and work on any difficult parts. When you feel that you've mastered the material, move on to the next part. At the end of your study session, briefly skim through your notes again.

But while review is helpful, cramming last minute is NOT. If at all possible, work ahead so that you won't need to fit all your study into the last day. Cramming overloads your brain with more information than it can process and retain, and your tired mind may struggle to recall even

Copyright © Mometrix Media. You have been licensed one copy of this document for personal use only. Any other reproduction or redistribution is strictly prohibited. All rights reserved.
This content is provided for test preparation purposes only and does not imply an endorsement by Mometrix of any particular political, scientific, or religious point of view.

previously learned information when it is overwhelmed with last-minute study. Also, the urgent nature of cramming and the stress placed on your brain contribute to anxiety. You'll be more likely to go to the test feeling unprepared and having trouble thinking clearly.

So don't cram, and don't stay up late before the test, even just to review your notes at a leisurely pace. Your brain needs rest more than it needs to go over the information again. In fact, plan to finish your studies by noon or early afternoon the day before the test. Give your brain the rest of the day to relax or focus on other things, and get a good night's sleep. Then you will be fresh for the test and better able to recall what you've studied.

Step 6: Take a Practice Test

Many courses offer sample tests, either online or in the study materials. This is an excellent resource to check whether you have mastered the material, as well as to prepare for the test format and environment.

Check the test format ahead of time: the number of questions, the type (multiple choice, free response, etc.), and the time limit. Then create a plan for working through them. For example, if you have 30 minutes to take a 60-question test, your limit is 30 seconds per question. Spend less time on the questions you know well so that you can take more time on the difficult ones.

If you have time to take several practice tests, take the first one open book, with no time limit. Work through the questions at your own pace and make sure you fully understand them. Gradually work up to taking a test under test conditions: sit at a desk with all study materials put away and set a timer. Pace yourself to make sure you finish the test with time to spare and go back to check your answers if you have time.

After each test, check your answers. On the questions you missed, be sure you understand why you missed them. Did you misread the question (tests can use tricky wording)? Did you forget the information? Or was it something you hadn't learned? Go back and study any shaky areas that the practice tests reveal.

Taking these tests not only helps with your grade, but also aids in combating test anxiety. If you're already used to the test conditions, you're less likely to worry about it, and working through tests until you're scoring well gives you a confidence boost. Go through the practice tests until you feel comfortable, and then you can go into the test knowing that you're ready for it.

Test Tips

On test day, you should be confident, knowing that you've prepared well and are ready to answer the questions. But aside from preparation, there are several test day strategies you can employ to maximize your performance.

First, as stated before, get a good night's sleep the night before the test (and for several nights before that, if possible). Go into the test with a fresh, alert mind rather than staying up late to study.

Try not to change too much about your normal routine on the day of the test. It's important to eat a nutritious breakfast, but if you normally don't eat breakfast at all, consider eating just a protein bar. If you're a coffee drinker, go ahead and have your normal coffee. Just make sure you time it so that the caffeine doesn't wear off right in the middle of your test. Avoid sugary beverages, and drink enough water to stay hydrated but not so much that you need a restroom break 10 minutes into the

Copyright © Mometrix Media. You have been licensed one copy of this document for personal use only. Any other reproduction or redistribution is strictly prohibited. All rights reserved.
This content is provided for test preparation purposes only and does not imply an endorsement by Mometrix of any particular political, scientific, or religious point of view.

test. If your test isn't first thing in the morning, consider going for a walk or doing a light workout before the test to get your blood flowing.

Allow yourself enough time to get ready, and leave for the test with plenty of time to spare so you won't have the anxiety of scrambling to arrive in time. Another reason to be early is to select a good seat. It's helpful to sit away from doors and windows, which can be distracting. Find a good seat, get out your supplies, and settle your mind before the test begins.

When the test begins, start by going over the instructions carefully, even if you already know what to expect. Make sure you avoid any careless mistakes by following the directions.

Then begin working through the questions, pacing yourself as you've practiced. If you're not sure on an answer, don't spend too much time on it, and don't let it shake your confidence. Either skip it and come back later, or eliminate as many wrong answers as possible and guess among the remaining ones. Don't dwell on these questions as you continue—put them out of your mind and focus on what lies ahead.

Be sure to read all of the answer choices, even if you're sure the first one is the right answer. Sometimes you'll find a better one if you keep reading. But don't second-guess yourself if you do immediately know the answer. Your gut instinct is usually right. Don't let test anxiety rob you of the information you know.

If you have time at the end of the test (and if the test format allows), go back and review your answers. Be cautious about changing any, since your first instinct tends to be correct, but make sure you didn't misread any of the questions or accidentally mark the wrong answer choice. Look over any you skipped and make an educated guess.

At the end, leave the test feeling confident. You've done your best, so don't waste time worrying about your performance or wishing you could change anything. Instead, celebrate the successful completion of this test. And finally, use this test to learn how to deal with anxiety even better next time.

Review Video: Test Anxiety
Visit mometrix.com/academy and enter code: 100340

Important Qualification

Not all anxiety is created equal. If your test anxiety is causing major issues in your life beyond the classroom or testing center, or if you are experiencing troubling physical symptoms related to your anxiety, it may be a sign of a serious physiological or psychological condition. If this sounds like your situation, we strongly encourage you to seek professional help.

Copyright © Mometrix Media. You have been licensed one copy of this document for personal use only. Any other reproduction or redistribution is strictly prohibited. All rights reserved.
This content is provided for test preparation purposes only and does not imply an endorsement by Mometrix of any particular political, scientific, or religious point of view.

Online Resources

Due to our efforts to try to keep this book to a manageable length, we've created a link that will give you access to all of your online resources:

mometrix.com/resources719/mttcautismsd

It's Your Moment, Let's Celebrate It!

Share your story @mometrixtestpreparation

Copyright © Mometrix Media. You have been licensed one copy of this document for personal use only. Any other reproduction or redistribution is strictly prohibited. All rights reserved.
This content is provided for test preparation purposes only and does not imply an endorsement by Mometrix of any particular political, scientific, or religious point of view.